REDBRIDGE LI

To ren

My Life in the PLO
The Inside Story of the Palestinian Struggle

Shafiq al-Hout

Edited by Jean Said Makdisi and Martin Asser

Translated by Hader al-Hout and Laila Othman

PlutoPress
www.plutobooks.com

First published 2011 by Pluto Press
345 Archway Road, London N6 5AA and
175 Fifth Avenue, New York, NY 10010

www.plutobooks.com

Distributed in the United States of America exclusively by
Palgrave Macmillan, a division of St. Martin's Press LLC,
175 Fifth Avenue, New York, NY 10010

British Library Cataloguing in Publication Data
A catalogue record for this book is available from the British Library

ISBN   978 0 7453 2884 3   Hardback
ISBN   978 0 7453 2883 6   Paperback

Library of Congress Cataloging in Publication Data applied for

This book is printed on paper suitable for recycling and made from fully
managed and sustained forest sources. Logging, pulping and manufacturing
processes are expected to conform to the environmental standards of the country of origin.

10 9 8 7 6 5 4 3 2 1

Designed and produced for Pluto Press by
Curran Publishing Services, Norwich

Printed and bound in the European Union by
CPI Antony Rowe, Chippenham and Eastbourne

CONTENTS

PHOTOGRAPHS

LIST OF ACRONYMS

AADC	Arab-American Anti-Discrimination Committee
AAUG	Arab-American University Graduates
ALF	Arab Liberation Front
ANM	Arab Nationalist Movement
AUB	American University of Beirut
AUC	American University in Cairo
CIA	Central Intelligence Agency
DFLP	Democratic Front for the Liberation of Palestine
LF	Lebanese Forces (Phalange militia)
LNM	Lebanese National Movement
NAM	Non-Aligned Movement
PFLP	Popular Front for the Liberation of Palestine
PFLP-GC	Popular Front for the Liberation of Palestine General Command, group under Ahmad Jibril that split from the PFLP
PLA	Palestine Liberation Army
PLC	Palestinian Legislative Council
PLF	Palestine Liberation Front
PLO	Palestine Liberation Organization
PLO/EC	Palestine Liberation Organization / Executive Committee
PNA	Palestinian National Authority
PNC	Palestinian National Council
PNF	Palestine National Fund
PNLF	Palestine National Liberation Front
PRCS	Palestinian Red Crescent Society
PSP	Progressive Socialist Party (Lebanon)
RPG	rocket-propelled grenade
SSNP	Syrian Social Nationalist Party
UAR	United Arab Republic
UNRWA	United Nations Relief and Works Agency for Palestine Refugees in the Near East
WHO	World Health Organization

GLOSSARY

(Note: This glossary is not part of the author's original text but is added by the publisher to help readers unfamiliar with some of the events mentioned in the text.)

Beik   A title of high rank dating from the days of the Ottoman Empire.

Camps War   Between 1985 and 1987 the Amal militia made a series of assaults on the Sabra, Shatila, and Burj al-Barajineh refugee camps, with the fighting spreading to Sidon and Beirut.

Committee 23   Another name for the Committee for the Exercise of the Inalienable Rights of the Palestinian People, formed to pursue the implementation of UN resolutions on Palestine. It is known as Committee 23 because 23 states participated in it.

Deir Yassin   Village of around 600 Palestinian Arabs near Jerusalem which declared neutrality during the 1948 war. More than 100 of its people were massacred on April 9, 1948, by paramilitaries from the Irgun and Lehi groups.

Dunum   Measurement of land, c. 1,000 m2.

Entanglement   The strategy of uncoordinated attacks on Israel that aimed to force Egypt's hand and make it go to war, whether ready or not.

al-Fakhani   District in Beirut where Yasser Arafat's command center was located.

Gaza–Jericho First Agreement   Official name of the agreement between Israel and the PLO signed in Washington, D.C., on September 13, 1993. "The Declaration of Principles on Interim Self-Government Agreements: Gaza–Jericho First" became known as the Oslo accords, referring to the secret negotiations between the Israelis and the Palestinians that took place in Oslo (1991–93) and paved the way to the official agreement in Washington.

Jaysh al-Inqadh   Arab army of deliverance, formed by the Arab League in 1947.

al-Jihad al-Muqaddas   The sacred struggle.

Jujube tree   Deciduous tree with red or black fruits that are dried or eaten fresh as a snack.

October War   The fourth Arab–Israeli war, October 1973. Egyptian and Syrian forces advanced across the Suez Canal and in the Golan Heights, breaking through Israeli defences. Though later reversed, these early successes did much to restore Arab morale, which had suffered since their defeat in the Six Days War of 1967.

Palestine Liberation Front   The PLF founded in Beirut in 1961 should not be confused with the present organization of that name.

Sabra and Shatila   Between September 16 and 18, 1982, Phalange militia groups perpetrated a massacre in the refugee camps of Sabra and Shatila. The death toll is variously estimated at from 800 to 3,500. The Israeli army surrounding the camps did nothing to prevent this and an International Commission found that they were involved, directly or indirectly.

al-Saiqa   Organization representing the Syrian Ba'th party.

United Arab Republic (UAR)   Egypt and Syria joined in a single state under President Nasser in 1958, and the union lasted until 1961, when Syria seceded. The UAR was associated with North Yemen, which remained a sovereign state, in the United Arab States. Egypt continued to be known as the UAR until 1971.

FOREWORD

This story is not an autobiography in the traditional sense – nor is it even my story, although I am the writer of it and the narrative voice is mine. This is the story of a people at a certain point in their history, an ancient people living an ancient homeland, a cradle of civilization, theater of wars and conflict. It is the story of Palestine and the people of Palestine between the 1930s and the start of the third millennium. I was 16 years old when the Palestinians experienced the Nakba, or catastrophe, of 1948 when their land was usurped and they were uprooted. Citizen became refugee, homeland became cause.

There is no precedent in history for what Zionism inflicted on Palestine and the Palestinians, except perhaps what European colonialists did to the native population of the Americas 500 years ago. Any group of human beings which experiences a crime on this scale, and lives to tell the tale, is left with marks and scars which are hard to ignore and impossible to forget. Members of my generation are the victims of such a crime. What distinguishes those of us who are still alive is that we are the last of the Palestinians to be blessed with the memory of life in our homeland and cursed by the bitterness of life in exile. Each of our lives is identified with that experience. The story of the homeland became the inseparable story of every one of its citizens. So this is not one person's autobiography; it is the story of a whole generation, a generation that knew how to stand up to the hammer blow of fate, how to remain steadfast in the face of adversity and aggression, how to restore its respect, how to continue its struggle and hold up the banner of liberation and the reinstatement of inalienable rights. And it also found out how to pass on the legacy of its memory to children and grandchildren. The memory persists through some secret bond between people and homeland – perhaps sustained by Palestine's unique geography or its place in history.

* * *

After this introduction, there are some points I would like to make: Firstly, throughout my life writing has been both my hobby and my profession, and my gateway into the world of politics. Therefore, parts of this book have come not from memory but rather from articles that I wrote, statements and speeches I delivered, and interviews I gave. I have elected to leave these texts in their original form in order to preserve the integrity of contemporary events and circumstances. Thus, although the final manuscript was assembled between 2006 and 2007, this book is not the result of a single effort, but rather was written over a long period of time in many stages.

Secondly, this book is not subject to the conventions or methodology of academic history, and therefore requires neither objectivity nor impartiality from the author. It is the affirmation of my own personal experiences as lived by me, under the twin emotional burdens of exile and revolutionary struggle. Having said that, I have spoken the truth and stood with a clear conscience on the side of justice.

Thirdly, the events that I have recorded here are just the ones I have witnessed or experienced personally. However numerous and important they may be, these incidents are just a small part of the history of Palestine in the period we are dealing with. So if any prominent personalities have been left out, that does not detract from their role or significance. Everything here is what I know to be true from my own personal experience, not from testimony of other people. In the same vein, and while speaking of well-known figures in the Palestinian national movement, I truly believe the real heroes of Palestine – the ones deserving of all our respect and appreciation – are those men and women without names, the simple folk who gave up everything for Palestine and never asked for any recognition or reward, the martyrs, the prisoners and their families, and those who stayed loyal to them. During my time, I met two kinds of people – those who gave to Palestine and those who took from it and exploited it. I salute the former and the latter will have their just deserts on the Day of Judgment.

Finally I would like to apologize in advance to any person, agency, or organization that may feel aggrieved about being treated harshly or unfairly by me in this book. As I have already said, I have tried my hardest to speak the truth as I saw it and only to recount what I witnessed myself. So if what I have written hurts your feelings in some way, remember that I have really been quite kind and considerate to you. In fact I have barely scratched the surface of truth and reality.

The aim of this book, its single objective, is to transfer the experience of one generation to the next, so that we do not repeat our mistakes and history does not repeat its tragedies.

Shafiq al-Hout
Beirut, January, 2007

1

JAFFA, MY CITY

I was born in the city of Jaffa in Palestine, on January 13, 1932. My name is Shafiq, my father's name was Ibrahim, my mother's was Tohfa, and our family name is al-Hout. Two official documents issued by the British Mandate Government in Palestine bear witness to these facts: the first is my birth certificate, issued by the Ministry of Health, and the second my Palestinian passport, No. 212023, issued by the Immigration and Travel Service.

Neither of these documents is in my possession any more. My birth certificate I left in the drawer of my desk in our house in Jaffa, when we had to abruptly leave the city in 1948 under the pressure of Zionist terrorism. My passport was seized by an Israeli officer who found it in my desk drawer in our house in Lebanon, when the Zionists burst into West Beirut in 1982.

(1)

Whenever we had a chance to meet and talk about our memories of the old days, my mother, who died in 1992, liked to recall the details of my birth. She said I was born on a rainy day, her labor pains beginning as the family sat at a low, round table having supper. Once when I asked her what was on the menu that night, she smiled and said: "*Muloukhia*" (Jew's mallow). And it was only then that I discovered why I used to sneeze whenever I ate that delicious dish!

My mother used to say that my birth was easy, not because I was her seventh child, but because I was the first to be delivered with the help of a licensed midwife. The shadow of that woman, Zainab Qabbani, remains vivid in my memory. She would frequently drop by our house, where she delivered all my younger siblings. Her presence aroused my curiosity as she was the first woman I had ever seen go around not wearing a veil. Instead of the usual black dress and head cover, she used to wear a long coat and wrap her hair in a white silk scarf. She was also a heavy and unapologetic smoker: indeed she used to show off by brazenly smoking in public. In those days, the conflict over clothing was not restricted to the question of whether or not women should wear veils, but was also about whether men should abandon the traditional male costume, the *kombaz*, for Western-style trousers – in other words the conflict was one between Arab and Western costume. My father remained loyal to his *kombaz* until his death in April 1971, although all his younger brothers adopted the new style. Once I asked my mother about the meaning of a scene which often came to my mind when I remembered my childhood: a blooming henna tree beside a well, underneath a dome that was open to the sky. Above the well a bucket was suspended from a rope wrapped around a log. She told me that the henna tree and the well were in the garden of the house where I was born, located in an alleyway off al-Alem Street, the second most important street in the Jaffa neighborhood of al-Manshiya. The house was a close by my father's shop; he was then a merchant.

Early in the last decade of the nineteenth century, my grandfather, Salim Youssef al-Hout, traveled from Beirut to Palestine to make a better living for himself and avoid being conscripted into the Ottoman army. He settled in the port city of Jaffa, where his older sister had married a well-known local merchant from the Saber family. My grandfather enjoyed life in Jaffa, which was becoming known as the "land of the newcomers," as it hosted so many outsiders, including many from other Arab lands and other parts of Palestine. As his standard of living improved, he became one of the main orange merchants in town, as well as the *mukhtar* (an administrative official) of the quarter where he lived. He acquired a solid reputation and great popularity, mainly because he used to stamp the documents required by his fellow citizens at no cost. Owing to his always detectable Beirut accent, he was known as Salim al-Bayruti rather than by his real last name. Just before his death at the end of 1948 in the Lebanese town of Souk al-Gharb, which he had chosen as a summer resort pending his eventual return to Jaffa, he gathered his sons around him. He told them about his plans for an orange grove he had planted 18 years earlier, in the village of Kastina, near the city of Majdal, north of Gaza. He then closed his eyes and passed away. He was buried in the Bachoura cemetery in Beirut, near his ancestors, including two noble sheikhs, Mohammad and Abdul Rahman al-Hout.

(2)

When I was about five years old, we moved from the house where I was born to another nearby which had a direct view over al-Alem Street. Our new home had a large garden with an old mulberry tree in one corner and a lofty jujube tree in the middle. I shall never forget my first day at school. I remember that I had been getting ready to attend the public school, but I ended up, though I do not remember why, at a private school belonging to the Association of Muslim Youth, which had been founded in Jaffa in the 1920s and played a great role in fostering education; however, in Palestine, it was the public rather than the private schools that had the better reputation, despite the fact that they were either free or charged only nominal tuition fees. At any rate, I did not regret what happened. When I sat for the first-year exam, not only did I pass but I was also promoted to a more senior class than expected, bypassing an entire academic year.

It was in our new house overlooking al-Alem Street that I had my first contact with my "problem" as a Palestinian. I was then around six. On the dawn of a summer's day in 1938, I was awakened by a terrifyingly violent knocking at our door. British soldiers accompanied by a Jewish woman recruit rushed in to the house; their commander ordered my father and my older brothers outside, where dozens of others were already gathered in an open space. One of the soldiers signaled to me with his rifle to go and sit on a straw mat near the garden. I did, but I kept a watchful eye on my mother who was struggling with the Jewish woman because she was refusing to be physically searched; the reason was that she had been fasting and had just finished her ablutions. The soldiers searched through the house, ripping open mattresses and tipping out oil, rice, grain, and kerosene together onto the floor, and even pocketing the money that they found, as well as some of my mother's wedding jewelry.

After sunset, and after the men had been standing in the burning sun for many long hours, my father and brothers were finally allowed to return home. My mother received them warmly and thanked God for their well-being. But after we were all reunited, and had made sure the soldiers had left the area, my mother brought out a strange object from underneath her clothes' chest that the soldiers had not found. Addressing my older brothers, Mustafa and Jamal, she asked: "What is this ... and which one of you does it belong to?"

"It's a bomb," my father said, taking it from her hands, while my brothers denied any knowledge of it. Yet I knew instinctively that it belonged to the younger one, Jamal, who was only 14 then. I became certain of this fact when I saw him weeping silently as he watched our father sneak out to hide the object away from the house.

That night, I sensed the danger we faced, not just as a family, but as a nation. I knew that we had a ruthless enemy. But I also realized that this enemy could be resisted, that there were already people resisting, and that my brother was one of those. When I woke up the following morning, I saw Jamal in a new light: he became my mentor and he was to leave an indelible mark on my life.

From that day on, I had a growing interest in politics and, as I got older, I began to understand newspaper articles and would follow radio broadcasts more closely. Whenever I failed to understand something, I would ask my brother. By that time, World War Two had erupted, and people used to gather in cafes to listen, carefully and silently, to the radio news. Occasionally, someone would whisper a prayer for the victory of Hitler, or *Abu al-Nimr* (Father of the Tiger), as some people called him, believing in the maxim that "my enemy's enemy is my friend." I shall never forget the sight of groups of men sitting around a radio in the cafe near our house every evening, listening to the news from Ankara. Turkey's neutrality allowed it to broadcast news that Arab stations could not. The news from Berlin, on the other hand, was banned, and anyone found violating the ban would immediately be dragged off to the detention camps at Sarafand or Acre.

Two men served as headmasters of the Manshiya Elementary School for Boys during the five years that I spent there. The first was a Lebanese man from Sidon, Said Sabbagh, who designed and drafted atlases that are still in print to this very day. The second was Jamal al-Alami, a Palestinian from Gaza. Both were extremely stern, and we used to quake whenever we ran into either of them in the playground or the classroom, or out on the street. The boys were often given beatings, and some instructors even became experts in the selection of the best wood for the purpose, as well as the most appropriate length and width.

All my elementary school teachers had a salutary influence on me during that period, yet one of them above all had a particular impact on me. Zaki al-Dirhalli had an amicable yet firm personality, and more importantly, he was one of the most famous football players in the Islamic Athletic Club of Jaffa. He used to play on the right wing, and was known by his fans as "the Golden Foot." He made training in all kinds of sports enjoyable – especially football – despite the shortage of equipment and playing fields. Fortunately, though, there was a spacious deserted area that divided the outskirts of our quarter of Jaffa from Tel Aviv. This space became a permanent bone of contention between us and the Jews of Tel Aviv. As if there were some unwritten agreement imposed by the balance of power, we used at first to leave the playground to them on Saturday, their weekend holiday. Later, however, when our team became more organized and in need of a proper playing field, we cancelled the agreement and no longer allowed them to monopolize the playground on Saturdays. In this we were supported by Mr Dirhalli, who believed that the land was ours and no one else's. In 1947, he was martyred in a Zionist terrorist attack on the Jaffa District Court.

(3)

Al-Ameriya was one of the best and most beautiful schools in Palestine. It was the only government secondary school in the Jaffa area, and only the top students from local elementary schools could gain entrance to it. It also recruited the best teachers, who had graduated from the élite academies of Palestine, as well as the universities of Egypt and the American University of Beirut. Al-Ameriya, which I entered when I was twelve years old, was one of the most significant milestones in my educational and public life.

It had a twin school, al-Zahraa for Girls, which was on the opposite side of the street. The building was painted the same green as my school, with the same yellow porcelain sign hanging over the gate and the same style of fence surrounding it with orange and lemon trees. No doubt this proximity was a major incentive for us to start talking about that "other sex" hiding behind the fence. It was the beginning of adolescence, with all of the changes, transitions, curiosity, and problems that normally accompany this phase in one's life. Unfortunately, there was no educational counselor, no therapist, and not even a useful textbook to help satisfy our natural curiosity.

One day we came across a book in the school library entitled *The Old Man's Return to His Youth*, which delved into sexual matters more graphically than some of today's pornographic magazines. It may be part of our Arabic literary heritage, but I have no idea how it ever made its way into the school's collection. When the librarian found us eagerly perusing it, he confiscated it.

Our homes were no less conservative than our schools. The only way for adolescents to learn about sex was from one another. Sometimes we would consult with older and more mature friends. At other times we would entice some rascal to provoke a religion or Islamic law teacher into broaching the subject in class. I recall one of those teachers who used to occasionally engage in something approaching free speech. When asked embarrassing questions posed by young men in the earliest awareness of sexual instinct, he would fidget and then say in a trembling tone: "Boys, there should be no timidity when it comes to religion." He would then haltingly elaborate on what is permitted by our religion and what is not, but with no physiological, psychological, or social explanation for these rules. This restricted sexual education did little to eliminate our obsessions and fears regarding a number of matters that were in dire need of explanation.

I can remember at least four of these worries. The first was masturbation, and what was being said about the dangers of this "secret" habit. The second was gonorrhea (fortunately penicillin had become available following the end of World War Two in 1945). The third was syphilis, whose reputation was terrifying, similar to that of AIDS nowadays. And the fourth was homosexuality, warnings against which were delivered with the utmost severity, as it was considered illegitimate, shameful, and the source of all terminal diseases. We used to ostracize anyone suspected of being gay. Had our religion teacher at the time imagined that the day would come when homosexuality would become legal and even acceptable, he would have pulled out what was left of his hair and declared it signified the end of the world.

Not only did al-Ameriya reflect the country's social reality, it also reflected its national character, as it was the most prestigious of all Jaffa's schools. It was a crucible that could galvanize the masses and incite the people to rebel against the British–Zionist alliance so as to vanquish colonialism and prevent the establishment of a national homeland for the Jews on Palestinian soil. There were several reasons for this which I shall carefully note, lest I be accused of being too biased towards Jaffa and my school.

The first reason for the school's influence was Jaffa's geographic proximity to Tel Aviv; whenever an Arab would slap or stab a Jew, or vice versa, the city would become immediately mobilized. Rallies

Photo 1 Graduates of al-Ameriyah school in Jaffa (1947). Al-Hout is standing in the middle, wearing a dark shirt and a beige jacket.

and demonstrations would be launched, and calls for struggle and opposition intensified. The second reason was Jaffa's position as the center of the Palestinian press. This gave the city a pioneering role in the orientation of the nation. The third reason was that, unlike other Arab cities whose élite families, with their wealth or inherited feudal power, monopolized political life, Jaffa's political decision makers were the masses, with students and laborers at the forefront. The fourth reason was that several schoolteachers, particularly in al-Ameriya, were intellectuals who had an important role to play in political life.

The influence of several of these teachers was felt strongly by my generation. Shafiq Abu Gharbieh, from Hebron, used to teach English and Latin. He showed us around the country and introduced us to places we had never visited, taking us either on foot or by bicycle. Not once did a lecture of his exclude some aspect or another of the national issues. He fell as a martyr while wiring a bomb which he was planning to deliver to his comrades in Hebron.

I also recall Abdallah al-Rimawi and Ahmad al-Sabe', who were close friends, sharing the same pan-Arab views, and who went on to join the Arab Ba'th Party. Both were graduates of the American University of Beirut, and together they contributed to the formation of our personalities and helped shape our political convictions.

Then there was Zuhdi Jar-Allah, a critical history instructor, who, though he did not always impress us with his own views, used to arouse our curiosity and instill skepticism in our minds, so we would not take any statement or rumor at face value.

I cannot forget Hasan al-Dabbagh, whose influence on us was both academic and behavioral: his concern was to make us into men who were qualified to deal with the future. He was particularly interested in planning ahead, and he thought that although the country might have enough fighting men, it surely was still in need of thousands of scholars and specialists.

(4)

There were a number of sports, social, and cultural clubs in Jaffa. The club that provided us with the means to carry out patriotic activities was the Islamic Youth Club. We used to gather there to make plans, prepare placards and flags, and make phone contact with other student representatives in order to coordinate rallies, agree on slogans, and so on. It was from there that we founded the first Palestinian students' union. The principal driver behind the initiative was Ibrahim Abu Lughod, who went on to become Professor of Political Science at Northwestern University, and the rest of us were his assistants.

We later found out that the club had played a major role in organizing the Arab Palestinian resistance, some of whose members fell in the battlefield, while others joined the Jaysh al-Inqadh, or Arab army of deliverance.

The municipality of Jaffa played an important role in the development of the city. It was presided over by four distinguished chairmen, who were, in order: Assem Beik Said, Omar Bitar, Abdul Raouf Bitar, and Dr Youssef Haykal. In his second term, Dr Haykal was elected rather than appointed to his position, thereby setting an important precedent.

I actually remember this election, which offered an occasion to hold patriotic festivals. The candidates would rush to build good relationships with the charismatic mufti of Jerusalem, Hajj Amin al-Husseini, who at that time resided in Egypt. According to his opponents, Dr Haykal's election victory would have been impossible had he not been appointed as chairman of the municipality earlier, because he was not associated with Hajj Amin al-Husseini, as other chairmen were.

Actually, the liveliest aspect of life in Jaffa was its journalism, and in my generation certain journalists and men of literature and poetry attained great prominence and fame. Among them were Rashad al-Bibi, Mahmoud al-Afghani, Mahmoud al-Hout, Kanaan Abu Khadra, owner of *al-Sha'b* (The People) newspaper, Ibrahim al-Shanti, owner of *al-Difaa* (The Defense) newspaper, and Hashem al-Sabe', the sharp-tongued owner of *al-Sareeh* (The Frank) newspaper. Indisputably, Jaffa was the center of the Arab Palestinian press: *al-Difaa*, *Falasteen*, *al-Sha'b*, *al-Sirat al-Mustaqeem* (The Straight Path), and *al-Wihda* (Unity) were all published there. Those newspapers were considered among the most important in the Arab world, second only to the Egyptian press.

Another interesting thing about my ancestral city was that while all of the many Palestinian political parties had their headquarters in Jerusalem, the Communist Party's headquarters was in Jaffa. The Communists were well known for their deeply rooted history in Palestine. They included men like Fouad Nassar, Emil Touma, Rushdi Shahin, Mukhles Amr, and others, who held regular educational seminars to stimulate democratic dialogue, and always made sure to invite us students. Sometimes we would help them selling their newspaper *al-Ittihad* (Union), which is in print in Haifa to this day.

(5)

By the academic year of 1947–48, my classmates and I had reached the Fourth Secondary, the last class before the final matriculation exams which would qualify us to enter college at the sophomore level. Passing these examinations was not easy and the odds were against success even during times of normality, let alone during such troubled times as we lived, with the country entering a state of war.

Following some preliminary basic training, many of us began to carry weapons. Young men joined groups in the quarter or street where they lived, and the leader of each group would assign the guard shifts. Most weapons were light – rifles or submachine guns. You could sometimes see a group of five or six boys carrying a motley collection of old equipment, including Ottoman, English, German, and even Italian weapons. The most common submachine guns were the Sten gun, which we used to manufacture locally, and the Thompson submachine gun, or tommy gun. Some of us left Jaffa and joined the *Jaysh al-Inqadh* in Damascus, where some became professional soldiers and integral members of the Syrian army following the 1948 *Nakba*, or catastrophe. These men eventually became the nucleus of the first command of the Palestine Liberation Army.

At that time, we were not aware that our leaders lacked wisdom, and that those in charge were at best incapable or lacked the means to undertake wise and effective leadership. For example, Abdul Qader al-Husseini, the brave and accomplished leader of *al-Jihad al-Muqaddas* (the sacred struggle), was turned away by the military committee of the Arab League in Damascus. He nevertheless decided to go on fighting with his men with whatever weapons they had at hand, although the balance of power was stacked against them. He fought until his martyrdom in the battle of al-Qastal, on April 8, 1948.

I do not wish to judge too harshly the members of the National Committee who were in charge of Jaffa, as most of them had good intentions and reputations, people like Hajj Khaled al-Farkh, Kamel al-Dajani, Ahmad Abdul Rahim, Hajj Ahmad Abu Laban. The problem was that both their qualifications and their abilities were limited, and they had few resources.

There was no military operations center, no media office, not even an official spokesman. We would read in the press that a battalion of the deliverance army would be arriving in a day or two, with thousands of properly armed Arab volunteers. The day would come, and instead of an army we would see 20 men led by a determined but ultimately impotent commander.

The bitterness I feel now in revealing these shameful truths does not prevent me from recognizing that the people of the Arab nations were different from their leaders. Throughout the decades, there has not been a single Arab nation whose members have not shed their blood for Palestine. Also, I must acknowledge the role of the Muslim fighters who came from various countries, especially Bosnian Muslims from Yugoslavia. I actually saw a group of those freedom fighters in the main square near our house in Manshiya, and I am still impressed when I remember their heroic fighting, their skill, courage, and religious faith. They were professional soldiers, some of whom elected to remain in Palestine even after the war.

However, the enemy knew all the details of our daily lives and they knew how to use that knowledge in their psychological warfare. The massacre of Deir Yassin was accompanied by incessant Zionist propaganda that instilled the spirit of defeat. At the same time, the Zionists began random and deliberate artillery shelling of residential areas, thereby intensifying fear and terror among the Palestinians.

Despite the gravity of the situation, Jaffa remained proudly steadfast until all her means of resistance were exhausted. I still remember the day I heard women's cries of joy and children's songs when some laborers from the Palestinian Casting Company succeeded in manufacturing a weapon with which to counter the Zionist mortar batteries. They called it the "mine launcher," and carried it around the city in an attempt to raise morale among the inhabitants. In the event, this weapon was never used successfully; on the contrary it caused the death of several members of the launch crews and so production was stopped.

During the month of April, political, military, and security circumstances deteriorated dramatically, and the daily pressures and difficulties increased. As far as we matriculation students were concerned, the most important challenge was to pass the final exams, whose date had been moved forward from June by the government. This decision was due to Britain's determination to end its mandate and withdraw from Palestine on May 15, 1948.

My patience and endurance were further put to the test: at noon on 2 April, I was shocked to learn of the martyrdom of my brother and mentor Jamal, who was then 24. At first I could not believe the news, although we had all been aware of the major role he played in the resistance movement. He was then the leader of an underground group which specialized in planting mines and bombs on the roads that linked Zionist settlements over a wide area. He had often been exposed to counter-attacks and more than once he had been injured and his car damaged. The leader of all the underground groups was a Sudanese officer, known as Tareq the African.

I shall never forget the friends who stood by me during those terrible moments following my brother's death, especially my oldest friend Ibrahim Abu Lughod, who insisted that I carry on with my exams.

The day after Jamal's martyrdom, I had to sit for the Arabic Exam: it took place in one of the halls of the Frères School on al-Ajami Street. The senior proctor in the hall was my uncle, Mahmoud al-Hout, who was an inspector in the Board of Education.

I opened the exam paper and read the questions: we had to pick out one title out of three and write an essay about it. One of the three options read: "Write about an event that shocked you." I couldn't believe my eyes. It felt as if the subject had been specially selected for me. I looked towards my uncle, who was somehow hiding his eyes behind his black-rimmed spectacles. My seat was next to the window overlooking the street; and I started to watch the casket that was wrapped in the flag of Palestine, carried by a crowd of angry men.

After I managed to get something down on the paper, Ibrahim and I rushed to bid farewell to my dead brother, who was buried in the red soil of the hill overlooking the Mediterranean shore. Ironic as it may sound, this very cemetery, which was later locked up by the Israelis, was opened again in 2001, under public pressure, to receive a Palestinian from Jaffa who had refused to be buried outside his homeland, after living in exile for more than 50 years. This lover of Jaffa was none other than the dear friend of my childhood, maturity, and old age: Ibrahim Abu Lughod.

(6)

On April 23, 1948, I was on the deck of the Greek ship *Dolores*, heading from Jaffa to Beirut.

I picked a spot in the prow, and began talking to myself like a madman, wondering aloud what had happened to us and why, whether we would ever make a return trip from the journey we were now making, or whether this was going to be a last, farewell journey.

No way! No way was this going to be a farewell to Jaffa. It couldn't be anything more than a short vacation. Had it been otherwise my father would not have made sure that our departure was entirely legal. The first thing he had done was to get us all a visa from the Lebanese Consulate, signed by the Consul, Edmund Roque. Had it been otherwise, we would not have left behind all the young men in the family capable of carrying guns: my brothers, cousins, and several others.

No doubt we would be going back. Two or three weeks at the most and we would be back. Beirut was not unfamiliar to me: we frequently used to visit our relatives there and spend our summers in the Lebanese mountains, always returning to Jaffa in the end.

No doubt we would be going back, as we had gone back so many times before, and Jaffa would be waiting for us. The boat would lead us back to our city near the spring known as Sabil Abu Nabut, surrounded by boundless orange groves.

Yet this time things seemed different. With my eyes fixed on Jaffa and its historic port, I watched sadly as the city gradually but inexorably faded into the distance, the ship mercilessly carrying me away. By sunset of April 23, 1948, Jaffa was no longer visible, and there was only seawater around us.

Yet insight is indeed more powerful than eyesight, and the heart is fonder than the eye. I make such a statement having lived through all the years since that day with memories of Jaffa overwhelming me. Not once have I run into an old friend without us discussing the good old days and our memories, such as the name of a particular street or alley, or who used to live in which quarter of the city, or in which particular spot this or that restaurant or club was located. We would sometimes astonish ourselves by suddenly recalling details that had seemed insignificant to us when we actually lived in Jaffa: the color of a specific building, or the name of a pastry salesman.

I once wrote the following in my introduction to the Book *Men From Palestine*, by the historian Ajaj Nuwayhed:

> Oppressive forces may be able to annex territory, assassinate individuals, or annihilate armies and institutions; but, despite their might, they cannot annex the homeland, assassinate the people, or annihilate a nation or its national character. They may be able to falsify a book or an atlas, or erase a landmark, or eliminate a flag, but they cannot falsify history, or geography, or eliminate heritage. When, under conditions of oppression and occupation, the land itself fails in its mission to protect its own landmarks and values and testify to its own history, thereby losing its role as the solid base for the notion of homeland, it becomes the duty of the citizen to take over this mission. The citizen now becomes the new base, and memory replaces the land as the embodiment of the homeland. There is no force capable of defeating memories or sentiments. By definition, memory is the enemy of dispossession.

If someone had asked me, before the land of Palestine was usurped, about that street in Jaffa that connected my home to my school, that I had walked thousands of times, I would perhaps not have been able to describe it to my own satisfaction. But, try me now: test my memory, and despite the passage of time and the coercion of historic events, you'd be surprised.

(7)

Indeed, there is no harm now in trying to recollect one of those journeys.

There were no bus stops on al-Alem Street, and only small horse-drawn carts could pass through the narrow thoroughfare. Consequently, I had to walk westwards to reach the parallel and rival Hasan Beik Street, whose residents used to boast that the busses passed through it. Hasan Beik came from Aleppo, and became well known after he built a mosque in Jaffa, which was also named after him and which stands to this day, despite dozens of Zionist attempts to bring about its downfall. It is a spacious mosque, surrounded by gardens and vineyards.

Bus Number 2 stopped right next to the mosque; there we used to wait for it as it approached us from its last stop on the outskirts of Tel Aviv, heading southwards towards downtown Jaffa, to Clock Tower Square. The first stop was on the Hamra Hill, or Baydas Hill as it was known, named after the wealthy Baydas family, who had built a high ceilinged palace on the brow of the hill that resembled an old British fortress.

After school, we usually came back to play football on the red sand on the west side of Hamra Hill (hamra means "red" in Arabic), which led down to the seashore. After the game, we would throw down our clothes on the beach and swim in the blue sea.

Bus Number 2 would continue down the wide road and arrive at the Manshiya police station, where the diminutive and unpopular Officer Abdallah was stationed; he often used to strut arrogantly alongside the British soldiers. We held many demonstrations against Abdallah, calling for his resignation. Past the police station, the Manshiya quarter ends, and the Irsheid quarter begins: at this point the bus, unable to negotiate the narrow alleys, would turn and take Mahatta Street, after passing the Khalaf bakery. The next turn was near al-Da'ifi butcher's shop, where the smell of fresh meat on the barbecue used to whet our appetites. Mahatta Street was lined with stores and cafés, of which Inshirah Cafe was the nicest. Among its regular customers was Sheikh Issa Abul Jibein, who, it was rumored, had supported a boycott of Rotenberg Electricity Company, leading to its being monopolized by the Jews. The interesting thing about Mahatta Street was that both horse-drawn carriages and buses passed through it; often a bus driver who had once driven carriages would wave at a former colleague and would toss him a dirty joke. I used to side with the carriages and their drivers; the sound of the carriage bells was always soothing; I also liked the sound of the horses' hooves, and even the sound of the whip wasn't too bad.

After passing the railway station to our left we would proceed to

Iskandar Awad Street. I do not know who Iskandar Awad was, or why his name had been given to this prestigious commercial street, but I do know that in Jaffa there used to be, apart from the Awads, several élite Christian families such as the Khayyats, the Homsis, the Roques, the Baroudis, the Gharghours, and the Andrawis. Most of them lived in the Ajami quarter, where churches of the various Christian sects were located. Old as it was, Iskandar Awad Street was one of the most beautiful streets of Jaffa: a striking variety of commercial premises, shop windows and stores. Above the stores were lawyers' offices or doctors' clinics.

This street ended at Clock Tower Square, the oldest and most important square in Jaffa. In its center was the tall clock tower, which had witnessed angry demonstrations as crowds left the Grand Mosque after prayers. There was also the prison fortress of Kishleh, surrounded by barbed wire on all sides, facing the port and the sea to the west, and overlooking a spacious yard to the east. In front of the Kishleh was the building that housed the District Court, which was blown up by Zionist terrorists in 1947, killing several decent young men. Further south, you could see a whole collection of stores and groceries, as well as the best *fuul* (fava bean) restaurant in all of Jaffa, Fathallah's. Mr Fathallah was more of an artist than a chef, and if you were wise you did not criticize his dishes or make any special requests; you either ate whatever he offered without complaint, or you might as well just leave! Behind Fathallah's was the Deir Market, where Jaffa's most reputable merchants would trade their wares. Beyond Clock Tower Square was the road down to the port of Jaffa, from where the best oranges in the world were exported. The quality of this product led the Israelis to retain the Arabic appellation "Jaffa oranges," fearing that to change it would risk the loss of the fruit's worldwide reputation, even though they had changed the names of each and every Palestinian town and village, including Jaffa itself, whose new name became Yaffo.

Further down the street was the *al-Madfa'* (Artillery) Café, which was named after the Turkish cannon stationed immediately in front of it pointing out towards the sea. The cannon was used during the month of Ramadan to signal the moment of sunset. The café's original customers were the tough Jaffa sailors, who were to play a significant role in the history of the national struggle. Adjacent to the cafe was the Muslim Youth Club, which had become a meeting place for students and scholars, and one of the places in town in which political decisions were taken.

To the south of this club rose the Rumayleh Hill, where Old Jaffa was located. At the foot of the hill were Jaffa's renowned shish kebab restaurants, as well as the pastry and ice cream shops that were especially popular during Ramadan nights.

By now the very same Number 2 Bus would have arrived at the port itself, and here passengers had to pay another piaster as a new section of the route was about to begin.

The bus would cross the yard and turn left into Salahi market, another famous commercial area of Jaffa, where the most knowl-edgeable orange merchants and brokers used to meet, as did those traders dealing in paper, wood, nails, and other commodities. There the Jaffa orange merchants used to start their day with a cup of coffee at the spacious David Café, or perhaps with a breakfast of *fuul* at Kalha restaurant.

At the end of Salahi market began the vegetable *souq*; most of the vendors here were of rural origin or from Gaza, which had close business ties with Jaffa. From here, if one remained on Bus Number 2 one would eventually reach Jaffa's Municipality Square, with its beautiful garden. This is where we used to get off the bus and walk towards al-Ameriya in the Nuzha Quarter, whose name (which means picnic) was well deserved thanks to its beautiful landscape and its many trees. Municipality Square was Jaffa's main entrance from both the east and the south; you could see buses coming from Jerusalem, Gaza, and practically all of Palestine, with the exception of Haifa, whose access route led through Tel Aviv. At the Municipality Café, merchants, senior employees, and members of the few élite families of Jaffa used to meet. Unlike Jerusalem, Gaza, Nablus, and Acre, Jaffa was not rich with "old families." The population was actually more Palestinian than specifically "Jaffan," while on a wider scale it was as much an Arab as a Palestinian city, due to the presence of people from various Arab regions. But the roots of the few old Jaffa families – in particular the Bitars and Haykals – supposedly dated back hundreds of years.

National political rallies were often held in Municipality Square, especially when public festivals were held at the nearby Hamra Movie Theater. This large and prestigious theater was then almost unique in the Middle East. We often walked the return journey from al-Ameriya: groups of young male and female students milling around, talking and joking, crossing back and forth across the street. As I look back on the scene I feel we were like a floral bouquet of youth and happiness.

My friends from Manshiya and I would walk past Municipality Square and then along the beautiful King George Street, which before the British Mandate had been Jamal Pasha Street. We used to call it Nuzha Street, in protest against both the Turks and the British. We would go past the theater, to the road that led into the Bassa sports ground. This is where seasonal sports festivals, including football matches between the various Palestinian teams, were held. The Islamic Club and the Orthodox Club were the two most famous teams in Jaffa. On the rare occasion when these clubs hosted Jewish teams, like Maccabi or Hapoel, thousands of spectators attended. In addition, the Bassa fields were the venue for festivals and shows put on by the Najjada Party, headed then, in the absence of Hajj Amin al-Husseini, by Mohammed Nimr al-Hawari. When Hajj Amin's cousin Jamal al-Husseini returned from his exile he founded an organization called *Shabab al-Futtuwa* (Youth Club), and just before the 1948 *Nakba*, an unsuccessful attempt was made to unite the two paramilitary organizations, although in any case neither group proved to be effective in the 1948 War.

On the opposite side of the same street stood the Continental Hotel, which was the meeting place for writers and poets, whose numbers had increased in Jaffa following the establishment of the Near East Radio Station there. At the Continental, we became acquainted with several Palestinian writers as well as some from the Arab World, particularly Egypt, such as Tawfiq al-Hakim, Abbas al-Aqqad, and Abdul Rahman al-Khamisi. Several famous singers and artists came to the Continental as well, such as Muhammad Abdul Wahhab and Youssef Wahbe.

Continuing out walk along the same road, we would arrive at the Post Office, a charming building with a white façade and spacious halls with glitteringly clean floors. I would excuse myself for a minute to check if there were any letters in our mailbox, P.O. Box 416; it was to this mailbox that my passport, No. 212023, had been delivered, after I had applied for it in the hope of going to Britain to study law. Thirty-four years later, when the Israeli army entered Beirut during their invasion of Lebanon in 1982, it was this same passport that was confiscated by the Israeli officer. Facing the Post Office was the Boasta nightclub, which was more prestigious than its counterpart, the Zarifiya nightclub, at Clock Tower Square. Local artists as well as some from Egypt and Lebanon, including the then-rising Lebanese star Siham Rifqi, performed at the Boasta.

Past the club was a busy intersection where Iskandar Awad Street, the Jaffa-Tel Aviv road, and al-Mahatta Street met. A policeman regulated traffic from his perch underneath a steel shelter in the center of the intersection, which was so spacious as almost to form a square. On one side of this square was the Nabil Theater, and facing it across the street was the al-Rashid Theater; between the two were the offices of the Jerusalem Bus Company.

I shall end my journey of memory here at this intersection: we had to take al-Mahatta and Iskandar Awad Streets to get us to school; the Jaffa-Tel Aviv road marked the beginning of the area shared by Arab residents of Jaffa and the Jews of Tel Aviv. Here too stood the governor's headquarters, and the Criminal Investigating Department (CID), in whose cells hundreds of Palestinians were tortured as they struggled for their national cause.

What I have written about here are snapshots from, rather than the whole record impressed on, my memory. There are still hundreds of images and names that I did not include as I have tried to restrict myself to those images associated with meaningful landmarks, especially for those who do not know Jaffa, a city still remembered as the Bride of Palestine

If I were to be asked now whether I was still sure of our return to my homeland, nearly 60 years after that disastrous day when I was uprooted from it, I would not hesitate one second before answering "Yes."

Not for one moment has Jaffa, a symbol of the entire homeland, ever been forgotten, and the memory of the place has been passed on from one generation to the next. Never has a single Palestinian in the Diaspora ever admitted to an alternative homeland. Am I sure? Just ask any child born in any of the Diaspora refugee camps, including those in the West Bank or the Gaza Strip, about his or her home, and he or she will immediately recollect the name of the ancestral town or village: I'm from Jaffa; I'm from Haifa; I'm from al-Lid; I'm from al-Ramleh.

I shall certainly return to Palestine and Palestine will certainly be restored to me. It is only a matter of time, but no matter how long it takes, the outcome is certain.

2

FROM HOMELAND TO EXILE

Beirut received us with good grace. Her weather-beaten seafarers, who would often express themselves in coarse language with a generous sprinkling of curses, felt sorrow mixed with anger over the situation in Palestine. Crowds of refugees coming from Jaffa and Palestine's other seaports used whatever vessels they could find to reach Lebanon, although many also did not make it. In a short time, schools, mosques, and monasteries throughout Lebanon were filled with refugees. Tents were provided for them by the United Nations, the very international institution that was to blame for their displacement. The tents were set up at different locations in what became known as the refugee camps. Most of these camps are in place to this very day, with the exception of al-Nabatiyeh Camp, which was completely destroyed by Israeli shelling in 1974, and Jisr al-Basha and Tel al-Zaatar, which were wiped out in 1976 during the civil war with the loss of thousands of their inhabitants. The main camps in the south are al-Rashidieh, al-Bass, Bourj al-Shamali, Ein al-Helweh, and al-Miyeh wa Miyeh; in Beirut, the camps are Shatila, Mar Elias, Bourj al-Barajneh, and Dbayyeh; in the Bekaa Valley there are Goureau, Weifel, and Taalbaya; and finally in the north, the camps of al-Beddawi and Nahr al-Bared. In 2007 Nahr al-Bared was also virtually wiped out and its people displaced during fighting between the Lebanese army and members of the Fatah al-Islam extremist group.

It was in the aftermath of the 1948 war that the Palestinian people's wanderings began: here refugees were looking for shelter, there others were searching for their relatives, while others were trying to find some source of income to support themselves and their families. All, however, lived in the hope of returning to their homes within a month, perhaps two or three if the worse came to the worst. But everyone expected to go home.

Luckily, we had relatives in Beirut, so we did not need to look for the sort of refuge that others less fortunate than ourselves had to endure. After that, so sure was my father that we would be returning home soon, we rented a furnished apartment rather than finding a more permanent dwelling. Our choice of residence was Souq al-Gharb, a friendly mountain town that was overflowing with Palestinians, mostly from Jaffa. All of us, especially the young, developed solid friendships with the local people. We were to spend two years in Souq al-Gharb.

During the summer of 1948, I enrolled at the American University of Beirut (AUB), for the 1948–49 academic year. The results of the matriculation exams had been released by then, and I had received a telegram from Ibrahim Abu Lughod, congratulating me on having passed.

(1)

The AUB was one of the best academic institutions in the Arab world. Students came to study from Palestine, Jordan, Iraq, the Gulf, and even Egypt. Students from other Arab countries actually outnumbered their Lebanese counterparts, who tended to favor Francophone education and pursued their higher studies at the Jesuit St Joseph University. The AUB also had a solid record of pan-Arab nationalist activism. During my time, the key activists of the Arab Nationalist Movement (ANM) were George Habash, Wadie Haddad, and Hani al-Hindi, who together went on to found the Popular Front for the Liberation of Palestine (PFLP). There was also another Arab nationalist party, the Ba'th, whose goals and plans had been set by two young men from Syria: Michel Aflaq and Salah al-Din al-Bitar.

While at AUB I became acquainted with another new party, new to me at least because I had not heard of it in Jaffa, although I did recall having read a few things about its leader, Antoun Saadeh. This party was the Syrian Social Nationalist Party (SSNP), branches of which, I later discovered, had in fact been established in northern Palestine, particularly in Haifa and Acre. What intrigued me about this party was the extremely intense feelings of its members regarding Palestine, which they considered part of the Greater Syrian homeland.

In addition to the parties I have mentioned, I was surprised to discover a considerable number of communists from all Arab nations, who were united in a single organization under the leadership of Mansour Armali, a medical student from Shafa Amr in Palestine.

Mansour was later expelled from the university and eventually went to the United States where he became a famous ophthalmologist. Many other communist students who were expelled from the AUB and deported from Lebanon were imprisoned in their respective homelands.

It was only natural that senior student activists should welcome newcomers and try to recruit them into their respective organizations. The Palestinian cause was then at the vanguard of political activity and consequently was the fulcrum around which parties tried to attract new members. At the same time, students from Palestine were zealously searching for a political path to lead them back home: thus they constituted a noticeable presence in all of the parties, and were usually more radical and fervent than any of the other new recruits. *Al-Urwa al Wuthqa* (Solid Bond Union) and the University Student Council were the two most important political forums in which loyalty towards certain student activists was tested: victory for any electoral list in the leadership elections meant its members were extremely popular. Before elections, students would vie with each other delivering speeches and issuing statements, and given that there were not that many female students, it was considered a great achievement to attract young women to one's list.

Looking back, I am ashamed to say the spirit among students was not truly up to scratch: we often resorted to violence and physical clashes, and our fanaticism far exceeded our maturity. I say this only now, more than half a century later, perhaps because this perception is an inevitable aspect of the wisdom of old age, acquired after the passage of a great deal of time and many years' experience.

(2)

When I went up to university in 1948, I had promised my parents and myself that I would study medicine. My freshman year was not exciting, as most of my connections were outside AUB, mostly with friends from Palestine whose financial situation did not allow them to pursue their studies. We believed the best way to organize our people was to establish a physical location for our meetings and so we created *Nadi Filistiin* (the Palestine Club) and in the summer of 1949 we applied for official recognition from the Lebanese Ministry of Interior. Having submitted the required documents we headed to the office of the Arab Higher Committee, where we met with the

Mufti of Jerusalem, Hajj Amin al-Husseini, until 1948 the most important leader of Palestine. We presented him with our idea and requested his help. This venerable figure showed little interest and led us to understand indirectly that we were free to do whatever we wanted, as long as we kept his name out of whatever we did. Despite our disappointment, we were not that sorry about his refusal to support us, as deep inside us we held him, along with the entire Palestinian leadership, responsible for the tragedy that had befallen our people. In any case, as we expected, our project never made it through the official channels: the Ministry of Interior received our request and ignored it.

Coincidentally, during that year of 1949, there were serious developments in Lebanon: the SSNP attempted a coup against President Beshara al-Khoury and his government, headed at the time by Riad al-Solh. The government's reaction was so severe that it instilled a profound fear into the hearts of anyone thinking of undertaking serious political work. We realized we had no choice but to resort to underground activity, and so we founded what we called the Conference of Dispossessed Palestinians. We intentionally chose the word "dispossessed" to declare our rejection of the customary epithet "refugee," which we associated with humiliation and ignominy.

We began visiting one Palestinian camp after another in the various Lebanese provinces, which at the time were still composed entirely of tents. We wanted to mobilize our people and organize them into political structures that were capable of providing mature leadership. But things did not go very smoothly, largely because of the presence of the older generation of people still loyal to Hajj Amin al-Husseini. I remember one time some Husseini supporters laid an ambush for us at Bourj al-Barajneh Camp; they sent some of their men to provoke us and then summoned the gendarmes, accusing us of being communists. An accusation of communist sympathies was then the most common pretext used by the authorities to thwart nationalist movements. Around that time, we met some other young men who were also trying to organize the Palestinian people politically. Most of those were, or later became, closely associated with the ANM.

At university, the communists in particular attracted my attention because they concentrated on the students' demands for better living conditions: Palestinian students suffered the most in this regard. Feeling myself closer to the communists than to other groups, I joined their electoral list for the student elections and even became one of their representatives. Needless to say my activities were welcomed neither by the university administration nor the Lebanese security authorities; this led to my detention and imprisonment for the first time in my life. The story begins at noon, one day in the middle of the 1950–51 academic year.

I remember I was working in the chemistry lab when someone came by and told me I had to go and see the AUB vice president, Archie Crawford. The president at the time was Stephen Penrose; it was when I heard people talking about him that I first learned of the existence of the CIA. It is possible that Penrose was not a CIA agent, but he surely was more than just a university president, given that he seemed to be more influential in Lebanon than the US ambassador himself! In addition, he had solid ties with a number of powerful institutions in the United States that were at the time under the sway of McCarthyism.

I entered Crawford's secretary's office, and she asked me to wait, as the vice president was busy with some visitors. As I sat I noticed strange movements in the room and felt as though I was being watched.

The secretary finally asked me to go through. Mr Crawford stood up and greeted me in his broken Arabic. He then started questioning me about my extracurricular activities, both inside and outside the university. He expressed the view that what he called my "undesirable activities" could lead to "unrest and provocation," and said the Lebanese authorities agreed with his stand. I had just begun to defend myself, frankly and confidently, when I was surprised by the sudden appearance of two police inspectors, who had been concealed behind the curtains. They put me in handcuffs and took me to a jeep that had been waiting on campus near the Medical Gate. I must have made a strange sight to the students watching on as I was dragged to the car still wearing my white medical gown.

On the way to the police cells, I recalled a front-page article I had read two days earlier in the daily al-Hayat about the "exceptionally dangerous communist element among the Palestinians." I drew a connection between my arrest and this alleged communist activity. My hunch was right, as I saw two comrades from the Conference of the Dispossessed also being dragged to the jail on false grounds. When the interrogators could find nothing tangible with which to accuse me, they let me go, but that was after a whole week had passed. As for my comrades, they were immediately expelled and taken to the Lebanese–Palestinian (Israeli) border where they were dumped facing a fearsome dilemma: if they returned to Lebanon they would be wanted men, facing prison and torture, while if they entered Israel they faced an even worse threat. One of them managed to escape and eventually made it to Iraq, but I have heard nothing about him since then. The other was caught by the Syrian authorities, who handed him over to Jordan. He was taken to the Jafr Prison, where he spent more than eight years in jail.

I went back to the AUB, only to discover that I had been suspended for a whole year. There was no way I was going to meekly submit to this punishment, so I turned to my fellow students for support. They wrote several petitions on my behalf and even threatened to go on strike. But that particular year the university responded very harshly to political activism: more than 60 students were expelled, and later deported to their respective countries where they were imprisoned. Among those expelled, the unluckiest were the Iraqis: they were not released from the notorious Nuqrat al-Salman prison until the July 1958 revolution.

What made things worse for me was that my family's financial situation had become quite intolerable. We could no longer afford a furnished apartment and had to crowd together in a single room, in a property that had been designated as a religious endowment by Sheikh Abdul Rahman al-Hout, becoming a "camp" for the "refugees" of the family. Had it not been for a few dear friends, who always used to welcome me into their homes, I would have been crushed by despair at this time.

I began to look for a job, any job, but the accusation of being a communist was a serious obstacle. I worked for a time at a soap factory, which shortly thereafter went bankrupt; then I worked at an amusement park in Beirut; but these were temporary jobs that hardly paid for my cigarettes.

(3)

My most frequent haunt was the famous Faisal restaurant opposite the AUB main gate on Bliss Street. I would have my coffee there and they would kindly allow me to pay for it later, at my convenience. I would meet my friends and comrades there and feel the warm embrace of the university, despite the administration depriving me of my education that year. Faisal had acquired a reputation throughout the Arab world not only for its excellent food, but also as a gathering place for the student élite, many of whom later took up key positions in their respective countries. Strange as it may sound, some of them used to receive letters from their families at the following mailing address: "American University – opposite Faisal restaurant."

I was one of many who were deeply upset in the mid-1980s when Faisal closed its doors for the last time. That restaurant was like an intellectual club where students, academics, journalists, and party members, of diverse backgrounds and beliefs, would meet and interact. May God bless the soul of its owners, Farid Faisal and Najib Baroudi, who were among the most generous people I ever met in Lebanon. No doubt dozens of AUB graduates share my feelings; some of them paid their bills only years later, without ever having received a complaint or a reminder from these kind creditors.

Sitting at Faisal restaurant, I sometimes used to make arrangements with some well-off idler to make extra money by writing term papers for him on any subject. But that is how disaster eventually struck.

One day, I finished writing a study entitled *The Concept of Freedom in Capitalist and Communist Regimes* for an AUB political science student. I liked the paper, so I kept a copy for myself. At noon, I went to East Hall restaurant, which was located on Jeanne d'Arc Street near the university. For once I was quite sure I could pay for my meal, from the fee I had received for writing the paper. As I was eating, I felt a strong hand grasp my shoulder and I heard a voice asking me to identify myself. When I did so, I was told to get up, and I obeyed.

I was desperate to get rid of the papers in my pocket, but it was too late: they were quickly transferred to the officer's pocket and he asked me how it was that I was still in Lebanon. Apparently, a presidential decree calling for my deportation, signed by both the President of the Republic Beshara al-Khoury and Prime Minister Abdallah al-Yafi had recently been issued.

I replied: "I was never properly informed of this. I may have read something about it in the press but I thought there must have been a mistake. The proof of my good faith is that you found me here, in one of my usual haunts." Then I asked them where they expected me to go: I was a Palestinian whose homeland was occupied and who had no passport. The inspector nodded to his colleague and without another word they marched me to their car.

I was surprised when the car stopped in front of a restaurant in the Zaytouna quarter, right opposite the famous Kit Kat nightclub. The chief of police was there, drinking a glass of *arak* and smoking a *narguileh*. The officer whispered in his ear and handed him the papers he had found in my pocket. The commander said: "Take him to the lockup cell of the Sureté Générale. This is a dangerous leaflet! We shall hand it over to the court before he is deported."

The situation had become even worse than before: now I had two disasters to worry about instead of just one. The following day, they transferred me from the lockup to al-Raml Prison, where I was locked up with robbers, smugglers, and killers. The Lebanese branch of my family summoned its collective energy and knocked on the doors of all possible political leaders, ministers, and members of parliament. All of them washed their hands of me, as though I were a murderer or something.

As my trial approached, my family was happy to hear that the case was going to be heard by Judge Mahmoud Noman, whose wife was my father's cousin. However, a few hours before the first hearing, my father received a surprise visit from Judge Noman, who said: "I'm sorry but I have come to tell you that I have excused myself from Shafiq's case. I have asked that it be transferred to another judge. Verdicts for this kind of case are always made in advance of the trial. We receive them written and sealed in envelopes: we just open the envelope and read the verdict. I'm afraid this is politics at the highest level."

When I entered the courtroom and saw Judge Jean Baz sitting there, I looked towards my father, brothers, and friends, and I knew that I was done for.

In my defense, I could not tell the story of the term paper for fear it would hurt the friend for whom I had written it. So I said that the study was purely academic and it had nothing to do with the "instigation of sectarianism," which is what the prosecutor had accused me of. The judge then delivered the prescribed verdict: "Three months' imprisonment, following which the deportation decree will be put in effect."

In prison, I ran into a fellow student, Mustafa Madani from Sudan, who also faced deportation and had been waiting for his father to come to bail him out. Ironically, Mustafa returned to Lebanon years later as chargé d'affaires and, even later on, as ambassador, at the time when I had become the representative of the PLO in Lebanon.

I was finally released from prison in April 1951. In the meantime, my family's efforts had paid off with the new Prime Minister, Sami al-Solh, who had succeeded Abdallah al-Yafi and had promised to suspend the decree for my deportation. Nevertheless, my persecution did not end then and the decree was not rescinded until much later.

Pending the end of my interrupted scholastic year, I worked at the Makassed High School. My return to university was no straightforward matter however, as I had to go through a tough interrogation by the Disciplinary Committee, most of whose members were chairs of departments. In the end, they granted me re-admission, but under the following conditions: first of all, two warnings were entered into my file, which meant that if I were to commit any infraction incurring a third warning I would be expelled; secondly, I was not to participate in any kind of activism whatsoever, and I no longer had the right to run for election in any student organization; thirdly, I was asked to transfer my major to a subject which would secure my graduation with only a Bachelor's degree: I was no longer allowed to study medicine, regardless of my grades, as that would necessitate a further five years of study, something the university administration was not prepared to permit.

I had no choice but to accept these conditions, and selected psychology and biology as major and minor fields respectively. Dr Terry Prothro, a liberal anti-McCarthyist professor from the United States who was head of the Psychology Department and a member of the Disciplinary Committee, had stood very bravely in my defense, and that had influenced my choice of major.

My final year at university was uneventful, and I received my diploma in the graduation ceremony of the academic year 1952–53. On that day, I recall that Dr Constantine Zurayk, then acting president, said to me with a smile as he handed me my degree: "Now at last we can rest assured that we are done with your troubles!"

(4)

After graduating from university, I joined Ali Bin Abi Taleb Makassed High School again as a teacher. I stayed there for three years before I was suspended, for refusing to use my authority as a superintendent to prevent the students from demonstrating and striking against France, which had exiled King Mohammad V of Morocco from his own country.

Today I am proud of the solid friendships I maintain with a number of highly distinguished men in Lebanon who were students of mine, and I understand their warm feelings towards me, because I hold the same warm feelings towards my own teachers. One of my students was Nabih Berri, the current Speaker of the Lebanese Parliament and one of the most distinguished Lebanese political figures; whenever we get together he reminds me of those good old days.

Despite the harshness of the three years that I spent as a teacher – my financial resources were limited, my political persecution continued and the political situation was deteriorating – this period witnessed my first serious experience of love. I shall spare my reader details of this experience, but I should mention two lessons which I learned as a result. First, having been almost completely demoralized by my life up until this point, I regained confidence in both myself and the world in which I lived. Second, I discovered my inclination towards writing and my ability to develop into a profession something that could have remained a mere hobby. Surely there is nothing in life greater than love!

My main concern at the time was once and for all to be rid of that presidential decree ordering my deportation. I had tried all kinds of mediation, but all had failed. Then, I realized that the decree would simply become void if I obtained Lebanese citizenship, as the Lebanese constitution did not grant any official authority the right to deport people who were Lebanese citizens.

I was delighted with this discovery, knowing that my grandfather had always made sure to register his children in the official Lebanese records. All my father had to do was to go to the Census Office and obtain a certificate showing his name in the records; that would enable him to acquire a Lebanese identity card. I would then be eligible for my card as well and the accursed decree would be revoked.

But my father – God rest his soul – refused to apply, as he thought that the establishment of his Lebanese citizenship implied abandoning his Palestinian one and he found this prospect unthinkable. I admit that I was flabbergasted by his stand, especially as my father had never turned down any of our requests. One spring evening of that same year, while we were sitting on the balcony at sunset, he took a deep breath and said: "Oh God! Do you smell the oranges?" A few seconds later, he continued: "This is orange blossom time!" I always knew that one could recall images from the past, but I had no idea that a vivid remembrance of a certain smell was equally possible! This moment helped me understand the mysterious nature of the relationship between a man and the land. My father refused to be naturalized as a Lebanese citizen decades before the Lebanese leaders became aware of the dangerous implications of such a move!

So I still had to get around this problem. What did I do? I filed a legal claim.

One Wednesday, which was the day dedicated to citizenship cases, the judge opened my file and looked through the papers. A minute later, he adjourned the case to another Wednesday, weeks later. Though frustrated and feeling hopeless, I went to the court on the appointed day. This time the judge opened my file and was about to postpone my case again, but hesitated for a second and then asked me: "Why you don't have a lawyer to handle your case?" I made the well-known Arab hand gesture indicating that I had no money and could therefore not afford such assistance. He contemplated me further, and then he said: "Come back next Wednesday, but I want to see you after the sessions are over: wait for me in front of my chambers."

Later on this brave judge, Henry Shaghoury, received me with a smile, and asked: "What's the problem, son? Don't you know that your documents are practically worthless? They are incomplete and uncertified. So what's your story? Tell me and don't worry: this will be off the record."

I told him the whole story and, although he tried to hide it, I could see that he was profoundly affected by my plight. He said: "I'll see you next Wednesday and hopefully everything will be fine." And as I was heading towards the door, I heard him say: "And there is no need for the documents I asked you for this morning."

That week was probably the longest in my life; I worried night and day, until Wednesday finally arrived: it was the day in which the impartial Lebanese judicial system, on behalf of the Lebanese people, granted me my Lebanese citizenship.

With tears streaming down my face, I stammered a whispered "Thank you" to the judge who changed the course of my life.

Outside the Hall of Justice, one of the janitors was waiting, and expressed his joy at the verdict. He told me that Judge Shaghoury had asked him to check with the Census Office and verify the presence of a document concerning my father; he had managed to obtain a copy of this document for the judge but only after investing considerable effort. I understood what he meant, and I gave him all the money I had in my pocket, which was very little. I then continued on my way, almost flying with joy.

(5)

I was awakened one day in 1956 by the noise of a workman banging away with his hammer as he hung a sign for a new office in front of my house. The sign consisted of a single word, in big red letters: *Al-Hawadeth* (The Events). Underneath it, there were three words in smaller print and black ink: "Arabic – Political – Weekly." That morning marked another turning point in my life, and the beginning of long-term relief from my problems. I had met the owner of the magazine, Salim al-Lawzi, through a common friend, Subhi Abu Lughod, a broadcaster whose connection with al-Lawzi dated back to the Near East Broadcasting Station in Jaffa.

I began work at *al-Hawadeth* on the first rung of the professional ladder. I started to write, draft, and draw, and I carried the wooden printing plates to the print shops. I loved the ambiance there and made friends with the printers and type-setters. One worry remained, however: my family's financial situation. Despite Salim al-Lawzi's appreciation of my efforts, he was not able to offer generous remuneration, especially as his magazine was still in its infancy. Seeking a more lucrative job began to seem like a good idea. The Kingdom of Saudi Arabia and Kuwait had by that time started to produce oil in massive quantities and they had an exponentially increasing need for manpower. Thousands of Arabs, especially unemployed Palestinians who had been forced from their homes in 1948, went to play their part in the oil revolution, as manual workers, professionals, and teachers.

But in order to travel to the Gulf, I had to get a passport, and a new torture began. According to the law, I had first to obtain an identification card, which proved my Lebanese citizenship. I launched the process, but was told that I had to wait a month during which the attorney general could appeal against the decision to grant me a card. If he did, then I would have to wait for the verdict of the Appeals Court; if he didn't, then the decision would become final and not subject to any future appeals.

The attorney general at that time was Judge Othman Beik al-Dana, later a deputy and a friend. Othman Beik was a member of the Council of Education of the Makassed. He was also aware, as I discovered later, of all my previous troubles, including my quarrels with the Makassed administration and the termination of my tenure at Ali Bin Abi Taleb High School. When I requested permission to enter his office, he received me stiffly and said: "I won't appeal against you, but don't imagine that I will sign my approval before the end of the month." I tried to persuade him to do it sooner, as I might lose several employment opportunities abroad because of this delay, but he did not budge.

I did not lose hope, and I continued to visit the Palace of Justice on an almost daily basis, searching for a way out. One day, I ran into one of Othman Beik's aides, who had taken maximum advantage of his contacts with the attorney general, who was at that time aggressively pursuing a seat in parliament. This man's role was to facilitate transactions. Having noticed the frequency of my visits, he enquired about the nature of my problem, and I told him. He coughed, then said: "Have you got £25 on you?" I answered: "No," which was the truth. "Never mind the 25, give me £10!" he said. Finally, his price went all the way down to £5, which was all I had. He left the room, but within less than half an hour he was back, carrying the document, complete with Othman Beik's signature!

Years later, I asked Othman Beik what had happened, and he said: "Actually, I had already signed your papers but delayed their submission. This man knew that, so he must have stolen them from the file and handed them over to you."

On August 25, 1955, I finally received my Lebanese identity card. I placed it in my pocket and guarded it carefully till I made it home.

(6)

My prospects improved radically in spring 1956, when a committee from the Kuwaiti Ministry of Education came to Beirut in order to recruit teachers from all disciplines. The committee's chairman was Abdul Aziz al-Hussein, a Kuwaiti, and it included two Palestinian members: Darwish al-Meqdadi, one of the senior Arab educators, and Hasan al-Dabbagh, who had taught me at al-Ameriya in Jaffa and had earned my utmost respect.

I made it through the interview, and managed to secure a contract. I was overjoyed, for several reasons: first, I felt that my family's finances might now improve; second, I had a number of Palestinian friends in Kuwait; and third, I was keen on pursuing higher studies, including a PhD in psychology, and so I had to make – and save – money.

Since I had to be in Kuwait by early September, I went straight to the headquarters of the Sureté Générale and submitted my application for a passport, including all necessary support documents and attachments. Theoretically, I should have been able to collect my passport within days, after the routine paperwork was done.

On the appointed day, I went to the headquarters and stood in line along with dozens of other applicants. At about 12 o'clock, an employee began calling out names. As soon as an applicant heard his name called, he would go up and be handed his passport by the employee, and then sign the receipt. My turn came, and I rushed to the man, holding a pen in my hand ready to sign, but he withdrew the receipt and put it back in the supposedly approved passport. He said abruptly: "There is a question about your application, and the director did not sign it."

I asked what I should do, and he answered unsympathetically: "I don't know. Sort it out yourself!"

Lebanese security during the time of President Beshara al-Khoury, as well as his successor Camille Chamoun, was organized in a single unit: the Sureté Générale. Its director was Farid Shehab, from a family whose princely heritage earned them the honorary title of *Amir* (prince). Shehab had maintained an ironfisted policy, and he was well connected with the British, French, and American embassies, and would often obey their instructions with alacrity, especially when it came to communists and Palestinians.

I knew I was about to confront the most difficult man in Lebanon, tougher than any of the prosecutors I had faced up until then. Despite that, I tried desperately to win him over and convince him to abandon his opposition and leave me in peace, but I failed. Time was running out, and September was approaching with no apparent hope.

One day, I met an old friend of mine at Faisal's: he was a member of the Andrawos family from Zahleh. I told him about my problem, and just as I finished, he said: "I can help you. Get up. Let's go." I asked: "Where to?" He said: "To Zahleh, to see my uncle, Bishop Niveen Saba, as he's the only one whose requests are never turned down by Prince Farid." We talked on the journey and I learned that

Farid Shehab had owed the Bishop a major favor because the latter had facilitated the process of an inter-sectarian marriage between a Greek Orthodox lady and a Maronite man. I do not remember whether this marriage involved Farid himself or a friend of his.

Bishop Saba was a progressive man who was interested in world peace movements and other humanitarian activities. He received us warmly, and heard me out with interest and patience. The moment I finished, he went to his desk and took out a paper; he scribbled a few words on it, folded it, and put it in an open envelope. I recall every word he wrote:

> To my son, Amir Farid Shehab. Greetings .... Shafiq al-Hout is one of two things: either he is innocent and a victim of injustice, in which case he deserves to be treated justly, or he is really a threat to national security, as your reports claim. If your information is correct, granting him the passport and facilitating his departure would be good news for you.

I spent that long night waiting impatiently for sunrise, as I wanted to be the first person at the Sureté Générale headquarters.

Prince Farid had read the letter before he received me. The minute I stepped into his office, he shouted: "I want to know just who was that son of a (...) who helped you reach the Bishop?" I froze, trying to take in what was happening and trying to keep calm. I quoted the proverb: "Ask no questions, hear no lies." He shouted again: "You will tell me who it was ... immediately." I stood still once more, and then said: "Just someone who cares for the bishop, for you, and for me." Perceiving that I was not to be browbeaten, he cooled down a little and said: "The bishop is dear to us, and we can't let him down. But you must issue a statement to the Lebanese newspapers distancing yourself from the Communist Party."

I knew that such a declaration would tarnish my reputation and highlight my defeat, especially as this demand had by that time become habitual, particularly for people accused of being commu-nists, although later it came to include others, including adherents of the Arab nationalist parties.

I can't remember what I felt at that moment, whether threatened or desperate. Whichever it was, something made me say bluntly that I would do no such thing, as I was not a member of the Communist Party, and the declaration of my innocence would confirm rather than negate the accusation. Before I excused myself and left, I felt a strong hand pushing me out the door by the shoulder, and the director's voice thundered at me again: "Don't you ever let me see your face here again. I have no passport for you."

A new go-between entered my life at this time. He approached me one day and, in a strong Beiruti dialect, said: "I've been watching you go back and forth to the Sureté Générale many times. What's your problem?" History was repeating itself and even the amount of the requested bribe was the same. The man asked me whether I had £25 on me, and added that he had intended to help me for nothing, but there were others who had to be taken care of. This time I did not try to lower the price, and borrowed some money from a friend of mine who had accompanied me.

A few minutes later, the passport, valid for a period of five years and for visits to all countries, was done, signed.

After I ascertained that the passport and the signature were genuine, I said to the go-between: "Give me your name and address, and I swear that I will send you a gift of £100, on condition that you tell me how you managed to get the signature."

In fact, the man was decent, as he said: "You need neither my name nor my address, and I don't want your gift. The whole story is that the director general usually signs the passports at around twelve noon, at which time the employee responsible for them would have placed all the passports in a pile, each open to the approval page. The passports that have a problem don't even make it to his office, but remain on the dusty shelves awaiting solutions. What happened today is that one of the employees managed to place your passport in the stack awaiting formal approval, and the director signed it without looking."

(7)

I was thrilled to get my passport, which implied freedom and the restoration of my personal dignity. But this joy did little to help me to forget the insult I had felt as a result of Farid Shehab's treatment, not only of me but also all those who valued freedom of thought. Several years passed, but the wound never healed. In the early 1960s, I had become the editor of *al-Hawadeth* (reporting to Salim al-Lawzi, its founder), and Prince Farid had been relieved of his position at the Sureté Générale, and was now Lebanese ambassador in Tunisia.

Once again, destiny played a major role in the following episode: Prince Farid was suspected of misusing his diplomatic immunity in pursuit of personal financial gains. *Al-Hawadeth* had published news of this, and I personally followed up the case, gathered all its details, and prepared to publish the story in several installments. As I had been expecting, Shehab contacted the Editor-in-Chief, Salim al-Lawzi, and set up an appointment to see him in our office. Salim had no knowledge of our previous encounter. When he asked me to put off the publication of anything relating to the scandal until we had heard what the man had to say, I asked him to invite me to sit in on the meeting. He agreed.

Shehab arrived and, protesting his innocence, contended that the story being circulated was based on nothing but one-sided rumors spread around by his political opponents. He asked us to stop our campaign. Before answering, Salim asked the Amir, who clearly had not recognized the passport applicant of four years earlier, to hear me out, and I said: "I just want to ask the Amir why he is so keen on suppressing the news related to his accusation, given that he is innocent and able to prove his innocence."

He answered haughtily: "Because I don't want to tarnish my reputation, as my dignity is more important than anything." I responded: "In that case, what about the dignity of other people? Does that mean nothing to you? When you were in charge of the Sureté Générale, did you verify the reports you had in your hands before having people detained or expelled from the country, or preventing them from traveling abroad?"

At this point Amir Farid appeared to begin feeling a little uneasy. He sat up, put on his eyeglasses and stared at me for a long time. Finally, recognizing me, he said: "It's you!" He smiled an artificial smile in an effort to calm me down and said: "Maybe we were a bit unfair with you. But what do you want now? This is all in the past and behind us."

I replied: "I want you to issue a statement in which you deny all the accusations against you and express your defiance of everyone who stands behind them. We will then print it on the front page of the magazine."

"No ... no ..." he remonstrated. "Let us not make a big deal of this. As I told you, bringing up such news would tarnish my reputation and my dignity."

At that point, I got up and shouted at him:

"And how come you didn't think of my reputation or dignity when you asked me to proclaim in the press my innocence of any relation with Communism, and when you deprived me of my right to obtain a passport?"

Salim al-Lawzi got up from his chair and pressed my shoulders to make me sit down. Then he addressed the Amir:

"I think you owe Shafiq an apology. And I hope you do that, not for his sake, but for yours, so that he can regain inner peace and be able to forgive and forget."

And so it was.

(8)

Let me, after this digression, return to the autumn of 1956.

By the time I had a passport, I had missed the beginning of the academic year in Kuwait by more than a week, but I traveled nevertheless. The day after I received my passport, I bade farewell to my family and my colleagues at *al-Hawadeth*. I had an agreement with Salim al-Lawzi to continue working with him as a reporter, but from Kuwait. I headed to the airport and boarded a Shiarco Airlines plane, which was used for the delivery of both passengers and cargo.

Back in the 1950s, Kuwait was quite different from the way it is today: architectural evolution in the Gulf states was still in its infancy at that time. Although Kuwait was just beginning to enjoy its boom, its old architectural style and ancient walls still stood. There was no air conditioning at the time; we had to make do with fans, when we could find them. We also used to buy water from tankers and had to filter it using a large funnel stuffed with white cotton, which would become muddy in no time. The best restaurants were those of the Pakistanis and Indians, and those were quite crowded, especially at lunchtime.

Life in Kuwait was harsh, but those who worked there were happy they had a job and so ignored the hardships. In this regard, Palestinians were pioneers: having lost their homeland, identity, and rights, they were struggling to get their lives back on track. There is no doubt that Kuwait, like Saudi Arabia, was one of the early venues that witnessed the birth of a new and diversified kind of Palestinian society, following the Palestinians' arbitrary scattering around the lands of exile. One could run into Palestinians from Jordan, Syria, the West Bank, the Gaza Strip and other places. These people were not referred to as "refugees," but *wafidoun* (newcomers).

My Gulf experience lasted less than two years, from 1956 to 1958, but it was nevertheless quite rewarding, at both a personal and a public level. Those years coincided with the first serious beginnings of the modern renaissance of Arab nationalism as well as the first strategic Arab reaction to the Palestinian debacle of 1948. The July 1952 revolution had succeeded in Egypt, and in July 1956 enthusiasm for the Arab Nationalist movement reached its peak when Abdul Nasser declared the nationalization of the Suez Canal, thereby challenging two of the great powers of the time: Great Britain and France. I lived through the repercussions of this event, the most important of which was the Tripartite Aggression – British, French, and Israeli – against Egypt. Prior to that, Abdul Nasser had already defied the entire Western world when he struck the famous arms deal with Czechoslovakia and broke the Western monopoly of Middle East arms sales which had been in place since the end of World War One.

I continued my work as a correspondent of *al-Hawadeth*, reporting mainly on public and official reactions in the Gulf. Like Lebanon, Kuwait was a lively arena of disputes and dialogue, as it included all kinds of diverse political views. The Kuwaiti press then was not like it is today, either in quantity or quality, and therefore there was plenty of space for coverage in the other Arab media, especially the Egyptian and Lebanese.

The main prerequisites of journalism are transparency and openness that allow readers to assess a writer quite quickly. I used to feel positive reaction to my writing, which encouraged me to invest more effort in it, as it was finally clear to me that I had a real chance of becoming a professional writer. Despite the temptations offered by my comparatively good salary, I remained in the Gulf only for a relatively short time, electing to return to Lebanon to work as a journalist there. I cannot deny that the national problems that were spreading throughout the Arab World at that time, in parallel with the continuing struggle for Palestine, doubled my eagerness to take this crucial step.

3

FROM JOURNALISM TO POLITICS

I returned to Beirut in mid-May 1958. At that time, the tension between President Chamoun and the opposition, which included an alliance between Prime Minister Saeb Salam and the leader of the Progressive Socialist Party (PSP), Kamal Jumblatt, reached its peak. *Al-Hawadeth* was politically neutral at the time because Salim al-Lawzi's inclination was towards socio-cultural journalism rather than politics. But he had clashed personally with President Chamoun and as a result of this he found himself constantly persecuted and threatened. Eventually he sought refuge in Damascus.

All of a sudden I found myself responsible for bringing out the entire magazine, from cover to cover. Having myself naturally been drawn towards politics, I now moved more firmly towards this calling. Consequently, and for the first time in the history of *al-Hawadeth*, well-established political writers such as Munah al-Solh, Maurice Saqr, and Bassem al-Jisr joined the editorial family. The magazine was now set upon a serious path, and the moral force of the articles, photographs, and caricatures led to increased sales and distribution. This was good news for Salim, who was still writing from Damascus and enjoying the recognition. When he returned to Beirut, his political zeal was rekindled; Chamoun had been defeated and the opposition had prevailed. This led Salim to open up new avenues to promote the further development and progress of the magazine.

(1)

As the magazine grew, so did I. I met key people in politics, economics, in the trade unions, and the arts. At the time, Beirut prided itself on its hotels and restaurants, nightclubs, and cafés. The city became the social hub for Arab public life, a gathering place for people engaged in politics from widely disparate political views. Its periodicals of the time reflected this. The political classes also used to respect – even fear – the well-known journalists. No member of parliament, minister, or public servant of any rank could start the day without reading the views of Ghassan Tuweini, Michael Abu Jawdeh, George Nakkash, Said Frayha, Salim al-Lawzi, or Riad Taha. Beirut's nightlife was as rich as its political counterpart. This was especially true during summer, when Lebanon would be crammed with tourists and summer vacationers, not to mention political refugees or guests, whether writers or artists.

But there were other aspects to Beirut, which began to manifest themselves in the development of deep social and political divisions: firstly there was the presence of what used to be called the "poverty belt" surrounding the capital; secondly there were the opposing positions taken in regard to affairs across the Arab world, including the Palestinian cause, the Algerian revolution, and the aspirations of the nationalist movement regarding Arab unity.

Camille Chamoun's defeat and the fact that he was unable to run for a second term as president implied victory of a kind for nationalism and defeat for the colonialist intervention that Chamoun had supported. Unfortunately though, that victory did not produce similarly positive results, either in internal Lebanese politics or in the prevailing economic situation. There was no doubt however, that Chamoun's successor, General Fouad Chehab, intended radical reforms. His platform was concerned with the construction of a "state of independence" which he believed could be achieved by strengthening public institutions, for example the Office of Central Audits, the Central Inspection Office and the Ministry of Planning. He also sought help from Father Louis Joseph Lebret, founder of the Institut de Recherches et de Formation en vue de Developpement, resulting in the Lebret Report, whose main objectives were the proper direction of the economy and meeting the needs of the majority through social security and public health services. After adopting these policies however, President Chehab was faced with militant opposition from the conventional political cadres, which in turn provoked the Military Intelligence Organization to intervene in political affairs. The unfortunate consequences were more violence resorted to by the president's "military men" and more corruption at the heart of the very institutions that were meant to be the engines of reform.

Al-Hawadeth supported President Chehab in domestic policy, and

President Nasser in Arab affairs. As a consequence, the magazine
had no worries about contradictions in its editorial position, except
in one area: the unacceptably harsh treatment of the Palestinians at
the hands of the Lebanese Military Intelligence. It is important to
remember that successive Lebanese governments, from the *Nakba*
until this very day, have turned a blind eye to the presence of Palestinian refugees in Lebanon except in matters related to security.
Indeed the basis that has always underpinned Lebanese policy
towards the refugees has been fear. Al-Shu'ba al-Thaniya, or the
Deuxième Bureau – the commonly used terms for Military Intelligence – had become the absolute ruler of the Palestinian people in
Lebanon and all the cards were in the its hands. No single agreement
was made that laid out the Palestinians' rights or obligations as
refugees.

Thanks to my position at *al-Hawadeth*, I was fully aware of what
was going on inside the Palestinian refugee camps, including the
oppression and subjugation of people there, and how any effort to
establish any kind of collective action was crushed, even if it was just
an educational or sporting initiative.

I was unable to publish stories of the many sad and shameful acts
of violence committed against Palestinians by officers well known for
their brutality. I could only refer to them indirectly. But that did not
mean I spared any effort to mitigate some of these racist policies by
direct contact with political and military officials.

(2)

During President Chehab's term, the first public administration in
charge of Palestinian refugee affairs was established and it became
responsible for all their personal administrative transactions, such as
the registration of births and deaths, the issuing of travel documents,
and coordination with the UN relief agency, UNRWA. But in fact
this administration remained under the jurisdiction of the Deuxieme
Bureau, a representative of which even sat at a desk in one of its
offices.

Despite all of the above, the establishment of the United Arab
Republic of Egypt and Syria in early February 1958 brought some
hope to the Palestinians in Lebanon. The slogan *al-wahdah tareeq
al-tahreer* ("The road to liberation lies in unity") was heard above
all others. To the Palestinians, Arab unity was more than just a

dream that they, like other Arabs, yearned for; nor was it merely a cautious vision of a better future for the Arab world. To the Palestinians, Arab unity meant the end of the Zionist nightmare and the restoration of Arab Palestine. For them, a unified Arab state heralded a kind of massive pincer operation around the whole of occupied Palestine. Israel's Prime Minister, David Ben-Gurion, went further and described it as a "nutcracker."

The fact of the matter was that the Palestinians were inclined towards unity principally because they had never had a chance at independence or even autonomy, even as a mere formality, as other Arab peoples had. Because of this, Palestinian society had never engendered a social class which benefited from the partition of Greater Syria that was imposed by the Sykes–Picot Agreement in World War One; the people, therefore, remained committed to their unionist ideology. Furthermore, until the early 1960s, the Palestinians had never been chauvinistic: throughout their history they had always welcomed non-Palestinian Arab figures as military or political leaders, and their anthems used to praise such leaders as the Syrian-born martyr Sheikh Ezz Eddeen al-Qassam, commando leader Fawzi al-Kawekji, who was Lebanese, and the martyr Ahmad Abdul Aziz, who was born in Egypt. Today, there are still non-Palestinian Arab leaders of Palestinian factions.

Because of these attitudes, the Palestinians were deeply saddened and frustrated when in September 1961 the United Arab Republic split apart into its two national components, Syria and Egypt. The grief was enormous, and it particularly hit those Palestinians who belonged to pan-Arabist parties and factions such as the Ba'thists, the Nasserites, and the Arab Nationalists. Even the Palestinian communists were deeply hurt and blamed their Syrian and Iraqi comrades for not having been adequately conscious of the importance of preserving unity.

Nationalist and progressive Palestinians did not accept the arguments posited by their Syrian, Egyptian, or Iraqi counterparts justifying the split; though they admitted that the United Arab Republic had committed mistakes, they always argued that the "Disunion" was a sin, a great sin.

(3)

Beirut, with its press and its social and political clubs and cafès, was at the forefront of the intellectual debate about pan-Arabism. There were people who wished to add fuel to the raging political fire, as well as others of goodwill trying to reinforce the main Arab line and reverse the dissolution of the UAR by rectifying the mistakes that had led to the split.

From my position as editor of *al-Hawadeth*, which was known for its support of Nasserite Egypt, I had plenty of opportunity to see and hear what was going on, and I contributed to the defense of the Arab union as both idea and state. I was always keen on achieving rapprochement between the factions of the Arab nationalist movement. My office became a gathering place for Arab political figures, writers, poets, and freedom fighters. We used to debate the issues, write about them, carry messages between parties, travel from one capital to another, and meet with leaders and officials. Our aim was to help resolve the crisis, and we kept our fingers crossed that the state of division and disunity would not last long.

Our hopes were bolstered when a military coup was launched against the Syrian government of Nazem al-Qudsi who had presided over the dissolution of the Union. A new government, headed by Salah ad-Din al-Bitar, one of the pioneers of the Arab Socialist Ba'th Party, was formed. When I heard the news I got in my car and drove at breakneck speed towards Damascus. At al-Masnaa on the Lebanese–Syrian border, I met dozens of Arab and foreign reporters who like me had rushed from Beirut to cover the story. It was hard for me to hide my joy and not to gloat at those colleagues of mine who were obviously unhappy about the new state of affairs. But my joy ended when the Syrian border officer approached and told me that I was forbidden from entering Syria. I asked the man whether there was a possibility of some mistake, but he said "no." I asked him which blacklist he had based his decision on, as each era had its own lists, but he refused to answer. He handed me my passport and at that moment I happened to look at the wall behind him, only to see Nazem al-Qudsi's picture still hanging there. I took the passport and said: "In any case, it seems there is no need for my visit. I thought a coup had taken place in Damascus against the dissolution of the Union and those who supported it, but apparently this was just a rumor."

I went back to Beirut, as sad as I could have been. My colleague Wafiq al-Tibi, a well-known Nasserite who had traveled with me, had been given the same treatment at the border. We sent a telegram to Prime Minister al-Bitar to tell him what had happened and he replied with apologies and invited us to go again. But I did not go. My anguish was not personal: Arab citizens, and particularly journalists and writers, are used to being humiliated and insulted at Arab borders. It was rooted in the realization that what those who had broken up the Egyptian–Syrian Union had destroyed in one day would require decades to rebuild. Thousands of Palestinians had been aware of the depth of the tragedy and had tried, as I had, to find an alternative to the dissolution. The Union was a historic opportunity that the Arabs had wasted, because some officials in Damascus had been infiltrated and were actually working for anti-union Arab and Western powers. As for the Egyptians, Abdul Nasser had been surrounded with aides who had not understood the significance of the Union to the Arab world.

(4)

In the early 1960s, the need increased for the creation of a Palestinian organization to try to revive a Palestinian national entity. This was an inevitable result of the failure of the Arab nationalist ideal of union between Arab states, and the resurgence of a narrower and more local nationalism. Several movements towards the realization of this Palestinian organization arose in different geographical locations: concentrations in the West Bank and Gaza; refugee camps in Syria, Jordan, and Lebanon; communities in Saudi Arabia and Kuwait, as well as other Gulf states. The effect of these Palestinian national stirrings was felt as far away as the Americas. There was no doubt that the success of the Algerian revolution, which had earned the respect of the entire world, helped to intensify these movements. Consequently, it was only natural to expect that this trend would receive wide support, even from Palestinians committed to pan-Arab movements, such as Ba'thists, Arab Nationalists, and Nasserites. These found no contradiction between their main political commitments and involvement in nascent Palestinian organizations on a local level. As a matter of fact, they had already initiated the trend within their respective organizational structures by beginning to demand the creation of dedicated Palestinian units.

As part of this trend, in Beirut in 1961, we founded the Palestine Liberation Front, or PLF. (This group is unrelated to the one that currently bears the same name.) The original nucleus was composed of Khaled al-Yashruti, Abdul Muhsen Abu Mayzar, Nicola al-Durr,

Samira Azzam, Said Baraka, Raji Sahyoun, Shafiq al-Hout, and others. We concentrated our activities on a call for the establishment of a Palestinian national organization which would become part of the pan-Arab liberation movement. *Al-Hawadeth* was the main platform of our front, and it played a major role in disseminating this idea to areas with large concentrations of Palestinians. There was a notable increase in the number of letters to the editor, including questions about the new PLF, whether it was already active and, if so, how people could join it. I used to handle the mail both openly, that is in print on the pages of the magazine, and also privately, by responding personally to letters.

By the end of 1961, in the wake of the collapse of the UAR, disputes broke out among the founder members of the PLF, particularly those who belonged to pre-existing political parties who felt uneasy about their new dual commitment. As a matter of fact most of the expanded membership of the PLF were independents, people deeply committed to a single goal: the foundation of a Palestinian Arab organization that would be immune to the conflicts among members of various political parties and the contradictions in their different positions.

It was amicably agreed to dissolve the nucleus of the front. However, the independent members, Nicola al-Durr, Samira Azzam, Said Baraka, Abdul Qader al-Daher, and myself – decided to go ahead with the process of consolidating the front; with the help and support of new members we started to lay down the main principles and rules of the front in preparation for its official launch. After that was achieved, the first issue of a new periodical, *Tariq al-Awda* (Path of Return), was published in 1963. The front also set about developing branches in Gaza, Syria, Kuwait, Egypt, Algeria, and the United States, where several of our old friends resided, including some from al-Ameriya school in Jaffa. These were particularly active in distributing *Tariq al-Awda* and in recruiting students into the front.

The front also included some employees of UNRWA, which was a crucial hub for the Palestinian refugees. Hundreds of young men worked in the various departments of UNRWA, education, administration, health, and so on, and it became very important for us to concentrate on those who constituted its cadres. We managed to get to a large popular base, thanks to the help of a group of young men who expended great efforts in widening the communication network of the front, taking advantage of the means that UNRWA could offer, as well as their own contacts inside the camps. *Al-Hawadeth* was our bridge to the Gaza Strip, where the pioneering supporters included the well-known poet Mouin Bseyso, along with several other leftists, in addition to a group of young Nasserites who had been studying in Egyptian universities.

I was frequently asked about the identity of the leader of the Palestine Liberation Front, or its secretary general. My answer never satisfied the enquirers, but now I think it is time to clarify this matter. I was one of the founders, and actually the most senior of them, but I never considered this to be an organizational position or grounds for leadership. By my very nature I am uninterested in formal positions. Fame never meant much to me, especially that I had already enjoyed a degree of it as a journalist: my reputation in that field preceded my political reputation. In the group, we were all friends and comrades, true believers in the importance of teamwork and decentralized leadership, but circumstances always meant that I was sitting in the driver's seat. Prior to the foundation of the PLF, my position at *al-Hawadeth* was extremely important as a base for communication and meetings between the various Palestinian factions and their leaders. When I became director of the Palestine Liberation Organization office in Beirut, it was only natural that I should also become the head of the PLF, especially as I had represented it in 1968 and 1969 when I was a member of the Executive Committee of the PLO.

I wish to note here that the success of the PLF lay in our untiring efforts to unite the various Palestinian revolutionary factions in the 1960s. Later on we were to call for the dissolution of the factions as separate entities and for their integration into the overall framework of the PLO. Indeed, to provide an example, we went as far as to break up our own front, and placed all our facilities and human resources at the service of the PLO.

(5)

In the 1960s, the number of Palestinian fronts and organizations increased gradually until finally there were 17 of them, most of which had almost identical goals and programs relating to the liberation of Palestine and the rightful return of the refugees to their homes and properties. Of these 17 groups, Fatah was the most interesting, as it included leaders still unknown to most people, although information had leaked out that most of them had been closely associated with the Muslim Brotherhood or the Islamic Liberation Party. Their magazine *Filisteenuna* (Our Palestine) which was published in Beirut, substantiated this information.

The closest Palestinian nationalist group to us was one that carried an almost identical name to ours: the Palestine National Liberation Front, or PNLF. Very soon, we got together and coordinated our efforts, particularly in regard to our respective positions vis-à-vis the PLO, the foundation of which was imminent. In 1966 and 1967 we formed a coalition, and later, in 1968, we secured membership in the Third Executive Committee of the PLO for Ahmad al-Saadi, from PNLF, as well as Ahmad Sidqi al-Dajani and myself, from PLF.

Our relationship with the founders of Fatah was problematic and we were in constant disputes with them. We used to publish comments on their literature which appeared in *Filisteenuna* as well as in various Gulf newspapers, usually in our own periodical *Tariq al-Awda* as well as in *al-Hawadeth* and elsewhere. The most significant points of conflict were the dialectical relationship between the Palestinian cause and the pan-Arab nationalist struggle, for example in Algeria, and the nature of the armed struggle which the Palestinians should adopt. We rejected the theory of "entanglement" (getting Arab regimes involved in a war against Israel) initiated by Khaled al-Hassan, one of the founders of Fatah, for we believed that decisions of war or peace should be taken only on a pan-Arab level, governed by a united Arab strategy and administered by a responsible leadership. These disagreements never caused serious conflict between us and Fatah, and we discovered that we still needed extra time to get to know one another better and reinforce our mutual friendship and trust.

My first meeting with Khalil al-Wazir, "Abu Jihad" (general commander of al-Assifa, the military force linked to Fatah), took place in mid-1961. A mutual friend, the artist Ismail Shammout, arranged the meeting. I was impressed by Abu Jihad's sincerity and modesty. His beliefs were quite simple: Palestine belonged to the Palestinian people but had been usurped by the enemy, and so we had to retrieve it by force. If you were to ask him about the ideological or financial bases necessary for any national military action, he would answer that the revolution they were planning would impose its own ideas and theories in due course through practice and experience.

A few months after my meeting with Abu Jihad, Yasser Arafat paid a surprise first visit to my office in *al-Hawadeth* in Beirut. He refused to identify himself to the secretary and our meeting was necessarily brief as he was on his way to Algeria, so we agreed to follow up with other meetings and activities, and he suggested that Salah Khalaf, "Abu Iyad," who was the second-in-command of Fatah, should be the link between us in the future. When it was time for him to leave, I walked him to the door and we stood there talking for a moment. Although I knew that he was unwelcome in Cairo because of his earlier association with the banned Muslim Brotherhood, I asked him: "Are you planning to stop in Cairo on your way to Algiers?"

Having understood the implication of my question, he answered: "Soon enough I will, *inshallah* [God willing]. We are counting on you to pave the way for such a visit, because the leaders in Cairo have a distorted image of us in Fatah."

Communication later actually was conducted with Abu Youssef al-Najjar, whose family had maintained good business relations with mine. He was from Yebna, a town south of Jaffa well known for its fine oranges and solid heritage. Personal relations used to have the deepest impact in Palestinian political work, and they still do, because they are based in our conservative traditions and habits. These personal contacts helped clear up several misunderstandings between Fatah and ourselves, and negative discourse was transformed into positive communication and fruitful agreement because of them.

Our relationship with the Popular Front for the Liberation of Palestine (PFLP) and its forerunner, the Movement of Arab Nationalism, ranged between the courteous and the negative. Courtesy sprang from our common stand against the dissolution of the United Arab Republic and the separation of Egypt and Syria, while the difference in our positions regarding the appointment of Ahmad al-Shuqayri, the representative of Palestine at the Arab League as coordinator of Palestinian policy, led to the negative aspects of our relationship. The movement, as we found out later, had been going through internal problems of an ideological nature. It had never cut off relations with al-Shuqayri, though its reactions to his political moves were clearly negative.

Two influential organizations remain to be discussed: al-Saiqa and the Arab Liberation Front (ALF), representing the Syrian and Iraqi

Ba'th parties respectively. Our relationships with those two were always contingent on our respective positions towards Damascus and Baghdad. Later on, in 1968, Ahmad Jibril, along with some of his supporters, split from the PFLP and added the words "General Command" to its name, becoming the PFLP-GC. Jibril was also pro-Syrian, and perhaps one might say that he was sometimes closer to the Syrian regime than the Ba'th Party itself.

Prior to the birth of the PLO, the link between our front, the PLF, and Ahmad al-Shuqayri, was Hamed Abu-Sitteh, an engineer from the Tarabeen clan in the Negev, whose family was widely respected among the Bedouin of Palestine. One week after I met him, I invited al-Shuqayri to my house in Beirut. I gathered all the leaders of the front, in addition to various Palestinian figures who resided in the Lebanese capital. We had all heard of al-Shuqayri, but this was the first time we had met openly with him. There is no doubt that he was an exceptionally able man. Because of his experience as a lawyer and diplomat, he was so much of an expert in addressing others that he ended up monopolizing the conversation.

The meetings between our front and al-Shuqayri went on for some time, and through *al-Hawadeth* I managed to shed light on his movements and meetings. My intention was to market the idea of the establishment of an independent Palestinian entity, which later came to be known as the Palestine Liberation Organization, or PLO. My writing also brought in the PLF's vision regarding the structure, aims, and policy of this entity.

It was an inevitable consequence of my deep involvement in this kind of activity that I resigned from the press and began my formal induction into politics, becoming fully dedicated to the PLO.

4

THE BIRTH OF THE PALESTINE LIBERATION ORGANIZATION

Between 1948 and 1964, the Arab world witnessed a number of revolutions, military coups, and other major political events, the most significant of which was the union between Egypt and Syria in the United Arab Republic and the subsequent dissolution of that union. As to the Palestinian question, four separate political movements developed. These were the local/regional movement, which had isolated itself from any collaboration with nationalist efforts in the wider Arab world; the Marxist/Leninist movement, which addressed the cause from the perspective of class struggle; the Islamic movement, which dealt with it from a religious perspective; and the pan-Arab nationalist movement, which was a continuation of the pre-*Nakba* political mainstream, upholding its belief that Palestine and its people were an integral and inseparable part of the Arab world, making the problem of Palestine the central cause of the Arab nation.

(1)

Throughout those years, all the efforts by the Arabs and Palestinians to find an effective path to liberate Palestine had come to naught. A first turning point however came when Gamal Abdul Nasser addressed the Arab peoples on the afternoon of December 23, 1963. His speech that day was seen as a major step forward for the Palestinian cause. In it, Abdul Nasser called for an Arab summit, the first after a long period of dormancy in the Arab League owing to various inter-Arab conflicts that had almost reached the point of conflagration. Also at that time, Israel was busy trying to take over Arab waters and was diverting the flow of the Jordan River. After a frank and harsh presentation of the deteriorating state of inter-Arab relations, Abdul Nasser concluded: "But irrespective of all these problems, we are ready to meet with anyone, for the sake of Palestine." The summit meeting was set for January 13, 1964. Everyone came, except the King of Libya, who sent his crown prince, Prince Reda, to attend on his behalf.

Until that summit meeting, the League Council had selected a representative for Palestine to participate in its activities, an unsatisfactory arrangement that was supposed to last until such time as Palestine became independent and was capable of appointing its own representatives. The position had been occupied by Moussa al-Alami, Hajj Amin al-Husseini, and Ahmad Hilmi Pasha, who headed the so-called Hukumat 'Umum Filastin (All-Palestine government) based in Gaza. This body had been set up in September 1948, but it soon foundered and was downgraded to a minor and powerless bureaucratic irrelevance. Consequently the condition of Palestine remained in a state of permanent neglect in the offices of the Arab League.

In September 1963, three months prior to President Nasser's call for a summit, the Secretariat General of the Arab League had contacted Ahmad al-Shuqayri and informed him that the majority of Arab states had recommended him as representative of Palestine at the Arab League. Al-Shuqayri had been vice president of the Saudi delegation at the United Nations but had by then resigned from this post – or, to put it more accurately, had been asked to resign. He had been in conflict with King Faisal over the war between Egypt and Saudi Arabia in Yemen, because he had refused – as we were once told – to lodge a complaint against Cairo and its military intervention there.

Intelligent and ambitious, al-Shuqayri was well aware of the Palestinians' needs, and he knew all their organizations and movements very well. He was also quite familiar with the ins and outs of politics within the Arab League, as he had represented Syria for a few years before he had moved to Saudi Arabia. Surprisingly though, some Arab states protested against his nomination, under the general pretext that he was neither a president nor a king. In fact, each protesting nation had its own set of reasons for rejecting his nomination, but the United Arab Republic and Algeria, acting in concert, managed to put an end to the dispute, and al-Shuqayri was finally invited to represent Palestine. However, a note concerning the protocol for his seating arrangements was attached to the appointment: he was not permitted to use the same type of chair as the one allocated to the heads of states, and he was to be seated a certain distance behind them.

I would never have believed the story of the protocol had I not heard later of what happened when al-Shuqayri was to deliver his first speech. Before he began, he pushed his chair forward until it came into line with the row of other seats, emphasizing his equal status and making the point that Palestine, even though it remained under occupation, was not to be regarded as in any way lesser than the other Arab countries. I witnessed a similar complication in protocol procedures during the Khartoum summit in August 1967, when the Sudanese government placed al-Shuqayri in a different hotel from the heads of the other Arab delegations. The entire Palestinian delegation threatened to leave the hotel and stay with Sudanese friends in Khartoum. However, the Sudanese Prime Minister, Mohammad Ahmad Mahjoub, called and assured us that no slight had been intended, and that he had already seen to it that some rooms originally reserved for the Sudanese delegation had been vacated to allow al-Shuqayri to stay in the same hotel as the Arab kings, princes, and presidents.

Indeed, al-Shuqayri had to overcome many obstacles put in the way by both official Arab circles and local Palestinian ones. A number of Arab nations had reservations about him personally that had nothing to do with their attitudes towards the Palestinian cause. For example, Tunisian President al-Habib Bourguiba simply did not like him; this was simply a case of bad chemistry between two men. Syria, on the other hand, then ruled by Amin al-Hafez, did not take al-Shuqayri seriously and considered him a mere instrument of Abdul Nasser, whose relations with Syria had deteriorated since the Disunion in 1961. Meanwhile, Jordan, over half of whose population was Palestinian, was deeply concerned about the implications of al-Shuqayri's appointment. At the same time as defending himself against these Arab antagonisms, al-Shuqayri had to win over and maintain the support of the majority of his own people, the Palestinians, and defeat the campaign against him that was being spearheaded by the Movement of Arab Nationalists, the Ba'thist organizations, and others.

During the period that preceded the Cairo summit of January 1964, al-Shuqayri traveled to the Arab states which had sizable Palestinian populations and held dozens of meetings. He also addressed the masses in the refugee camps, where he proved his eloquence

and charisma. He managed to win the overwhelming majority of
the people over to his side in support of his vision. His strong belief
was that the Palestinian national identity needed to be restored,
and to do that it had to acquire the recognition of Arab leaders
through the establishment of an independent entity that authenti-
cally represented Palestinians. Various members of the Palestinian
public, including nationalists, intellectuals, and businessmen, played
a major role in supporting the project of building up such an entity.
They did this either directly, by backing al-Shuqayri's movement, or
indirectly, through constructive criticism. But there were also others
who completely rejected the project, fearing that this entity would
end up in the same way as the ill-fated Hukumat 'Umum Filastin
(All-Palestine Government) in Gaza.

Those who opposed al-Shuqayri and his project differed among
themselves as well. Amman and Damascus, for instance, differed
in their positions on more than one point. The Jordanians explicitly rejected the idea of an independent entity, considering that it
would endanger the security of their kingdom, in which the West
Bank would no longer be a part. On the other hand, Syrian Prime
Minister Amin al-Hafez insisted that there could be no entity without
territory, but that would mean King Hussein giving up Jordanian
control of the West Bank, while Nasser would have to relinquish the
Gaza Strip; Syria itself was prepared to give up the Himma zone,
which was under its control.

But, using his considerable patience and communication skills,
al-Shuqayri finally managed to form the Preparatory Committee
for the Formation of the Palestine National Council (PNC), which
in turn undertook the selection of the PNC members, and adopted
a draft National Charter and a statute for what came to be known
later as the Palestine Liberation Organization.

(2)

On January 13, 1964, the Arab Summit in Cairo passed several resolutions, the most important of which was only a few lines in length,
and read as follows:

> Mr Ahmad al-Shuqayri, Representative of Palestine at the Arab
> League, shall continue to communicate with the member states
> and the Palestinian people, with the intention of setting the proper

foundations for the organization of the Palestinian people, so that they can play their role in the liberation of their nation and acquire self-determination.

The wording of the resolution was generic and subtle, and lacked any precise prescription of the mechanisms necessary for the fulfillment of a Palestinian national entity. Furthermore, it gave the Arab nations custody over the Palestinian people, despite the fact that it was the Palestinians themselves who were the bearers of their cause and had the right to self-determination.

The Palestinians reacted negatively to the resolution: the various political groups considered it nothing more than an attempt by Arab leaders to divert people from the true path of the revolution already adopted in the mid-1960s by many Palestinian organizations which had raised the banner of military struggle and rejected the suzerainty of the Arab leaders and their League. Nonetheless, al-Shuqayri carried the few lines of the Cairo resolution (above) in his briefcase, determined to convert the words into a tangible reality, and he went on another tour to visit Palestinians wherever they were gathered in large numbers, preparing the ground for the upcoming historic event: the establishment of a Palestinian national entity. Following several frustrating rounds of talks with Arab and Palestinian leaders, it was decided that the Palestine National Council would hold its first meeting on May 28, 1964.

Under the auspices of King Hussein of Jordan, the conference was held at the InterContinental Hotel in East Jerusalem. The place was saturated with Jordanian intelligence officers, headed by Mohammad Rassoul al-Kilani, a character well known to thousands of Palestinian and Jordanian political prisoners. But the conference delegates stood up to this sort of pressure and managed to achieve the declaration of their entity: the birth of the Palestine Liberation Organization. At the time, I had the feeling that we were all endowed with a spiritual, metaphysical strength which gave us the power to resist the pressures of intimidation, to overcome all obstacles and eliminate all doubts, so that we could move forward. We knew we should not waste the opportunity at hand, as we might never have another chance as good as this to manage our own destiny.

Those were historic days: there was constant motion and continuous debate; doubts and illusions jostled with one another; threats were heard and temptations offered and overcome. Committees would discuss an issue, make a record, strike it out, renegotiate, print it up, and then drop everything they had already done and begin all over again. At last we reached the concluding session: al-Shuqayri, as chairman of the conference, announced the creation of the PLO after its charter and statute were set down, and he was elected its chairman.

When we left Jerusalem, we did not fully understand that what we had just achieved, in May 1964, was the beginning of a serious strategic reaction to what had happened to us and to Palestine in May 1948. Today, looking back over the years since the *Nakba*, I think this moment was the Palestinians' most significant achievement in their six decades of national struggle.

Four months after the meeting at the InterContinental Hotel in Jerusalem we moved to the Palestine Hotel in Alexandria, where Arab kings and presidents convened on September 5, 1964, for a second summit meeting. Al-Shuqayri delivered a long presentation with the hope of achieving legitimacy for the PLO within an Arab framework.

Things could have got out of hand because of the various inter-Arab conflicts, especially as every Arab government had its own vision of the anticipated role of the PLO. Some wanted it to be merely an empty shell with the name of Palestine attached, others wanted to abuse it for their own benefit, and yet others wanted to tame it and use it as a bargaining chip. The issue might not have been resolved and the PLO might never have achieved the official recognition of the Arab world had it not been for the intervention of Presidents Nasser of Egypt and Ahmad Ben Bella of Algeria. Iraqi President Abdul Salam Aref added his vote to theirs. Indeed, he went even further and offered, with typical Iraqi generosity, the first payment into the PLO's bank account. Discussions were then concluded, and the establishment of the PLO was approved.

(3)

Al-Shuqayri started to build up this new entity from scratch. He equipped it with civil organizations, institutions, and military forces. Shortly thereafter, he headed to Jerusalem, where he raised the Palestinian flag over the official headquarters of the PLO. He also announced the names of those who were going to assist him in creating the organizational structure, beginning with its various units and offices in the Arab host states; and finally he declared the foundation of the Palestine Liberation Army (the PLA).

In addition to the chairman, Ahmad al-Shuqayri, and the President of the Palestinian National Treasury, Abdul Majeed Shouman, who were to be directly elected by the Palestinian National Council, the first Executive Committee included the following members: Bahjat Abu Gharbiyah, Hamed Abu Sitteh, Nicola al-Durr, Haidar Abdul Shafi, Khaled al-Fahoum, Farouk al-Husseini, Abdul Khalek Yaghmoor, Falah al-Madi, Walid Qamhawi, Qosai al-Abadleh, Qassem al-Rimawi, and Abdul Rahman Siksik.

Early in October 1964, the Executive Committee decided to appoint me as its representative to the Lebanese Republic and as director of the PLO Office in Beirut. We, in the PLF (Palestine Liberation Front – Path of Return), had already declared our support for the PLO and our determination to place all our facilities at its disposal. Accordingly, I accepted my appointment, resigned from my post at *al-Hawadeth*, and moved to my new office on Corniche al-Mazraa, one of Beirut's main thoroughfares.

Having brought in some new members to the PLO, I immediately set about organizing the office. At that time, there was no financial inducement to dedicate oneself to the PLO, and other Palestinian factions had not yet even admitted the principle of cooperation with the newborn organization. From the very start, I was keen on establishing positive diplomatic relations between our office and the Lebanese government, in a manner similar to all other Arab embassies. This was not an easy task, and it required popular support by both Lebanese and Palestinians. We had to invest a great deal of effort in convincing the Lebanese government of our right to raise the Palestinian flag over the front entrance of the building. Thankfully, the then Prime Minister, Hajj Hussein al-Oweini, was cooperative, and we reached an agreement: the office of the PLO would be considered a diplomatic mission like any other Arab embassy, with all privileges and obligations prescribed by normal diplomatic protocol. The PLO Beirut Office was the first in any Arab capital to acquire this status.

We took it upon ourselves to unite the various and disparate Palestinian factions, believing that the PLO was not a conventional organization, but rather a temporary homeland pending the liberation of the Occupied Territories. We believed that its civilian and military units were the proper framework for the emancipation of our people, regardless of their intellectual or political differences.

(4)

On January 1, 1965, Fatah was officially launched. This caused a great deal of political turmoil in Palestinian circles. Our mission to achieve Palestinian unity became more complicated, especially when the dispute over the nature of the military struggle was brought up in discussions. The United Arab Command had warned against the dangers of skirmishes with Israel without prior coordination with the Arab states, as its chairman, Brigadier Ali Ali Amer, has recorded. In the PLF, we were always against the theory of "entanglement" and we did not tolerate anyone trying to goad Nasser into action. After the breakup of the Union, several of Nasser's enemies started to take advantage of the presence of United Nations peacekeepers in Sharm al-Sheikh and the Gulf of al-Aqaba, and challenge Nasser by questioning his patriotism in terms of the Palestinian cause. Even some Nasserites at the time were seduced by these calls for military struggle, and filled the newspapers with bellicose articles which seemed to suggest that all Cairo needed to do was to declare a war against Israel in order to be victorious. Even worse, it was suggested the newborn PLO, along with other Palestinian factions, was immediately capable of standing up to Israel all by itself, with no official support from even a single Arab nation!

As a result of this internal struggle, we in the PLF, as well as some others, felt as if we were caught, as the old Arabic saying goes, between a hammer and an anvil: the hammer was the conventional al-Shuqayri policy and the anvil the newly born struggle of the Palestinian *fedayeen*. This impossible situation persisted until the June 1967 War, when our worst fears became painful realities. What had been left of Palestine, including East Jerusalem, was lost, along with the Sinai peninsula in Egypt, and the Syrian Golan Heights.

In the meantime, however, al-Shuqayri tried to absorb the inter-Palestinian problems by forming a new Executive Committee, which was intended to bring in the two generations – the traditional bureaucratic one and the young revolutionary one which was keen on initiating new practices – and to be capable of absorbing the factions that were still refusing to participate in the various elements of the PLO. On August 10, 1964, the second Executive Committee was formed, and, in addition to al-Shuqayri and Abdul Majeed Shouman, it included Ibrahim Abu Sitteh, Sayyed Bakr, Jamal al-Sourani, Najib Rsheidat, Ahmad Srouri, Faez Sayegh, Daoud al-Husseini, Said al-Ezzeh, and

Abdul Hameed Yassine. Unfortunately, however, this committee lasted only for a year and failed to heal the wounds between the two generations. During the third round of the Palestinian National Council, held in Gaza, in May 1966, debates intensified between the conventionalists and the newcomers, and finally al-Shuqayri was forced to accept new members of the Executive Committee from the younger generation. The new committee consisted of: al-Shuqayri (President), Abdul Majeed Shouman (President of the National Treasury), Said al-Ezzeh, Ibrahim Abu Sitteh, Jamal al-Sourani, Nimr al-Masri, Abdul Fattah Younis, Shafiq al-Hout, Ahmad al-Saadi, Ahmad Sidqi al-Dajani, Ussama al-Naqeeb, Abdul Khaleq Yaghmour, Bahjat Abu Gharbiyeh, and Rifaat Awdeh.

We did our best in this leadership to implement some of the PNC resolutions adopted during the third round, particularly those related to the configurations within the Palestine Liberation Army, which was scattered between the Gaza Strip, Syria, Iraq, and Egypt. The army's commander, Brigadier Wajeeh al-Madani, largely agreed with us. We often coordinated military activities with him through an underground unit known as *Abtal al-Awda* (Heroes of Return). During this period, Israel perpetrated a massacre in the West Bank village of al-Samou, which strained the relationship between the PLO and the Jordanian government.

Things went from bad to worse within the PLO as a result of al-Shuqayri's autocratic methods. He single-handedly initiated a virtual coup within the organization when he announced from the PLO Radio Station in Cairo that the Executive Committee had been relieved of its duties and replaced by a secret Revolutionary Council. He then announced a series of decisions that affected several officers of the Palestine Liberation Army who had opposed his coup. As for me, al-Shuqayri went as far as threatening to remove me from Beirut and relocate me, choosing India of all places, where the PLO did not even have an office. On February 15, 1967, Ahmad al-Saadi, Ahmad Sidqi al-Dajani, and I sent a telegram to al-Shuqayri protesting against his actions and declaring them illegitimate. We appended to the telegram a memo explaining the reasons we had rejected his decisions and what we saw as his violations of the Charter, and we expressed our respect for democracy and collective decision-making. In conclusion, we asked him to nullify his decisions and initiate the formation of a new Executive Committee.

The magnitude of the opposition increased, and several new

members joined the Executive Committee, including Dr Haydar
Abdul Shafi, Dr Rifaat Awdeh, Dr Salah al-Dabbagh as Director
General of the Foreign Affairs Unit, Khalil Owaidah, Director of the
Education Affairs Unit, and Raji Sahyoun, a senior official at the
Media Affairs Unit.

(5)

On February 17, 1967, two days after we sent the memo, I was
subjected to the first attempt on my life; a gunman fired from a
car parked front of my house, hitting me in the leg. I feared that
our people, especially those living in the camps, would draw a link
between this cowardly attempt and my conflict with al-Shuqayri.
Consequently, the first thing I did upon my arrival at the American
University Hospital was to reiterate what I had said to the Lebanese
Gendarmes who had delivered me there, that I blamed Jordanian
Intelligence for the attempted assassination. My hunch turned out to
be correct, as Egyptian Intelligence managed to intercept a phone call
that night between the Jordanian ambassador and one of the participants in the attack. I later heard from trustworthy Arab sources that
the Jordanian intelligence official in charge of the operation was so
angry at its failure that he sent someone to the hospital to finish me
off, but the Lebanese government had tightened security around my
hospital room and I was spared.

After leaving hospital, I spent some time recovering before
beginning going back to my office in Beirut. (I did not go to India.)

It was only natural that the 1967 war would have dramatic
repercussions throughout the Arab world, including for the PLO.
Several Arab capitals rushed to take advantage of the situation and
avoid taking responsibility: the PLO became the scapegoat, as if it
had been responsible for the massive defeat. We therefore chose to
suspend our internal divisions and reunite behind the PLO leadership, and al-Shuqayri in particular, in defense of our newborn entity,
the liquidation of which seemed alarmingly imminent. We had also
noticed that some Arab states had been trying to prevent the PLO
from participating in the next Arab summit, which was scheduled
to take place in Khartoum at the end of August of that year. Earlier
al-Shuqayri had sent me a letter through the Head of Foreign Affairs
at that time, Mohammad Nimr al-Masri, in which he informed me
that he had deferred his decision to transfer me to India, and that

I should return to exercise all my privileges as director of the PLO office in Lebanon. He then asked me to go to the Sudanese capital to participate in a preliminary meeting of the Arab ministers of foreign affairs, in preparation for the anticipated summit.

(6)

The Khartoum meeting in early August 1967 was my first political mission at such a senior level. It was during those meetings that I lost my political virginity: I discovered that the first basic fact of Arab politics is that the highest official in any Arab state, regardless of whether he is king or president, is the sole decision maker, leaving very little margin in which his ministers could maneuver. I also found out that there was no black and white in politics: gray was the prevalent color. What hurt me most however, were the mutual grudges between Arab states, which were more intense than those against the common enemy. The only thing that saved me from complete despair was the thundering demonstrations of the Sudanese people, who had come to Khartoum from all parts of the country to receive the Arab leaders and encourage them to fight back and avenge the defeat.

The meetings lasted for five days, and produced two resolutions: the first set up a meeting for the Arab ministers of economy, finance and oil in Baghdad, in an attempt to consider strategic retaliatory action; and the second called for another meeting of the ministers of foreign affairs to precede the summit by just a few days, this time to finalize its agenda. Although the Sudanese prime minister reassured me that the PLO was going to be invited to the summit, I still had my doubts, especially when I learned that we were not even invited to participate in the Baghdad Conference, under the pretext that "the Palestinians had neither money nor economy nor oil"! I returned to Beirut deeply worried that we would not participate in the summit, especially after I heard the statements directed against al-Shuqayri, who was continuously being targeted on a political and personal level. I shared my concerns with the Executive Committee.

The date of the meeting of the Arab foreign ministers came, but we had still not received an invitation to the summit. In reaction, al-Shuqayri sent me to Khartoum again, with a message to Prime Minister Mahjoub, and with special instructions to be followed in the event the Sudanese government did not go back on its decision.

The night was cold, and I was extremely tense; my heart would skip a beat whenever the plane experienced turbulence. I just could not stop thinking: Is it possible that the people of Palestine would not be invited to participate in an Arab conference that was going to be held in the name of Palestine and the Palestinian cause?

Khartoum finally started to appear on the horizon, like an ebony-colored beauty with a diamond necklace. Two people were waiting at the airport, my dear old friend, fellow student, and fellow prisoner Mustafa Madani, who was then an ambassador at Sudan's Foreign Ministry, and Said al-Sabe', the PLO representative in Khartoum. The latter immediately launched into a description of the pressures being applied to Sudan not to invite the PLO. When I asked about Mahjoub's position, Mustafa said: "Mahjoub is cornered, but he is doing his best to sort things out, especially as Sudan is the host state. But for now he is keeping silent, trying to put off the declaration of his government's position till the last moment." He then added: "In any case, he is waiting for you." I asked: "When? Tomorrow, *inshallah*?" It was already past midnight, but Mustafa smiled and said: "Right now!"

Mahjoub received me in the main hall of his home, feigning anger at the Palestinian position: "What's with this al-Shuqayri of yours? Always firing off at us in the press and broadcasters. What the hell does he want?" I answered: "He's not asking for anything that is not just. He only wants the Palestine delegation to be invited to the Conference."

He then took me by surprise: "Have you had your supper?" He ordered snacks and then said to me: "Done, my friend. We shall ask our embassy in Beirut to extend an invitation to the chairman of the PLO." Mahjoub then recited the names of all the countries opposed to the participation of the PLO and he expressed his concerns about their likely reactions to any change in the decision not to invite us

My mission ended at that point, but Mahjoub's troubles were far from over. He still had to convince Syria to reverse its stance and he had to pull off a miracle to bring together President Nasser and King Faisal, in order to stop the war between Egypt and Saudi Arabia in Yemen. In the end, Mahjoub proved that he was more of a statesman than a poet, perhaps contrary to his own wishes or beliefs.

(7)

I shall not dwell on the details of the 1967 Summit Conference, but will focus on the important points:

- The results of the conference reflected the change in the balance of power within the Arab states following the 1967 war, and that was clearly detectable in the phrasing of the resolutions. The famous "Three Nos" – No Conciliation, No Coexistence, and No Negotiations with Israel – were in fact compromised by the goals that the Arab regimes agreed upon, which were the elimination of the consequences of the Israeli aggression and the liberation of the "recently occupied Arab territories." This was the first official indication in Arabic of an indirect and implicit recognition of Israel's existence in the Palestinian territories occupied in 1948.

- The Palestinian delegation withdrew from the summit conference in the closing session, because of its reservations about the decision of the Three Nos, mentioned above. In the original Palestinian proposal there were four Nos, but the fourth was dropped from the final document. Al-Shuqayri, in an immediate press conference, announced the substance of the fourth No – No unilateral acceptance by any Arab state of a solution for the Palestine question. Such a solution should be subject to discussion at high-level Arab meetings, which should and must include the Palestine Liberation Organization.

  Now, more than 40 years later it is only fair to note that al-Shuqayri's reservations were entirely justified, as his fears at the time were later borne out. Egypt acted alone in 1978 when it signed the Camp David Accords. And 15 years later, ironic though this may be, the PLO itself also unilaterally signed the 1993 Oslo Agreement. Last but not least, Jordan acted on its own by concluding the 1994 Wadi Araba Agreement.

- Israel's Foreign Minister at the time Abba Eban considered the conclusions and resolutions of this summit a "declaration of war against Israel."

Which of the various evaluations and analyses of the outcome of the 1967 summit, or of the three Nos, was true? It is not easy to arrive at an answer to this question: herein lies the importance of language in politics. The presence or absence of a single word may uncover dangerous intentions or expose positions to the possibility of misinterpretation.

The 1967 Khartoum summit conference was a critical turning point in the course of the Palestinian struggle and it put an end to al-Shuqayri's era. Four months after the conference, in a broadcast on PLO Radio in Cairo on December 25, 1967, al-Shuqayri submitted his resignation to the Palestinian people. There followed a new phase in the history of the struggle that might be called "the phase of factionalization."

(8)

When al-Shuqayri resigned in late 1967, the Lebanese president was Charles Helou, whose tenure was considered an extension of that of his immediate predecessor, Fouad Chehab. The refugee camps were still under the iron fist of the Lebanese army's Deuxieme Bureau, suffering various forms of oppression and terrorization; indeed, the Palestinian camps were more like detention camps than centers for refugees. And just for the historical record I shall mention a couple of incidents that I personally witnessed in my capacity as head of the PLO Office in Beirut.

The first incident I recall took place before the end of 1964, when I started visiting the camps in order to introduce the refugees to the PLO, and explain to them its policies and programs. Al-Rashidieh camp in the south near Tyre was the first I visited, but when I entered the camp just before noon I was surprised to find that no one was waiting for me. In fact, there was no one on the streets at all: it was as if the camp had been completely deserted. As we passed the headquarters of the Bureau, we saw some of their men outside, their eyes exuding hostility and belligerence. We were not scared off by this and headed towards the square where the meeting was supposed to be held. Though we found the chairs lined up, there were no people sitting in them, only some children, who soon surrounded us and stared at us curiously. I was carrying a portable megaphone, so I switched it on and started talking to the children as a kind of a game. I would ask them a question and they would answer; I would make a statement, and they would echo it, and so on. I soon noticed that there were men and women listening to us from behind their doors and windows. Little by little, the adults began to emerge and, within less than a quarter of an hour, the public space was packed with oppressed and angry people. It was an opportunity to tell them things they would not dare to whisper within earshot of the men of the Deuxieme Bureau or the Gendarmerie.

Barely had I returned to my office in Beirut, when Major Sami al-Khatib, the second in command of the Bureau, was on the line asking me about "the hell" that I had raised at al-Rashidiya Camp. I had had decent and friendly relations with Major al-Khatib going back to the late 1950s when I was working at *al-Hawadeth*, so I did not hesitate to tell him directly that his organization should begin taking seriously the significance of the birth of the PLO, and put an end to its policy of repression and terrorization, and that there was urgent need to grant the Palestinians their civil, human, and national rights.

The second incident took place at Ein al-Helweh Camp in Sidon on May 15, 1965, where I was to participate in the commemoration of the 1948 *Nakba*. The moment I arrived, I sensed serious tension and I noticed that at least a hundred soldiers in uniform had deployed the camp. In spite of that, and paying no attention to the armed presence at all, I saw no harm in proceeding with our program. Then, a young man carrying the Palestinian flag approached me. He handed me the flag and said, with tears in his eyes: "The officer has prevented us from raising it on the flagpole, and then we tried to place it on the platform where you were going to speak, but he refused that also."

I grabbed the flag and headed to the microphone. I delivered a speech devoted exclusively to the flag itself: "Wasn't this flag the reason why our fathers and grandfathers died? Would we have tolerated all that misery and suffering had it not been for this flag? Didn't the PLO emerge in order to reinstate dignity and pride in this flag?" By the time I had finished my speech, which had fired up the emotions of thousands of people, the officer had withdrawn all of his soldiers, which was a wise decision on his part.

Of course, this incident did not pass without consequence: several young men were arrested and subjected to beatings and torture, but this time there was no contact between me and Major al-Khatib. I knew that I needed to talk with the real decision makers in the country and that, although Fouad Chehab's term as president had ended, he still had a lot of influence in the army. I had already met the former president, again thanks to the old days of *al-Hawadeth*, which had supported him fully against his enemies among the corrupt ruling class in Lebanon, whom he used to call *Fromagistes*. I visited him at his home in Ajaltoun, accompanied by my assistant, Abdul Qader al-Daher.

I complained to him about the suffering of the Palestinians, especially the political activists. Then I told him in detail some of the incidents that were taking place at the time, such as the beatings, the torture, and the repression. I also added, trying to mitigate the impact of what I had said, that I did not think those practices were the result of a political strategy, but rather misconduct by individuals, which should therefore not be allowed to continue.

President Chehab did not interrupt me even once and started to talk only after I had had my say. "I am well aware of the situation you have described, though I must admit, based on what you just told me, that the 'boys' may have gone a bit too far. But I want you to know that this is indeed a deliberate policy."

He noticed our astonishment at his words, and continued: "In this part of the world, we are all backward. Each person is backed by a community or a sect of about 40 or 50,000 people, and so you cannot control such an issue as yours that easily. You people," he said, referring to the Palestinians, "number about 150,000, all homeless and desperate. You can see your country across the border with the naked eye, and yet cannot go to it. You turn on the radio and hear that everybody is with you and wants to liberate Palestine, but the truth of the matter is that no one wants to lift a finger."

He was silent for a moment, then he said: "I am the one who established this policy and I am the one who issued strict orders to the officers, particularly in the south, in the camps and villages, and on the border with occupied Palestine. I have even banned shooting in the air at their wedding celebrations." Smiling, he added: "Those people in Israel don't know our customs. Imagine how things might turn out if they were to think we were waging an attack against them, just because a young couple were getting married!" He then returned to his serious mood, and talked about the situation in Lebanon, its sectarian composition and its corrupt political class. In the end, he promised that he would make sure that "the boys" would behave with less severity and ease off the violations that we had reported to him.

Fouad Chehab was a man of his word and would never give a promise he could not keep. After this visit, we noted that the Deuxieme Bureau loosened its grip and began to build bridges with the various Palestinian factions that had started to surface in the Lebanese arena, especially Fatah, which had begun to establish military bases in the south.

Lebanese–Palestinian relations continued to ebb and flow at the official level, but amongst the general public and in most areas, if not all, the relationship was positive. In the 1960s, the whole world was infected by the spirit of revolution and change, from South

East Asia to Latin America, through Africa and the Arab region. All Lebanese and Palestinian veterans living in Lebanon will remember that glorious day in 1968 when the body of the first Lebanese martyr of the Palestinian revolution, Khalil al-Jamal, was brought home from the Syrian–Lebanese border to Beirut. A member of Fatah, he was one of the first Lebanese to join the Palestinian revolution, and died alongside two Palestinian comrades fighting the Israelis at al-Aghwar, in Jordan. Crowds lined the streets to salute the martyr's convoy. Church bells rang, together with the calls from the minarets to the greatness of God, *Allahu Akbar*. A great funeral was held in Beirut for Khalil al-Jamal.

As time passed, however, things radically changed. One of the major changes, in the wake of the 1967 defeat and the fall of Jerusalem, the West Bank, and the Gaza Strip, was the fact that a new group of approximately 800,000 Palestinians became displaced.

Photo 2 The author (left) with Arafat in Lebanon (early 1970s)

Most of these new refugees were absorbed by Jordan, while the rest went to other Arab countries, particularly Syria and Lebanon. This new wave of Palestinians perturbed the Lebanese government, which had always feared an increase in the number of refugees in Lebanon. To make matters worse, this time most of them had entered the country illegally with the help of the Palestinian factions. Consequently, a segment of Lebanese society, concerned for the safety and destiny of their country, began to re-evaluate their original support of the PLO and the revolutionary units.

Thus Lebanese–Palestinian relations began to deteriorate and clashes took place between the *fedayeen* and Lebanese army units in the south. Had it not been for the efforts of decent people on both sides, things would have spun out of control there and then.

5

THE FACTIONS GAIN CONTROL OF THE PLO

After the 1967 defeat, the Arab regimes accepted the ceasefire in full compliance with Security Council Resolution 242. By contrast, the Palestinian military factions denounced this resolution, and this led to an immense rise in their public support. Palestinians began to talk again about the need to replace the leadership of the PLO with one that reflected the views of the military factions.

(1)

As members of the Palestine Liberation Front – Path of Return (PLF), we had repeatedly warned against the dangers of not coordinating with the unified Arab military command, but at this point we had no choice but to join this new military trend, especially after the worst had already taken place, namely the fall of the West Bank, Jerusalem, and the Gaza Strip. The Central Command of the PLF held a meeting in late September 1967, in which we discussed the repercussions of the recent war. Our general conclusions included the following points:

- On the international level: we noted the deeply rooted interdependence of Zionism and imperialism, and hence of Israel and the United States. We also noted that the call for Israel's destruction had been rejected by the Soviet Union and the Eastern Bloc, and that the Palestinian leaderships should take this into account, especially when it came to strategic policies and international relations.
- On the Arab regional level: we pointed out the extremely inaccurate estimate by the PLO and all Palestinian factions of the relative strengths of the Arab states vis-à-vis Israel. But in spite of the imbroglio and consequent defeat, we maintained our position: challenging the state of Israel remained our patriotic duty.
- On the Palestinian level: we warned against the inherent dangers in the refusal of some Palestinian activists and organizations to support the PLO, especially the Fatah faction, which had

refused to join it. We asked that all factions unite under the PLO umbrella.

I must say that people who used this kind of political discourse were swimming against a strong current. Even within our organization, the PLF, some of my comrades and I had to struggle to establish an internal compromise between those among us who called for the unity of all Palestinian factions and those who favored autonomy and the strengthening of our own organization. The latter group competed enthusiastically with other factions in crossing the Jordan from the East Bank to the West and claiming military successes. Eventually, we managed to reconcile the two philosophies, this time in cooperation with the leadership of the Palestine Liberation Army (PLA), which had created a brigade called the Popular Liberation Forces and had begun training its soldiers at the Khau Camp, in the Jordan Valley. Many of our members joined this squad. Unlike other factions, we never got into the habit of releasing frequent military statements, most of which turned to dust as soon as they were issued. Playing that game called for capabilities that we did not possess in the PLF, as it would require making ourselves dependent on one Arab regime or another, which we categorically refused to do. President Nasser, whom we appreciated and had faith in, was never eager to establish a "Nasserite" organization in the Palestinian arena, though he always provided logistical support and military training.

Internal dialogue at the PLF continued at various levels until we finally decided to dissolve the organization altogether. Five years after the first edition of our periodical *Path of Return*, it was discontinued.

(2)

Many people were surprised when al-Shuqayri resigned, though others had seen it coming. It even caused confusion among the very Palestinian leaders and members of the Executive Committee who had demanded that he go. Because of the president's resignation, the committee could not carry out its obligations and convene the National Council to a special session in order to assess the new developments. All it did was to appoint one of its members, Yahya Hammoudeh, as "temporary" PLO chairman. It even considered itself to be "temporary," pending the final results of the dialogue between the various factions. It was obvious that the Executive Committee had bent under the pressure of those factions that were demanding a totally new Palestinian National Council (PNC) with the object of taking full control over it.

In fact, all the factions had no choice but to accept this sudden legacy and they had to ponder how to distribute the spoils among themselves. Rather than the Executive Committee, the Palestine Liberation Army, an armed force to be reckoned with, became spokesman for the PLO. The PLA was made up of three brigades: the Ain Jalout brigade in Egypt; the Qadisiyah brigade in Iraq; and the Hittin brigade in Syria. The headquarters were in Damascus: most of its officers had served in the Deliverance Army, formed in 1947, but after the 1948 war they had joined the Syrian army. In addition to the three brigades I just mentioned, there was a brigade called the Popular Liberation Forces. This unit took it upon itself to establish a presence in the refugee camps, train volunteers, and maintain security, a role which was later transferred to the military police in the camps in Lebanon.

The Command Center for all Palestinian forces and groups was in Amman, while the camps for training the *Fedayeen* guerrillas were in the Jordan Valley; guerrilla operations were mounted across the Jordan River. On March 21, 1968, the first battle between the Palestinian forces and the fearsome Israeli army took place at the Karama refugee camp near Jericho. That was indeed an unforgettable day and that fierce battle, which became known as the Battle of Karama, energized most Arab nationalist sympathizers, who watched the brave heroes of Karama not only reclaim lost territory but also restore Arab pride, which had been deeply wounded in June 1967. I must not fail to mention here the remarkable role played by the Jordanian army personnel, whose artillery fired incessantly against the enemy and stood down only after the battle had ended and Israeli Defense Minister Moshe Dayan ordered his army to retreat.

Karama cleared the way for the guerrilla organizations, Fatah in particular, to take over leadership of the PLO. Convoys of young Arab and especially Palestinian volunteers began to flood into the Jordan Valley, with no objective in mind except to join in the armed struggle, restore pride in Arab fighters, and demonstrate that they could achieve victory if only their leaders were willing to fight on.

Finally, the leaders of all the factions, including the PLA, agreed to restructure the National Council on the basis of proportional representation, with each faction represented according to its size and strength. In addition, a number of independent and consensually agreed-upon members would be appointed, and representatives of associations, trade unions, and popular organizations would also join. Finally, the factional leaders agreed to convene a special session of the National Council in Cairo between July 10 and 17, 1968.

During this special PNC session, presided over by Abdul Mohsen al-Qattan, two important events took place. The first was the election of the first Executive Committee of the post-Shuqayri era. The new committee was headed by Yasser Arafat, but in contrast to past practice, when the PNC used to elect the chairman of the committee who would in turn select the members, this time the PNC did it the other way around and elected all members of the Executive Committee, who in turn chose one among them to be chairman. There is no doubt that this development was a sign of improved democratic practice. The second important event was the amendment of the PLO charter; even its title was changed from the *Pan-Arab Charter* to the *National Charter*. This deepened the undeclared division between the trend towards a pan-Arab identity and a narrower nationalist or chauvinistic one. The 1967 defeat, along with all the psychological repercussions that overwhelmed the Arabs and the Palestinians, undoubtedly contributed to the adoption of a number of amendments to the charter that were passed without serious, in-depth discussion, causing the PLO later to find itself trapped in intellectual and political paradoxes.

(3)

I started my official career with the new PLO chairman, Yasser Arafat, at a meeting in Amman, where he had invited representatives from all offices in Arab states and other friendly countries so that we could become better acquainted and able to cooperate more closely. At the top of the agenda which he had set was a discussion of the main points of the strategy for the immediate future. What happened was that Arafat began by welcoming us, and then he delivered a passionate speech and prepared to adjourn the meeting.

I requested permission to speak, and said: "To begin with, may I ask my brother Abu Ammar [Arafat's *nom de guerre*] to allow us to welcome him to the Palestine Liberation Organization. We value the position he took in Fatah when he resisted his narrow-minded Fatah comrades who had been set against joining the PLO and accepting their responsibilities." Then I spoke briefly of our concern about the policies adopted by the various factions, particularly the quota-based system for election of members of the National Council that had been agreed. When I had finished, I was surprised to hear Abu Ammar say: "Everything you said is true and I have no objection." A colleague interrupted: "We want you to issue a statement that explains things, in order to reassure everyone that we are on the right track." Abu Ammar stood up and addressed me directly: "I hereby ask Shafiq to write a statement as you request, to issue it on my behalf and I agree in advance to everything he says in it."

At that moment, I realized that the man in front of me was quite different from his predecessor. Arafat was just as charismatic as al-Shuqayri, but in a different and more unusual way. He was full of self-confidence, a man who once he had decided on something would take it all the way without ever stopping. This, I thought to myself, is a difficult man.

Two weeks later, as I was working in my office in Beirut, I was surprised by an unusual commotion in the street outside. I looked out from the balcony and saw a crowd of men, women, and children surrounding a man I recognized as Arafat from his checkered *kuffiyeh* headscarf, which would later become the symbol of Palestinian resistance. He was carrying a submachine gun over his shoulder, something he always did until he started wearing a pistol strapped around his waist some time later. The PLO office workers were quite shocked by his appearance, but they were charmed by his warmth. He treated each person as if he had known them for years. He went into the bathroom to freshen up after his journey and then asked me where he could perform his prayers. After praying, he requested a simple breakfast for his driver Abu Zaki, his two travel companions, and himself. He then excused himself, returned to the room where he had prayed and took a nap, as he had not slept since he had left Amman two days earlier. By the time he woke up, news of his presence had spread and hundreds of people from the camps of Beirut were crowding into the office to see him. Palestinian and Lebanese leaders rushed over as well, just to meet this man and shake his hand.

By now I realized that without doubt the man was a master of the art of public relations and winning friends and supporters. I also have to admit that I liked him on a personal level, but I remained hesitant about him on a professional level. Still, I decided that we should give him a chance and offer all the support he needed. From that day on we always remained good friends, despite all our open disagreements. This relationship was especially consolidated after an unfortunate experience which I have always refrained from recounting; now, however, I feel that keeping silent about it is no longer justified.

(4)

In the spring of 1969, a journalist colleague of mine, who was also a well-known painter, came to my office. This man, M, and I shared a deep admiration for Gamal Abdul Nasser and had participated together in a number of national events.

M did not seem his usual, cheerful self. Indeed, he looked sullen and on the verge of tears. I asked what was wrong; he took a copy of the Holy Qur'an out of his coat pocket, placed it in front of me and said: "Hold the Qur'an with your right hand and swear that you will not disclose a word of what I am about to tell you." I hesitated at first, but then I gave in to his request. I heard him out, listening with incredulity to what he had to say.

More than a month earlier, M had been ordered to assassinate me. Furthermore, he told me that a vegetable seller who had set up his cart on the pavement opposite my house was "one of us, waiting for my signal." With tears in his eyes he added: "It has been over a month now, and I have been delaying the order. I can no longer sleep at night. I keep thinking, how can I possibly order the murder of the man who taught me national loyalty and love of pan-Arabism and Nasser. But," he continued, trembling, "I have started to fear for my own life if I don't do what I have been told."

I was stunned. I tried to make things easier on him however, so I said jokingly: "Take it easy. Just shoot me in the shoulder and then I'll let you run off. This way, you'll have accomplished your mission, or at least had a go." Then I added: "But tell me, M, who are you really, and who are you working for? Who wants to assassinate me?"

He reminded me of my oath, and said: "Abu Ali Iyad." I knew about Abu Ali Iyad, whose real name was Walid Nimr, although I did not know him personally. He was one of the pioneer commanders of the Fatah forces known as *al-Assifa*, which had a reputation for ruthlessness, even ferocity. I asked M what he thought could have been the reason for Abu Ali Iyad's order, but he claimed not to know anything. I do recall him saying: "I thought that you were Fatah, one of their underground leaders!"

We were silent for a while, trying to think of a way out. M was extremely scared and confused. He finally spoke out and said that he had had no choice but to leave the country, at least for a while. And indeed, I learned later that he had traveled first to Turkey and then to Italy, from where he sent me a postcard to reassure me that he was well.

I had no idea what to do, but reckoned that in order to keep my promise to M, I first had to stay alive. I decided to bring up the matter with Abu Youssef al-Najjar, a member of the Fatah Command as well as a friend and neighbor of mine, who rented an office in the same building as the PLO office. I told him the whole story, of course without disclosing the name of my reluctant assassin. Abu Youssef found the news bizarre, though he expressed concern and said it was necessary to inform Abu Ammar and the members of the Fatah Command. He added: "I am afraid that someone must have provided false information to Abu Ali Iyad with seditious intent."

A few days later, Abu Youssef called me to a closed meeting. The top Fatah leadership were all there, Abu Ammar, Abu Youssef, Abu Jihad (Khalil al-Wazir), Abu Iyad (Salah Khalaf), as was, to my surprise, Abu Ali Iyad himself. Needless to say, I refused to shake hands with him. Abu Ammar opened the proceedings with an introduction in which he commended me, and then recited the popular saying: "Whoever throws water at Abu Hader shall have fire thrown at him" (My own nickname is Abu Hader). Then he asked Abu Ali directly if the allegations against him were true.

At first, Abu Ali tried to play down the issue, claiming that it had been just an empty threat. Abu Ammar did not accept that answer, so Abu Ali spoke again, this time making a great show of his agitation: "In fact, I have information that Mr Shafiq is an arms dealer; he deals with the Russians and frequents the Soviet Embassy."

Some comrades laughed, while the others just shook their heads. As for Abu Ammar, he spoke sharply and firmly: "Listen, Abu Ali, this arms dealing that you're talking about, it's something all our followers and friends are involved in. I know for a fact that the arms that Abu Hader owns do not exceed three or four Kalashnikovs, all of whose serial numbers are registered with the Lebanese army. As for his relations with the Russians and his visits to their embassy, please realize that that is exactly what we all strive for. I mean, I hope to live long enough to see Moscow recognize us as a national liberation movement."

And so the problem was solved. Abu Ali Iyad got up, kissed my forehead, and apologized. He admitted that he had fallen victim to a piece of malicious disinformation and he promised retribution against those behind it.

(5)

Arafat returned to Jordan with Abu Iyad, while Abu Jihad stayed behind to follow up on the situation in southern Lebanon, where tension had almost reached the level of armed confrontation between Palestinian factions and the Lebanese army. I went back to working with politicians and the news media, in an attempt to cool the situation down. But all of our endeavors failed to put an end to the trouble and fighting did indeed break out.

Once again I found myself in Ajaltoun, heading to the home of ex-President Fouad Chehab, hoping that he might be able to offer a way out. I had just come from a futile meeting between a Palestinian delegation composed of various factions and a Lebanese one composed of the commander of the Deuxieme Bureau, Gaby Lahoud, the Director of the Internal Security Forces, Mahmoud al-Banna, and the Director General of the Public Security, Joseph Salameh.

Chehab spoke as though he was continuing the conversation we had begun four years earlier, albeit taking into account the developments that had occurred since then. He said: "We no longer have any choice but to deal with your troops as though they were Allied Forces." He explained to me he meant conditions were like those in World War Two when the Allies had to take joint decisions under certain circumstances. I requested his help in securing this, assuring him that the Palestinian side would accept; he said: "I had already told President Charles Helou that was the optimum solution, even before the fighting began. But some people cannot imagine things in advance; events must take place first, and only then do they learn."

Soon after this meeting, I received a phone call from Sami al-Khatib, on behalf of the Deuxieme Bureau, to inform me that Lebanon was ready to reach an agreement with the Palestinians that would address their military and civil presence. Then he asked me whether I had had any ideas that could contribute to the success of this endeavor. I asked: "Don't you think that the 'mentor' [that was how the men of the Deuxième Bureau used to refer to President Chehab] needs another 'mentor' to help him realize this plan?" Sami exclaimed immediately: "There's no one else ... Abdul Nasser."

And so it was. On November 1, 1969, Palestinian and Lebanese delegations headed to Cairo, where they signed what became known as the Cairo Agreement. On the Lebanese side, the agreement was signed by General Emile Bustani, Lebanon's army commander, and Yasser Arafat, chairman of the Executive Committee of the PLO, signed on behalf of the Palestinians.

The Cairo Agreement, which was kept secret even from the members of the Lebanese parliament, was seen as a very controversial document and caused a great deal of turmoil between its supporters and opponents among Lebanon's politicians. Ironically, though, when the text of the agreement was fully disclosed, few people paid much attention to it and even if it had been fully implemented it would not have conferred any more rights on the Palestinians than those granted to any other human being. The terms of the agreement respected Lebanon's sovereignty and were to be implemented under the auspices of the Lebanese authorities, while the Lebanese army would have the final say in all matters. But, what it did do was respect the right of the Palestinian people to assemble, train, and prepare in Lebanon for the liberation of their own country.

In the end, partly due to the secrecy surrounding the agreement, none of the signatories complied with any of its clauses. But it did resolve an internal problem for the Lebanese, improving relations between the president of the republic and the prime minister and allowing government to resume its activities.

For the record, the agreement was later cancelled unilaterally by Lebanon in 1978.

(6)

On Wednesday, October 15, 1969, only two weeks after the signing of the Cairo Agreement, Beirut was subjected to an unprecedented terrorist attack by Israel. On that morning, I was in my office at Corniche al-Mazraa receiving some visitors with the office's legal adviser, Shawqi Armali.

It was almost 11 o'clock when we heard the sound of thundering explosions and the room where we were sitting was suddenly filled with suffocating smoke. Initially I was stunned but, once I recovered my senses and saw that everyone was alive, my first thought was that a bomb must have gone off inside the office. However, the office guards quickly discovered that the explosions were caused by four rockets fired from an apartment in a building right across the street from ours. When the guards broke into the apartment they found it empty: all that remained were the empty launchers which the rockets had been fired from and the remains of some tinned food, fruit, and so on. Later on, official and press reports showed that an Israeli agent with an Austrian passport, going under the name of Ahmad Raouf, had carried out the operation; he had wired the rockets to a timer and then had left Beirut for Frankfurt four hours before the explosions.

Later that day, I made a statement to the press accusing Israeli Intelligence of carrying out the attack. I added that a foreigner, who had claimed to have been a Dutch reporter, accompanied by a young woman, had visited the PLO office before the attack and requested permission to take photographs from inside it: the activities of the office were, allegedly, going to be the theme of his upcoming report. I also added that I had denied his request but told the reporter the PLO would provide him with the photos it had available and allow their publication. He insisted on taking photographs, and I saw no way out but to call the guards and have him removed by force. He still did not give up and tried to take some photos from outside. Impatiently, the guards forced him away again and threatened to get tougher. What I did not know at that time was that this third attempt on my life was not going to be the last, but one of a total of ten, with seven still to come.

Now we began to look forward impatiently to the end of the year and the end of Charles Helou's term as President of Lebanon. The rivals in the upcoming presidential elections were Suleiman Franjieh and Elias Sarkis.

(7)

I was in favor of Elias Sarkis, a loyal follower of Fouad Chehab. He was a highly qualified man of great integrity, more closely associated with the middle class than the aristocratic families, and closer to the younger generation than the older. I harbored fears about Suleiman Franjieh's ruthless nature and his readiness to take and implement fanatical decisions. At first the Lebanese pro-Palestinian movement, led by Kamal Jumblatt, made no decision about whom to back. Later on, Jumblatt declared that it was essential to scrutinize both candidates carefully before the movement would give its backing to one or the other. In the end, Suleiman Franjieh won the closely contested elections by the margin of a single vote.

Zuheir Mohsen (an official of the al-Saiqa faction, which used to follow the Syrian Ba'th Party), Abu Youssef al-Najjar (from Fatah) and I went together to congratulate Franjieh on his success. He was receiving congratulations at the Ministry of Foreign Affairs at Bustros Palace. From the very beginning Franjieh was as explicit as he could be. He put all courtesies aside and said: "I do not stab anyone in the back. When I decide to fight, I confront my opponent head on." Then he added: "I hold the utmost respect for Palestine, and Israel is an enemy we should all fight. But I have seen and read some things from your side that I do not appreciate. This talk of 'feudalism' and 'socialism' is unacceptable in Lebanon. Our regime is free and open, and every country is free in deciding its own political system. I shall allow no one to interfere in our domestic affairs."

Needless to say, Lebanon was not the only potential war zone. From the beginning of 1970, there were clear signs of coming upheavals in Jordan, where the main body of the Palestinian Revolution was based, with all of its various military, political, and media activities.

6

JORDANIAN–PALESTINIAN RELATIONS

The first time I visited Jordan was in the summer of 1949 as one of a group of Palestinian AUB students contracted by the World Health Organization (WHO) to work during the summer vacation as health advisers at the recently established refugee camps. I was assigned to work at Karama Camp in the Jordan Valley, where I met old school friends from Jaffa.

Karama was no different from the other camps. The buildings that there were, including the toilets, were all still made of tin. In the middle of the camp was a water tank that used to be filled on a daily basis, and people would collect the water they needed in plastic containers. At the edge of the camp in an abandoned mud house was a clinic in which a medical team, composed of two doctors and one Scottish nurse, resided. Located as it is below sea level, the valley, known as the *Ghawr* in Arabic, is unpleasantly hot. Abu Michel, the camp manager, was a patient and good-hearted man who tried continually to reassure people by saying: "This is just a temporary situation and soon everyone will return home."

I noticed that most of my friends were attracted to leftist thinking by then, and some had even joined the Communist Party. This was above all an expression of their anger at Britain and the United States, but also a result of the complete collapse of pre-*Nakba* Palestinian society and the huge increase in the number of the poor. At the time, there was a great deal of talk about the US "Clap Plan" to solve the water problems, including naturalizing the refugees wherever they found themselves outside their homeland. Everywhere people expressed their opposition to the Clap Plan, using every means at their disposal. One night, some of my friends and I sprayed anti-Clap slogans in red all over the camp: this angered the Jordanian security police, whose men tore the place up looking for "the vandals." My situation was looking precarious so I sneaked out of the camp to Amman one night and returned overland to Beirut.

My happiness at having avoided prison was offset by my sorrow at not having collected the wages that I badly needed at the time. I was blacklisted in Jordan until May 1964, when I was included in the Palestinian delegation from Lebanon to Jerusalem to participate in the first meeting of the Palestinian National Council (PNC).

(1)

The Lebanese national carrier, Middle East Airlines, used to offer a daily flight to Jerusalem which took less than an hour, landing at Qalandiya Airport. Qalandiya had been a military base during the British Mandate, but became a civil airport under Jordanian rule. On this particular day about 20 of us, members of the Palestinian delegation, including a number of women, awaited our flight in the departure hall of Beirut International Airport with a degree of anxiety despite the reassurances we had received from the Jordanian authorities. Almost immediately upon our arrival we were separated from the other travelers, most of whom were foreign tourists, and then were made to wait for ages for an intelligence officer to arrive. Everyone knew that no Palestinians were granted visas to Jordan until the Jordanian border control had received clearance from the central authorities in Amman; sometimes clearance had to come from the royal palace itself. The officer began to separate us according to a list of names he held in his hand which he consulted as he addressed each of us. This person may enter; this person may not; this person must wait for further clearance from Amman. At last, Nicola al-Durr, the most senior member of the delegation, said to him: "Please inform your superiors that we are here as a delegation: we are neither tourists nor ordinary visitors. We are here on a national mission that you had prior knowledge of. Either we all enter the country together, or none of us does."

Finally, a messenger from Prime Minister Bahjat al-Talhouni arrived and apologized to us on his behalf. The prime minister was "shocked," we were told, at our having been thus delayed and he promised to discipline the "imbecile public servant who did not understand the depth of the government's ardent desire to uphold the PNC, and see to its success in accordance with the orders of His Majesty the King."

In order to please us even further, the Jordanians assigned each of us a minder to accompany us day and night! Apparently, I was even more fortunate than the others, as no less a man than Mohammad Rasoul al-Kilani himself, the notorious head of General Intelligence, informed me that I was invited to attend a luncheon given by Sheikh Mohammad Ali al-Ja'bari in Hebron where I would have the honor of meeting His Majesty the King in person. Of course, this invitation was more in the nature of a summons than a friendly request. I followed my friends' advice and attended the luncheon rather than risk an unfortunate "incident." A short while later, I was escorted to a rooftop terrace at al-Ja'bari's house, with al-Kilani and several other intelligence officers all dressed in plain clothes in close attendance.

When we were within about three paces from the king, al-Kilani introduced me in a triumphant tone: "Your Majesty, this is Mr Shafiq al-Hout." The king smiled and welcomed me warmly, and I addressed him directly. "Your Majesty, I confess that I have written some articles criticizing your policies and those of your government. But I would like to assure you I have never written a single word in order to satisfy a third party or for my own personal gain. Everything I wrote was based on my convictions and my concern for the cause of Palestine. There is Palestine, Your Majesty, behind you," I added, pointing over the king's left shoulder at the hills to the west. "It would give me great honor to serve as a soldier in your army in order to liberate it."

"Let bygones be bygones," King Hussein responded in a reassuring tone. "We desire only the best for you, and we hope that you will be our guest in Amman."

"Amman and Jerusalem are the same, Your Majesty, and a genuine Arab can never differentiate between them," I replied. At that moment, al-Kilani nudged me to indicate that the meeting was over, and we left. No sooner had we withdrawn than he asked me:

"What did you think of our master?"

At first I did not know how to respond, as I dislike hypocrisy or answering questions under pressure, and so I just said:

"I liked him better than I like you, at least!"

(2)

I made a third visit to Amman in late 1968, after Abu Ammar had taken control of the PLO. Less than a year later, in summer 1969, I paid a fourth visit, and this one deserves a more elaborate narration.

In 1969 the attention of the news media was focused almost exclusively on the activities of the Palestinian *fedayeen*, despite the ferocity of the war of attrition being waged on the Egyptian front. A French television crew came to Beirut to arrange meetings with some of these fighters in order to provide audio-visual testimony of the new movement and to shed light on its leaders. Alia al-Solh, daughter of the former-Prime Minister, Riad al-Solh, accompanied them and she urged me to help them as much as possible. Having made all the necessary arrangements, I traveled with them to Jordan. I particularly wanted them to see the Khau Military Camp where the Popular Liberation Forces were being trained under the supervision of officers from the Palestine Liberation Army.

After they had witnessed the military training, the French crew members wanted to know whether the hundreds of young men they had seen had indeed volunteered to join in the struggle, and whether their number included dozens of students who had given up lives at university in the United States or Europe in order to join the *fedayeen*. I asked the crew leader to pick some of the men at random, and inquire of each why he had chosen to join up. He picked three men and asked to visit their parents in their homes. All three happened to be from the Jabal al-Hussein refugee camp in Amman and we set off at once to visit their families.

At one of the houses, we found no one at home except an elderly looking woman. In retrospect, she was perhaps only 60 years old, but years of anguish and subjugation can take a heavy toll, making people seem older than they really are. In any case, questions and answers followed one another as the interview took place, and the woman answered all the questions put to her openly and without hesitation. Finally the interviewer posed a critical question:

"Why did you leave your homeland in 1948?"

She replied instantly: "Because, sir, we were stupid!"

I hesitated for a moment before giving the translation, but sensing my reluctance she looked at me sternly and gave me no choice in the matter: "Tell him exactly what I said. Yes, we were stupid idiots."

I did as she said and looking back at the day my family and I left Jaffa, I thought to myself: Were we really as stupid as this woman has dared describe us? With reflection I concluded that she was partly right. It was true that all our subsequent destitution and suffering had stemmed directly from our flight from Palestine. But in 1948, we did not have any information about the reality of our situation other than what we read in the newspapers or heard on the radio. And so we believed what we believed, and thus did the *Nakba* take place. It was only later that the people of Palestine realized that they had been given no proper leadership. Our so-called leaders were no match for those of the enemy. And the other Arabs were no better off, as most of them were ruled by impotent leaders or agents of foreign powers.

So that old woman from Jabal al-Hussein Camp had spoken the truth. We had made a serious mistake in 1948 by seeking refuge outside our land, and we repeated this mistake in 1967 when many more of our people left the West Bank. As for those of our countrymen who remained in the territories occupied in 1948, they deserve our gratitude and recognition. Indeed we owe them our most sincere apologies for the harsh criticism we poured on them over the years because they decided to remain, steadfast and faithful, in their homes. We shunned them because they took Israeli citizenship, but today it is to them that we look for the prospect of liberating our land and restoring our rights. We made the same major mistake of fleeing twice, but, thank God, we finally learned our lesson. In 1982, when the Israelis invaded Lebanon, they tried to make us repeat our historic mistakes by committing brutal massacres and mass murder. This time, however, they failed, and instead faced stiff resistance. The Palestinians had finally understood the true meaning of being refugees and were determined not to repeat their own tragedy a third time. They remained in their camps in Lebanon even as the camps were reduced to ruins about them.

(3)

My fifth visit to Jordan took place in spring 1970, when tension between Palestinian factions and the Jordanian regime was reaching its peak and was dominating the political landscape.

I concluded the following from this visit:

- In principle, coexistence between a revolutionary movement and the governing host regime – whatever and wherever that regime – is effectively impossible unless extraordinary efforts are made to protect and preserve the relationship.
- Our comrades in the Palestinian factions misbehaved in ways that affected people's livelihood and daily affairs, costing them their popularity.

- The relationship between the two peoples had become character-ized by fanaticism on a local level that even infected members of the Jordanian National Movement, which had been a supporter of the Palestinian movement, and the Free Officers' group, several of whom had spent long years in Jordanian jails because of their political activities. These people did not appreciate what was happening on their soil without their being consulted or asked to participate, especially as their dedication to the libera-tion of Palestine was no less strong than that of the Palestinians themselves.
- The regime had taken advantage of the vicious campaign carried out by some Palestinian factions against Nasser for his acceptance of the Rogers Plan. (The plan, rejected by Israel, was devised by US Secretary of State William Rogers to secure Israel's withdrawal from the Sinai and end the war between Israel and Egypt.)

I met with Abu Ammar during this trip, and I conveyed to him my impressions, based on meetings with various friends in the Jordanian military and the National Movement, who were all quite pessimistic about the prospects of a peaceful solution. It was clear that the Jordanian government had regained the dynamism it had lost in the 1967 defeat. Military staff were being mobilized, including those who had already retired. In short Jordan was preparing itself for battle.

Abu Ammar seemed like a man caught in a raging sea, his ship battered by gales and massive waves from all directions. Many Arabs around the region wanted a showdown, not out of sympathy with the Palestinian revolution, but rather out of hatred for the Jordanian regime. Abu Ammar seemed to me to be more interested in negotia-tions and co-existence with Jordan, and was extremely angry with the provocative graffiti sprayed onto the walls of Amman, saying "Power, Absolute Power to Workers and Soldiers," "Yes to the Revolution, No to the Regime," and so on.

Abu Ammar promised me that he would exercise restraint and that he would go to Cairo in order to clear the air and end the Palestinian media campaign against President Abdul Nasser over the Rogers Plan.

I returned to Beirut feeling rather less pessimistic and immedi-ately set about contacting all the political and military factions in a further attempt to calm the situation. But tension had escalated beyond control, reaching a crescendo at the beginning of September

1970 when a number of airliners were hijacked simultaneously by
the PFLP and three of them were forced to land in Jordan, at the
Dawson's Field airbase, which the hijackers had renamed Revolution Airport. When the hostages had been taken off the planes the
hijackers dynamited them. It was an act of such blatant defiance that
the Jordanian regime decided it was time to carry out mass attacks
against the refugee camps and any infrastructure of the PFLP and
other factions within them.

(4)

In mid-August 1970, a Fatah delegation presided over by Abu Ammar
flew to Egypt and met President Nasser at his residence in al-Ma'moura
on the north coast. Abu Lutf (Farouk Qaddoumi) and Abu Iyad later
briefed me about what happened at that meeting, which I shall try to
summarize briefly.

According to Abu Lutf, Nasser arrived an hour late, which was
unusual for him. As soon as he entered the room he said: "I've been
walking on the beach for over an hour, trying to cleanse myself of
the feelings of bitterness which your campaigns against me have
caused, and I am keen not to say anything that might in turn hurt your
feelings."

He then addressed Abu Ammar and said: "What is it that you
want from Jordan?" And Abu Ammar replied: "A patriotic government." Nasser asked: "What do you mean by a patriotic government?"
One of those in attendance said: "A government led by Suleiman
al-Nabulsi."

Nasser smiled and said: "Is that the extent of your problem with
Jordan? OK, let me tell you something: there is no such thing as a
'number two man' in the Arab world. No prime minister nor anyone
else in office can do a thing without the consent of the head of state.
Only he can decide matters."

Showing that he had indeed regained his usual good humor, Nasser
added: "You can even ask Ali Sabri (Egypt's prime minister at the time),
if you don't believe me ... Of course, there are a few things they can do
on their own, such as official receptions, but nothing more."

He then turned to Abu Ammar and asked him: "By the way, I
have heard that the Iraqis gave an official reception in your honor in
Baghdad and that they received you with military bands. Would you
like us to do the same for you in Egypt? And while on the subject of

Iraq, I hope for your sake that the Iraqis remain neutral in the event of a clash between you and King Hussein."

In those days, an Iraqi brigade was positioned near the Syrian borders and the Iraqi regime was fomenting rebellion and revolution in Jordan, allowing factional leaders to believe that the Iraqi regime would be on their side. But Iraq's intervention could spark war on a wide scale.

Nasser concluded: "I ask you in your own interests to try to calm relations between yourselves and the Jordanians. The Israelis are not going to leave you in peace, and the US Sixth Fleet is monitoring every activity on the shores of our Arab region. I myself am busy building a missile shield to protect the Egyptian heartland from the enemy's air force. As for the Rogers Plan, I have repeatedly explained to you that even the United States does not want this plan any more, so its chances of success are less than half a percent. I also told you that you are free to turn it down: I even ask you to do that; but you have no right to hurt us or to level false accusations against us. Once again, I must warn you that I will not be able to send commando paratroopers into Jordan to help you out."

All of this was told me by Abul Lutf in the presence of Abu Iyad. As for Abu Ammar, I saw him while he was on his way from Beirut to Amman, and we had a brief conversation. I asked him about the position Fatah was taking after the meeting with Nasser vis-à-vis the Rogers Plan, and he said: "We are against it. Nasser assured us that his position is tactical, which is smart, as he knows that America won't dare stick to this plan."

I asked: "And what are you planning to do regarding this vicious campaign against Nasser?" He answered: "This campaign is both wrong and dangerous. The imbeciles who are inciting the demonstrations in Amman have no idea how popular Nasser is among both the Jordanian people and the Jordanian army. Nevertheless, I am going to Amman to try to put an end to this madness."

I learned later that he did try, but his attempt failed. Consequently, we agreed to hold an exceptional session of the National Council on August 27, 1970.

(5)

I arrived with a group of independent PNC members in Amman the day before the meeting. Someone met us at the airport and delivered us to Janah Firas Hotel at Jabal al-Lwebdeh. As he drove, he violated so many traffic regulations that we almost believed he and the faction to which he belonged were in a state of rebellion not only against the Jordanian political leaders, but against the entire traffic system, as well!

Delegations had begun to arrive from all over the world. Among them was a delegation from Cairo that included more than 20 well-known Egyptian personalities, including the authors Ahmad Bahaa al-Deen, Lutfi al-Khouli, Mahmoud Amin al-Alem, the diplomat Murad Ghaleb, and others, all of whom were supporters of the revolutionary movement. Hotel lobbies were jammed with people in discussions, and all of them warned against the dangers of bloody confrontation between Palestinians and Jordanians.

The questions preoccupying me during this period were these: What does the PLO want from Jordan, and what does Jordan want from the PLO? And, is there still a chance to define these demands, in order to meet them or at least come to a compromise over them? What worried me the most was that I saw no one qualified to mediate between the two sides. Even the Jordanian National Movement was confused and split, and slipping into chauvinism. The Jordanian armed forces were nowhere to be seen on the streets of Amman, which in itself seemed a worrying sign. Jordanian Intelligence, however, was on full alert, and reported all our conversations, meetings, and movements to the king's palace.

The PNC session began with a general discussion during which the conflicts and differences between the various factions became apparent. Each speaker presented demands and conditions, trying to outdo his rivals, and long applause followed speeches that made up in volume for what they lacked in wisdom. This session also witnessed a great deal of talk against Egypt and Nasser, which caused some members of the Egyptian delegation to walk out in protest.

In the end, the PNC produced a communiqué; although a few wise heads had edited it, trimming what was unnecessary and selecting more appropriate words, it had an enormous impact on the audience. But to my mind it was implicitly a declaration of war against the Jordanian regime.

The following day, several of us met at the house of a friend and conducted a sort of symposium in which several factions, including Fatah, participated. I asked the Fatah representative whether he agreed with me that the PNC statement was in effect an unofficial declaration of war, and he answered casually: "So be it. And what's wrong with that?" And then he lectured us at length on the nature and the history of relations between Palestinians and the Jordanian regime. When he was done, I asked him: "But what about the balance of power?" Winking in my direction he answered: "Aren't you the one who wrote that the 'path of liberation passes through Amman'? Or have you changed your mind?"

I said: "First of all, there's no shame in changing my mind, and I believe that doing so requires a courage that others more vain than I don't possess. Second, my opinion has not changed, and I still believe that the liberation of Palestine will not be possible without the liberation of Amman. But by liberation I mean liberation of the will of the people."

He replied, like an immature adolescent: "We, on the other hand [meaning Fatah], do have the means ..." He pointed to the mountain visible through a window and said: "Do you see the forest on that mountain? It has been transformed into a forest of guns. So don't worry."

Recognizing his ignorance, I did not allow myself to be angered by his words, but responded coldly: "If you think your speech has reassured me, please understand that on the contrary you have just doubled my worries. Just for the sake of argument, let us assume that we went ahead and won this war against the regime. What would you do then: crown Arafat as King of Jordan? Will Jordan become a substitute for Palestine? And what about the other half of this country's people, our Jordanian comrades and brothers? Have you thought of their position and what might be going on in their minds as they ponder the eventualities as you are thinking of?"

With a measure of despair he answered: "You have no idea what this regime is like, or what it has done to our young people and our countrymen. You live in Lebanon and your situation there is quite different from ours."

I spoke firmly, putting an end to the discussion by pointing to my wounded leg: "Although I live in Lebanon, a bullet is lodged right here in my leg: one of the supporters of this regime fired it at me three years ago. Where were you on that day?"

This conversation was a good example of the atmosphere in the Palestinian revolutionary arena in the early 1970s, and the character of the tense debates that took place at the time between leaders, cadres, and individuals in the movement. Some of these questions remain, critical and unanswered, to this very day, including the nature of the relationship between Jordan and Palestine, which is considered the most sensitive among all Arab peoples.

The war between Palestinian forces and the Jordanian army erupted in September, 1970. Thousands of people were killed and hundreds of houses were destroyed, and at the end of it the Palestinians suffered a third migration. Disaster had struck and the Iraqi brigade stationed in Jordan did not lift a finger in anyone's support. The Israeli air force monitored events on the ground, while Mr Nixon's fleet was on alert, ready to challenge any and all interventions from outside. But Nasser defied him. He called for an immediate Arab summit meeting, and dispatched President Ja'far al-Numairi of Sudan and the Kuwaiti Defense and Interior Minister, Sa'd al-Abdallah al-Sabah, to salvage the situation and rescue Abu Ammar from the siege, as well as to organize the release of Abu Iyad and Abu Lutf from Jordanian prisons. The summit convened, and the episode ended with the departure of the Palestinian revolutionary forces from Jordan.

On the last day of the summit, Nasser died, and all in all that accursed day marked the beginning of the end of the pan-Arab era.

The Palestinian factions migrated north, first to the fields of Jarash in Jordan, and then further north to the Syrian borders, where they were denied entry into the country. At the time Damascus was preoccupied with its own internal struggles, especially between the rival groups led by Salah al-Jadeed and Hafez al-Assad.

In the end the Palestinian factions had no alternative but to head west, towards Lebanon, there to open a new chapter in their struggle to find the right road to the liberation of Palestine.

(6)

I met King Hussein a second time in New York, in 1975, during the opening of the 30th Session of the General Assembly of the United Nations. His then prime minister, Sharif Abdul Hamid Sharaf, who had been with me at the AUB, received Abu Lutf and me at the entrance of his suite at the Waldorf Astoria Hotel, and escorted us to the reception room. The king greeted us with the utmost finesse and courtesy, as was his habit. Then he exchanged some general political talk with Abu Lutf.

When he noticed my silence, the king said smilingly: "We have heard nothing so far from Brother Shafiq." And so I said: "Your Majesty, you have talked with Brother Abu Lutf about the important things, and I have nothing to add but a small request: I want a visa to visit Amman!"

The King looked surprised and said: "You are most welcome at any time. Consider yourself my personal guest." I responded: "You see, Your Majesty, that is precisely the problem: not every Palestinian has the luxury of meeting you and receiving your personal invitation. I am talking on behalf of ordinary people." Here, Sharif Abdul Hamid intervened and said with heavy irony: "Your Majesty, Shafiq is especially sensitive to the workings of Jordanian Intelligence and the ins and outs of airport logistics ..." I interrupted Abdul Hamid and said to the King: "I wish Your Majesty would ask me why I want so badly to visit Amman? You may not believe this, but the truth of the matter is that I am hungry for a plate of *fuul* at Kalha Restaurant, as I have not tasted it since I left Jaffa in 1948."

The king shook his head and said in front of everyone: "Probably this is the most important thing we have heard in this meeting: we should not forget ordinary people."

7

NASSER AS I KNEW HIM

The intention of this chapter is not to enumerate the achievements of the Nasser era, which produced major changes both within the Arab world and outside. Nor is it to list its shortcomings, many of which have already been spelt out by others, some accurately and objectively, others with prejudice and unfairness. Indeed, the Nasser era has been the subject of a long and acrimonious debate, as though the man was still working away in his modest office at Manshiyat al-Bakri in Cairo rather than, as he has been since 1970, lying in an equally modest grave just a few meters away.

I wish in this chapter to describe "Nasser the man," as I knew him.

It is based on personal encounters I was fortunate enough to have had with a man I admired and respected, first as a journalist and editor of *al-Hawadeth* magazine between 1958 and 1964, and later as a politician working full-time with the Palestine Liberation Organization.

(1)

I met President Nasser six times in all, the first two occasions being chance encounters which need not detain us at length. In 1959, I was one of the thousands of supporters who set off in convoys from Lebanon to Damascus when Nasser paid a visit to the capital of the Northern Region of the United Arab Republic. I was at the time part of the *al-Hawadeth* family, which editorially was firmly in the pro-Nasser camp, and we were received in the Guest Palace to meet the president. Another meeting took place in 1961, during a conference of Arab journalists in Cairo, in which a special session had been arranged with him for Lebanese reporters. Then between 1962 and 1967 I was privileged to be called to his private office for three lengthy discussions. The third spontaneous encounter, and the last time I spoke to Nasser, was in Khartoum during the Arab summit of 1967.

(2)

The first interview: When I headed to Cairo in mid-April 1962, I was not on a reporting assignment. It had not even crossed my mind to seek an interview with the president. In fact, I was on my honeymoon. My friend, the well-known Egyptian author Ahmad Baha ad-Deen, met me and my new bride, Bayan Nuwayhed, at the airport and drove us to the Semiramis Hotel. I liked this hotel because of the wide diversity of its guests: politicians, artists, Egyptian and Arab journalists – as well as political refugees who had made it a forum for their meetings and debates, and sometimes their quarrels.

Two days after our arrival in Cairo, I was surprised by an unexpected visit from the president's secretary, Abdul Majid Farid, a gentleman I had met in Beirut. He told me he had been sent by President Nasser to congratulate me on my marriage and to inquire whether I was comfortable at the Semiramis or would rather move to another hotel. He also asked whether I needed a private car or had any other requests, as I was his guest in Egypt. After expressing my sincerest gratitude, I said: "I wish I could meet the president, if for only a few minutes, so that I can get to know him better and thank him in person for all he has done for the Arab nation."

Abdul Majid answered: "*Inshallah*. I will check the president's schedule and get back to you."

From that moment, I lived in the hope of a meeting, although I knew that there must have been a very long list of people waiting to see Nasser. On Friday evening, April 27, 1962, I was in the lobby with my wife when I was called to the telephone. When I returned Bayan could tell from the look on my face that my wish – a wish that must have been shared by countless millions across the Arab world – was going to come true.

I had a sleepless night, turning over in my mind which of the innumerable issues around the Arab world I should ask him about. It seemed impossible to prioritize. Should I flit from one subject to another, seeking a brief response by the president to each, or should I try to concentrate on a single question, delving more deeply into it with him?

The phone rang early the following morning. It was Abdul Majid Farid again, informing me that the meeting was to be that very day at noon. I saw the president for the first time in the study of his modest house in Manshiyat al-Bakri. He stood at the entrance of the room, tall and smiling, and I extended my hand to shake his. A day or two earlier the editor of *al-Ahram*, Mohammad Hassanein Heikal, had written that three Syrian officers had come to Nasser to propose a conditional return to the Union between Egypt and Syria, so I decided to open the conversation with the subject of the Union. But how should I begin?

The president noticed my hesitation and offered me a cigarette to help me loosen up. Although I was a smoker, I refused. Instead, I moved to light his, but he had already done so and took a long draft from the cigarette. He said warmly: "I see you are carrying a lighter, which means you smoke. Please, relax, go ahead and have a cigarette."

"Thank you, Mr President ... Frankly, sir, I could hardly sleep last night, so worried was I about how to conduct this interview. I wish I had listened to the advice of a friend of mine, who told me to take a sedative before meeting you."

The president laughed and said: "I'm sure the reason you didn't sleep and why you're so agitated now is because you are a bridegroom who has just got married. That's all!"

He laughed sincerely and repeated his warm congratulations on my marriage. At that point, I felt the ice had melted: it was as though I had known Nasser for many years and was now able to talk to him frankly, and ask whatever questions I wanted. I must say, having met most of the Arab leaders over the years, I never felt with any of them as I felt with Nasser. I found I could speak comfortably and with confidence about whatever I wanted. Indeed, as I look back at my conversations with him, I even feel a tinge of embarrassment because I permitted myself to say things that might normally be considered out of bounds, things I would never utter today in such circumstances.

I will give one example of this. As we were talking about the Union and all the problems it had experienced, we talked about what Mohammad Hassanein Heikal had written on the subject in *al-Ahram*. Despite my awareness of the deeply rooted friendship between Heikal and Nasser, I said: "In Beirut, we all read Heikal's articles and we regard him as being politically 'American.' What confuses us is that he's also considered your official spokesman."

Without the slightest surprise or annoyance, Nasser responded: "I have heard a lot of this sort of talk, although it is not true. Heikal happens to be close to me and he is in a decision-making position.

It is only natural that his themes are richer than others. He is also free to express his opinions, some of which I agree with, some of which I disagree with ... I also consider him a friend and I trust him only to quote the statements that I make which I don't mind being published."

Then, sensing perhaps that his answer had not fully convinced me, the president added: "Let me tell you something. A few weeks ago, you responded in *al-Hawadeth* to an article Heikal had written in *al-Ahram*. I read your piece and then I called Heikal and told him he was wrong and Shafiq was right." (Heikal's article had been entitled "We Are Alone on the Battlefield"; in it he wrote that the Union had been imposed on Egypt, and had exhausted the objectives for which it had been created, and that there was no longer a justification for its continuation. My reply was entitled "No, You Are Not Alone on the Battlefield.")

Although I was aware that the meeting was beginning to exceed the limits of courtesy, I found it hard to break away. I asked him: "Mr President, did you know that some people say that you're a cross between Stalin and Jesus Christ, and that's why you don't resolve matters as swiftly as necessary."

He smiled and said: "That's not true and not acceptable. I am neither Christ, peace be upon him, nor am I Stalin."

After a moment's silence, he continued by using his full name, which includes that of his grandfather, from upper Egyptian peasant stock, and his father, who was a postal worker: "I am Gamal ... Abdul Nasser ... Hussein. I am trying to pave the way for a better society that can guarantee development together with self-sufficiency and justice, inspired by the history, traditions, and tolerance of our people."

I responded: "Some of your supporters disagree with you regarding tolerance, as they think that you are too lenient with the enemies of the revolution."

Then he spoke at length about the Egyptian people, emphasizing his faith in them and respect for them. "With a stroke of my pen, I could suspend all our newspapers and permit just one single party newspaper. I could subject all cinemas, theaters, as well as the media, to strict regulations. But I assure you if I did that the Egyptian people would be angry. They like to criticize and at the same time they have a great sense of humor. Our people have been oppressed for thousands of years and they have the right to express themselves, even though some might take advantage of this freedom for their personal interests."

He then stared into space for a minute, as though reviewing history in his mind, and said: "Many people misunderstood me when I decided to redistribute the land and carry out agrarian reforms. They thought my primary objective was to increase productivity, but they were wrong. What motivated me was not economic expediency, but rather to restore to the Egyptian *fellahin* their dignity and pride. These people have been downtrodden for millennia. You may find it hard to believe – as so many others have done – that in the beginning many *fellahin* refused to accept their deeds of ownership. Some went so far as to think it would be blasphemy ... Can you see what I'm trying to say here?"

This was the first time I understood the true meaning of the Egyptian slogan "Raise your head, brother." I also saw Nasser's deeply ingrained feelings about the oppression of the landless *fellahin*, especially that there were still people in Egypt referred to as "transient laborers." No wonder the Egyptian people loved Nasser: he was one of them.

After this exchange, the president paused again, before discussing several other issues, including the need to have multi-party political platforms. I then asked him: "Is it acceptable that there were people in the United Arab Republic such as Farajallah al-Helou (member of the Political Bureau of the Communist Party in Damascus) who have been killed because of their opinions?"

Nasser was silent for a moment. His smile disappeared for the first time since the beginning of the interview and a look of regret appeared on his face. He said: "You may not believe this, but I assure you that I read the news in the papers like any ordinary Arab citizen and I was saddened and angered by this event. Indeed, we got in touch with the officials in Damascus for details on the case and asked them to carry out an investigation."

Today, looking back, I ask myself who would dare pose such a challenging question – or even a lesser one – to any Arab leader!

Suddenly realizing that I had taken already two whole hours of the leader's time, I wrapped up the interview and made my farewell. Nasser stood up and, striding towards the door, he called out: "Hassan ... Hassan." He then returned with a smile: "Don't you want to have a photograph taken with me?"

After the picture was taken he extended his hand to shake mine,

Photo 3 The author's first interview with President Nasser in Cairo (1962)

and congratulated me once again on my recent marriage. Before leaving, I enquired whether he wished to review the article I was going to write before its publication and he answered that I was free to publish without any clearance. And then he added: "This is what I normally do with Heikal."

(3)

The second interview: This interview was a very special occasion, and it deserves a little preface. On the evening of February 8, 1963, during the month of Ramadan, Mohammad Hassanein Heikal called me from Cairo and proposed that I head immediately to Baghdad as a special correspondent for *al-Ahram* to cover the news that had caught the attention of the whole world that day: the Iraqi *coup d'état* against Abdul Karim Qassem. "I'm not interested in the facts on the ground," he said. "We have already dispatched our correspondent to gather those. What I am after is analysis: the background of the coup, its future, the most influential forces, the balance of power, and so on."

I flew to Baghdad the following day. Signs of the coup's aftermath, smoke, blood, and physical destruction, were still visible throughout the Ministry of Defense, where Abdul Karim Qassem's office had been located. The news was still unclear and all kinds of rumors were circulating about the coup and who was behind it: Ba'th, the Arab Nationalist Movement, the Iraqi army, or one of its commanders like Abdul Salam Aref?

Thanks to my old AUB friendships with several Iraqi Ba'thists and Arab Nationalists, I managed to gather important details about what had happened and what might happen in the immediate future. The first thing I learnt was how Qassem had been liquidated. Seated at his desk, I took a photo of his bullet-ravaged office. I also learnt that his ministers and senior supporters had all been detained.

I reported all my findings to *al-Hawadeth* on a daily basis. Then I headed to Cairo to write the full story for *al-Ahram*. The morning following the publication of the first installment, Heikal called me and said: "The president wants to see you today." He picked me up and drove me to Nasser's house. He parked his car in a nearby spot then, looking at his watch, he said: "We have ten minutes before the appointment. How about taking a stroll? It'll be a chance to have a smoke before we see the president."

It was Ramadan, and most Muslims – from the president down – were fasting, which meant not eating, drinking, or smoking during daylight hours. As we walked, Heikal stopped a lad on a bicycle and exchanged a quick greeting with him. Two younger children were running alongside the older boy. Heikal looked at me and said: "Do you know these children? They are Nasser's. That is his eldest son,

Khaled." The children were playing in the street, unescorted and without guards!

The instant we entered the house, it was evident that Heikal was treated like one of the family and he behaved accordingly. We went straight into the president's office. When Nasser entered the room, dressed in simple clothes, a white shirt over his trousers, it seemed as though he had just woken up after a nap. When he saw us, he rubbed his nose as if he smelt something and I understood what was troubling him, so I said quickly: "Mr President, I am excused from fasting as I am traveling, and I can make up these days of the fast at a later time." I then looked towards Heikal and added: "I don't know why Heikal isn't fasting though!"

Once again, Nasser let out that genuine laugh of his and said: "You are free to do whatever you want. But let me tell you something: up there with God, there is no mediation, and no one can help you." A man of deep and sincere faith, he meant what he said.

Naturally, Nasser was interested in every detail related to the events in Iraq. He asked me to brief him on my impressions and frequently interrupted me to ask me to shed more light on this or that issue. He was annoyed and shook his head in disappointment when I described the scenes of violence, such as Qassem's surrender and summary execution. He did not utter a single word of gloating or revenge, despite all the insults and political attacks he had suffered during Qassem's era and despite his deep pain at the fall of Iraqi unionist martyrs at the battle at Um al-Toubol.

Once my account convinced him that the main player of the coup had been the Ba'th Party, and that Abdul Salam Aref had not yet achieved total power, he asked me what the leaders of the Arab Nationalist Movement were thinking and saying. He was especially interested in hearing the views of men like Bassel Qubaisi, who was one of the leaders of the Popular Front for the Liberation of Palestine. (Qubaisi was assassinated by Mossad in Paris years later.)

I was aware of the mutual sympathy between Nasser and the Arab Nationalist Movement, but I could not mislead him and report that they had played a major role in the coup, because their role had been quite minor. Rather I told him about the excuses they had produced; their version of the story was that the Ba'thists had preempted the very coup they themselves had been about to launch! I just said: "They are now quite frustrated, as they have no role to play. And they may end up having to wait a long time before reaching power."

As a joke, I added: "And I suggest to the bachelors among them that they consider this period an opportunity to take advantage of their free time and get married." Nasser appreciated the joke. He laughed and said: "Not a bad idea; perhaps this will help them increase the numbers of their supporters."

We resumed our talk and I recollect the following from what he said: "There are no problems between me and the Iraqi Ba'th. They knew perfectly well that from the inception of their coup Cairo would stand by them and give all the support they need. We can talk to them at any time about a plan for a union, with no pressure or coercion. I only hope that they will not take a stand with the Syrian Ba'th."

Political veterans like myself no doubt remember the days that followed the Iraqi coup and the later negotiations in Cairo between Egypt, Syria, and Iraq with the aim of establishing a new union between the three states. What few people know, however, is that there was also an Algerian delegation in Cairo at the time, authorized by its government to declare Algeria the fourth member of this new union in the event that an agreement was reached.

The February 1963 interview opened my eyes to a quality in Nasser I had not known before. Although a pan-Arab union was his greatest dream, the man detested the idea of violence being used as a means to achieve it. This was probably the main reason he backed away from getting entangled in armed conflict in Syria in order to re-establish the Union. Though he was a Unionist, Nasser was no "Bismarckist."

(4)

The third interview: At the end of 1966, two years after I had resigned from al-Hawadeth and become fully dedicated to the PLO and a member of its Third Executive Committee, the conflict between a group of us and Ahmad al-Shuqayri, the Chairman of the Committee, had reached its zenith. Al-Shuqayri had tried to pull off a coup when he declared on PLO Radio in Cairo the creation of a Revolutionary Council to replace the Executive Committee. His intention was to outflank the underground fedayeen factions, and as a result of his action a long media and institutional battle occurred between him and the rest of us. This was to dominate Palestinian politics for some time to come.

Coincidentally, as I have already mentioned, I suffered another attempt on my life on February 17, 1967, in Beirut: I was wounded in the thigh and was committed to hospital for a few days. The press saw a connection between the assassination attempt and the internal crisis of the PLO, though I categorically denied any such link. *Al-Ahram* published the news of the attempt on its front page. Almost every official of the Egyptian embassy in Beirut paid me a visit in hospital and I also received a telegram from President Nasser. When I got home, I received a visit from the Egyptian ambassador, Abdul Hamid Ghaleb, who was leaning on a cane. He apologized for not having visited me at the hospital as he had injured his foot. He then briefed me about the investigation that Cairo had begun into the attempt on my life, and invited me to spend my convalescence in Cairo.

I flew to Cairo in March 1967 and had another meeting with the president, along with my friend Mohammad Hassanein Heikal, who was always the link between the president and me.

The president greeted me with a smile, and the first thing he said was: "So how are you doing now ... Is your leg OK?" He then asked me about the family and what children I had produced. When I told him that I had had two daughters, he laughed and said: "We shall call you *Abu Banat* (Father of the Girls). You are just like Mohammad Ahmad [his private secretary, who was still standing at the door as we prepared to sit down]." He added, still laughing: "No ... no ... Mohammad is even luckier than you. He's got five girls already, isn't that so, Mohammad?"

We then had a serious talk, perhaps the most important I ever took part in. "What's going on between you and al-Shuqayri," he asked, "and why are you raising hell against the man?" He listened attentively as I recounted the whole story, and then said: "It is true that he talks too much, and every day he delivers a new statement or gives more interviews, but there is no harm in that. Let the man talk. Between you and me, I should mention that Shuqayri's statements and these operations by the *fedayeen* are needed to fill the void in anticipation of the real war which we must eventually wage, and which we shall win. But, in order to be victorious, we must ensure the necessary conditions are in place." He then elaborated on these conditions and concluded: "We should therefore wait for at least two or three years." And then, laughing, he added: "Is it reasonable to ask al-Shuqayri to keep his mouth shut for three years?"

Al-Ahram published the interview the following day. I also managed to publish parts of it in *al-Hawadeth*, in which I was still writing intermittently, especially on matters relating to Palestine. The significance of this particular interview lies in a mystery which became apparent only later, and for which I have never found an adequate explanation: how did Nasser fall into the trap laid for him in 1967? This matter is especially puzzling in light of the fact that he had explicitly told me in this interview, just three months before the June war, that he would only wage a war he was sure of winning and that the conditions for victory required three more years of preparation?

I had not at that point yet discovered that Nasser was overly keen on preserving his public image. In the critical months that preceded the 1967 war, the media campaigns against him escalated considerably. Their chief objective was to provoke Nasser at that vulnerable point in his thinking. In fact the provocations actually began earlier, when the Israelis first threatened to attack Syria, Nasser's favorite Arab nation. This provocation was later exacerbated by a continuous media campaign urging him to expel the United Nations forces from Sinai and close the Straits of Eilat, thereby egging him further and further towards war. Strangely enough, these campaigns were launched by Nasser's enemies and allies alike.

Perhaps the only explanation of why he fell into the trap, though he was a man of good sense and judgment, lies in his pride, which his enemies knew how to exploit.

In the end, Nasser courageously took full and sole responsibility for the defeat of 1967, from whose repercussions the Arab world suffers to this very day. Indeed he began his resignation speech with this admission of responsibility. Considering this stand, I do not think it possible that anyone can doubt the man's personal courage.

(5)

My third chance encounter with Nasser lasted less than a minute. It took place in Khartoum when I had the opportunity to participate in the activities of the Arab summit of August 28 and 29, 1967, as a member of the PLO delegation, headed then by al-Shuqayri.

Nothing could hide the bitter reality of Nasser's defeat, not even the crowds of Sudanese people who lined the streets from the airport to the official guest house, chanting with enormous enthusiasm:

"The Enemy of Nasser is the Enemy of God," although they did restore some lost pride to the tall knight.

At the opening session of the summit, all eyes were on him and everyone waited with bated breath to hear what he would say. But after the official opening remarks, he did not utter a word. The Sudanese president, Ismail al-Azhari, looked around at the kings and presidents gathered in the hall, searching for a raised hand requesting the floor, but not a single one of them showed any inclination to speak. Ignoring al-Azhari's embarrassment, everyone stared at Nasser, waiting for him to say something. I waited with the others to hear what he would say, wondering how he would address the kings and presidents. I knew how he addressed the masses of his people in their hundreds of thousands, and how he handled journalists in interviews, or in private meetings, but I had never heard him on such an occasion as this and so could not imagine how he would conduct himself.

At last, he spoke. His rhetorical style was quite different from any I had heard him use before: a balanced combination of diplomatic tact, revolutionary zeal, crowd-moving oratorical eloquence, and solemn analysis. The speech also included courageous self-criticism in which he recognized his mistakes without for a moment renouncing his principles and goals. His speech was improvised, delivered without interruption, yet it was as though he were reading from a book. Sometimes he reached a point in his presentation of the realities at hand, or the tricky questions surrounding them, and everyone expected him to pause, or cautiously sidestep the next difficult issue. Instead, he forged ahead, clearly presenting alternative courses of action and his various responses to them. He allowed his listeners to understand what they would, but was fully confident he had left them no alternative but to agree with the decisions he had taken.

The meetings of the summit continued, some open and public, some behind closed doors, including those dedicated to an attempt to achieve a reconciliation between Egypt and Saudi Arabia over their conflict in Yemen. There were serious concerns over the possible outcome of the summit. A few minutes before the concluding session, I was standing with some other participants in the lobby of the Sudan Hotel, unconsciously leaning against the elevator door. Suddenly, one of Nasser's bodyguards asked me to step aside as the president was on his way down. I barely had a moment to move out of the way, when the elevator door opened and Nasser appeared. I froze, not knowing what to do. Should I go ahead and shake hands with the man, or would a simple gesture be sufficient? Was it possible that Nasser, at this critical moment and under such circumstances, might not even remember me, especially after the hundreds of people that he had had contact with in the past two days?

He looked at me, as if wondering what I was doing there. And then he extended his hand in greeting and said: "How is your leg? Any better? Have you got yourself a boy yet, or are you still *Abu Banat*?" That was Nasser through and through: witty, alert, with an excellent memory, a sense of humor that despite everything remained intact, forgiving, never malicious, and always extremely sensitive to his public image.

I shook his hand firmly, and all I managed to say was: "May God be with you, Mr President .... May God be with you."

8

FRATRICIDAL WARS

The Palestinian freedom fighters' move from Jordan to Lebanon was not the result of an official or public invitation. The Palestinians did not single out Lebanon because it was more revolutionary or closer to pan-Arabism than other Arab nations. Rather, they headed there because it was open, like a garden without a fence. It would have made more sense for the fighters to move to a nearby Arab country that could play a role similar to that played by Hanoi with the rebels of South Vietnam. Egypt or Syria would have been a better choice than Lebanon, the weakest of the frontline Arab states bordering occupied Palestine. In addition to its small size and limited military capabilities, Lebanon is unusual for its multiplicity of sects and faiths, and the diversity of its people; these disparate groups are unable to settle on a common understanding of their country's past, or a common vision of its future.

What's more, the Lebanese government already had many reservations about the Palestinian presence on its soil. Palestinian–Lebanese relations were meant to be regulated by the Cairo Agreement of 1969, which had been in place for a year when the Palestinian revolution moved to Lebanon. As time unfolded, painful events were to inflict terrible damage on the relationship between the two peoples.

(1)

In the years before September 1970, an early and significant event in the history of Lebanese–Palestinian relations was the raid by four Israeli helicopters on Beirut International Airport on the evening of December 28, 1968. This attack resulted in extensive damage and the destruction of 13 aircraft belonging to Middle East Airlines, the Lebanese national carrier. Less than two years later, on March 26, 1970, a massacre occurred in Kahhaleh, a Christian suburb in the hills south of Beirut on the highway leading to Damascus and this almost dragged the country into a civil war. How did this happen?

The Palestinian unit al-Kifah al-Musallah (the armed struggle) had confronted a gang of Lebanese drug dealers who had been dressing like *fedayeen* as a disguise, including their trademark *kuffiyeh* head-scarves. They used to operate near the Sports City, stopping cars and selling narcotics and contraband cigarettes. I had even run into a few of them myself.

As soon as I heard of the stand-off in Kahhaleh, I called representatives of the Kifah al-Mussallah and asked them to do everything possible to avoid violence, because the reputation of the revolution was on the line. Regrettably though, armed confrontation was inevitable and several members of the gang were killed as well as an officer on the Palestinian side, Said Ghawwash. Following the incident, Raymond Eddeh, a prominent Maronite Christian leader, called and thanked me for having saved Beirut from a criminal gang that the Lebanese authorities themselves had failed to crack down on. He also offered his condolences for the martyrdom of Captain Ghawwash.

The next day, a funeral convoy of several cars carrying *fedayeen* headed to Damascus where the martyr's family was living. The men were in uniform and wearing red berets, and they were unarmed. Just as the convoy drove past Kahhaleh, it was ambushed by armed men who had been hiding on the roofs of the nearby houses and in the church steeple. All 14 *fedayeen* were killed. Kamal Jumblatt, then Minister of the Interior, immediately phoned and asked me to meet him in his office, in order to come up with an emergency plan to control the situation before a political volcano erupted. We met briefly and together headed towards the scene of the crime, where the bodies were still lying on the street. The head of the Kahhaleh municipality, Elias Abi Khalil, was waiting for the minister with a large group of local residents, all of whom denied that any local people had been involved and testified that the gunmen had infiltrated the town. Jumblatt warned that the criminals would be severely punished and then requested that I speak to the crowd. Angry as I was, I managed to stay calm and told them that we in the Palestinian revolution were aware of the intention of whoever had committed this crime in this place: to arouse sectarian passions and spark a civil war.

That same evening, Lebanese reporter and TV broadcaster George

Farshakh visited me in my office. He handed me a roll of film that he had managed to take during the Kahhaleh incident while on his way to Zahleh in the Beqaa Valley. When we had the film processed and the photos were enlarged, the truth became clear. Most of the shooters were identifiable and they included the Phalange leader Bashir al-Gemayyel, who was positioned near the church.

I took the photos to Kamal Jumblatt, who could scarcely believe his eyes. He asked that I keep it quiet to avoid the inevitable repercussions. A few days later, al-Gemayyel was ambushed and taken to one of the camps by the *fedayeen*. Once again, Kamal Jumblatt intervened and asked for my help in locating the hostage and returning him safely. I promised that I would and, although it was very difficult to convince the hostage-takers to deliver him to me, Bashir al-Gemayyel was returned in one piece. His car was also returned, but only after we had confiscated a machine gun from its trunk along with a number of red berets still covered in gore.

(2)

I reported to the PLO Command my assessment of the overall situation; I asked all factions to review their positions and engage in sincere self-criticism so that we could avoid a repetition of the tragedy of "Black September" in Jordan. This time, the first victims would be the freedom fighters who had survived the hellish heat of the Jordan Valley, only to come to the freezing Jabal al-Sheikh and Jabal al-Arkoub in Lebanon. I published my report in the Lebanese newspaper *al-Muharrer*, which had drawn me back to writing.

The introduction to my piece stated that revolution was impossible without a physical base. As long as our revolution was outside occupied Palestine, an alternative Arab territory bordering it had to be sought. We should, I continued, reinforce this new base by fostering the sympathy of its people, government, and influential forces. My second point was that armed confrontation between allies seemed alarmingly imminent, especially when the interests of individual Arab states were seen to supersede those of pan-Arab interests. My third point was that the greatest danger to the revolution was that its local opponents would exploit violations committed by the PLO's supporters or infiltrators to turn the host nation against it. Consequently, the Palestinian freedom fighter, though only human, must try to behave like an angel. My fourth and final point was to emphasize the importance of setting strict rules to control military operations and prohibit any organization from carrying them out unilaterally.

Palestinian newcomers had a great deal to learn about Lebanon, especially regarding its people, who were so drastically different from the Jordanians. In Lebanon, each district had its own set of values, each sect its own peculiarities, and each sector its own chieftains. Relations between citizens were governed by complex formulae whose origins dated back to Lebanon's early history. The Lebanese people's assessment of their country's past, present, and future were varied and complex. Accordingly, some Lebanese welcomed the "newcomers," while others resented the "foreign immigrants." Their views were informed not only by each person's attitudes towards Israel, but also by their hopes and fears for the political and demographic dimensions of Lebanon.

It was only natural, then, that the realities of Lebanon would be reflected in the fragile and hesitant Lebanese government, at least during the terms of Presidents Charles Helou, Suleiman Franjieh, and Elias Sarkis. I don't think I was exaggerating when I once said: "Beirut is the Arab capital that has loved us the most, and Beirut is the Arab capital that has hated us the most!"

(3)

The Palestinian revolution came to Lebanon in 1970, just at the beginning of Suleiman Franjieh's presidency. Israel had always hunted down Palestinian freedom fighters wherever they happened to be, but in Lebanon it adopted a more complex strategy: strike the Palestinians militarily and try to turn the Lebanese against them.

In the beginning, Israeli action was restricted to striking the *fedayeen*'s bases, thinking that this would be enough to neutralize the revolution and force it to cease its operations in the Upper Galilee region of northern Palestine. But our fighters were not weakened; instead, they grew braver and more capable of dealing with the enemy. Now, claiming that the Palestinian refugee camps throughout Lebanon were all military targets, the Israelis expanded their raids to strike deep into Lebanon, including Beirut and its suburbs, and the north. Israeli violation of Lebanese airspace became a routine event.

Israeli arrogance became intolerable. Abba Eban, who was Foreign

Minister at the time, was asked what he thought of the deaths of dozens of children as a result of an air raid on Nahr al-Bared Camp in northern Lebanon. He responded, unashamedly: "That was a strictly preventive measure: who can guarantee that these children will not become terrorists when they grow up?" Despite these attacks, successive Lebanese governments continued to turn a blind eye to this violation of their own country's sovereignty. No protests were lodged with the UN Security Council, not even for the sake of appearances.

For fear of turning Lebanese public opinion against the revolution, the leaders of the PLO decided drastically to reduce their guerrilla operations in the south. At the same time, they tried to persuade Lebanese officials to adopt a defense strategy that would deter Israel and end its violent blackmail. The PLO offered to help equip the Lebanese army, having received a promise from Libya's Colonel Qaddafi in that regard.

But, in spite of the reduction in operations from Lebanon, Israel continued its attacks against the camps, especially in the south, to drive people away and break the ties that had developed between the Lebanese and Palestinians. In addition to its direct military aggression, Israel never stopped its state terrorism, using Mossad agents who took up residence in Beirut's best hotels. On July 8, 1972, the novelist and PFLP member Ghassan Kanafani was blown up in a car bomb planted by Mossad. Ten days later, Mossad sent a flurry of letter bombs to Palestinian officials; one exploded in the hands of the academic and director of the Palestine Research Center, Dr Anis Sayigh, who was severely injured. They also sent one to me, but luckily it was detected before it could do any harm.

On April 10, 1973, Israeli commandos struck the PLO hard in an operation aimed at the heart of the Beirut leadership. A group of Israeli commandos led by the future prime minister, Ehud Barak, entered two buildings in Verdun Street near al-Snoubra and assassinated Kamal Nasser, Kamal Udwan, and Mohammad Youssef al-Najjar and his wife. That same night another attack, in al-Fakhani Street, targeted other members of the leadership, including Abu Ammar himself. The attack failed by sheer chance, as on that particular night a skirmish had taken place between two Palestinian factions that had occasioned a general alert in the area. When Barak's commandos approached, guards told them to halt. They ignored the order and the guards fired at them and they fled.

The incident shook the whole of Lebanon and Prime Minister Saeb Salam asked General Iskandar Ghanem, the head of the army, to step down. President Franjieh disagreed, and so it was Salam who resigned. Tensions grew and the government was almost torn asunder.

Just three weeks after the Verdun–Fakhani outrage, an armed clash took place between the Lebanese army and a group of *fedayeen* in Beirut. At that very moment, I happened to be taking Raymond Eddeh to visit Abu Ammar in the latter's office in al-Fakhani. The gunfire was quite clearly audible. Indeed, an artillery shell landed right behind the building in which we were meeting, shattering the windows. Eddeh picked up the phone and called General Ghanem to ask him what was happening. I could not hear what was said at the other end, but I did hear Eddeh quite clearly say: "I am talking to you from Abu Ammar's office and a shell has just hit us, so don't try to tell me that it's a simple operation against some uncontrolled elements." We let Eddeh make his telephone calls, while Abu Ammar got on another line to Damascus and put his Fatah comrades there in the picture, asking them to report the details to President Hafez al-Assad. In the meantime, the shelling continued uninterrupted. We heard that Lebanese planes had gone to raid the Sabra and Shatila camps, but the pilots had dropped their bombs in the sea in order not to jeopardize civilian lives.

All of a sudden, the guns fell silent, and shortly afterwards officials from both sides met. As a result of this meeting, the Cairo Agreement was supplemented with a new appendix, referred to as the Melkart Agreement, named after the hotel in which the deal was concluded. A discreet signal had passed between President Assad and both President Franjieh and Abu Ammar asking for an immediate ceasefire because the region was on the brink of a major development. Sure enough a few months later, the October 1973 war took place, with Egypt and Syria attacking Israel simultaneously in a bid to win back their occupied territory.

The outcome of the clashes in Lebanon was that the Lebanese authorities decided to relieve themselves of the responsibility for defending the refugee camps. If the Palestinians were insisting on warding off Israel, then they would have to take care of their own defense. The PLO began to arm the camps with as much equipment as possible, including anti-aircraft guns. This step was the cornerstone in the building of what some Lebanese began to refer to as the Palestinian "al-Fakhani State."

(4)

I feel a great sorrow when I think back to the painful events that befell Lebanon during the 1975–90 Civil War, as they inflicted deep wounds on us all, Lebanese and Palestinians. I am not keen on delving into the details of the bloody clashes between Lebanese and Palestinians, or the times when the Palestinians and Lebanese were against the Syrians, or the Lebanese and Syrians against the Palestinians, or Syrians and Palestinians against other Palestinians, or finally when it was the Lebanese against the Lebanese. The names of the episodes were never agreed upon and each party named them differently. But on the Palestinian side, we agreed ultimately that this period, whatever you wish to call it, was disastrous for all of us and benefited only our enemies. Although many years have elapsed since these events, their repercussions remain palpable and it seems there are still those who have not learned the lessons they taught us. As I was a Palestinian of Lebanese origin, my concern and pain was doubled throughout those years, especially as I was in close and constant contact with both sides, aware of their respective feelings and their bitterness about the civil and fraternal wars that were taking place.

In July 1975, around three months after the massacre of Palestinian bus passengers in Ain al-Remmaneh which sparked the "Two Year War," a seminar was held by the Palestine Research Center to discuss Palestinian–Lebanese relations in order to avert a total breakdown. The first speaker was Kamal Jumblatt, leader of the Progressive Socialist Party (PSP), who attributed the crisis to various factors, the first and most important of which, according to him, was the paranoia of the Lebanese Christians. Most Arab Christians, he said, suffer from this for various historic reasons. On the other hand, Jumblatt pointed out, there was also fear among Palestinians stemming from the refugees' memories of their travails and the harsh conditions under which they lived, as well as their harsh treatment by the Lebanese authorities, the Deuxieme Bureau in particular. Palestinians, he continued, had no confidence in the Lebanese government because of its absence of true patriotic feeling. Things would be different if the Palestinians could be assured that the government was truly motivated by national and patriotic priorities.

Jumblatt discussed another major factor in Lebanese–Palestinian relations: the nature of the Lebanese political regime, which had always been extremely conservative and inimical to change. Fouad

Chehab had tried to impose social reforms, but he was confronted by an oligarchy which felt it had an inalienable right to use the system to secure its own private interests. It was horrified by the demographic changes that had tilted the scales against it, and by the progressive ideas and leftist movements that had begun to spread throughout Lebanon. By contrast, it was only natural that a number of Lebanese reformers with nationalist tendencies should stand by the Palestinians and support their revolution. Jumblatt concluded his speech by pointing to the presence of undisciplined members of the Palestinian movements. Untoward activities were being committed and attributed to the revolution, defying the law, damaging the image of the revolution, and allowing its opponents to exploit the situation in their own favor.

As well as being president of the PSP, Kamal Jumblatt was chair of the Lebanese National Movement (LNM), which had gathered together the forces, parties, factions, and personalities in support of the Palestinian cause. Among these forces there were some who were even more enthusiastic and motivated than Kamal Jumblatt himself. Indeed, those who sympathized with the Palestinian cause were not restricted to the members of the LNM; there were many others, both Christian and Muslim.

Opposite the LNM that afternoon there was the Lebanese Front bloc, composed of Sheikh Pierre Gemayyel, Camille Chamoun, Suleiman Franjieh, Charles Malek, Fouad Efram al-Boustani, Edward Honein, Father Sharbel Qassis, Said Aql, and other rightwing leaders and warlords who were trying to convert their anti-revolutionary positions into an ideology. In fact, as I have written elsewhere, the text of the document issued at the launch of the bloc in the town of Awkar was broadly similar in form and substance to the ideology of Zionism in terms of its discrimination and racism, and its view of religion as the basis of nationality.

This artificial ideology did not endure and less than two years after the Lebanese Front was founded, Suleiman Franjieh withdrew from it. In addition, the Vatican instructed Father Boulos Numan, who had succeeded Father Sharbel Qassis, to refrain from political activities. The only significant figures left were Pierre Gemayyel and Camille Chamoun and their political movements, al-Kataeb (Phalange) and al-Ahrar (Liberal Nationals) respectively. But the power of both these two elderly leaders had already begun to decline in favor of their sons, Bashir Gemayyel and Dani Chamoun. After his assassination of Toni Franjieh, the president's son, and his attempt on the life of Dani Chamoun, Bashir Gemayyel took over and monopolized the direction of the Christian constituency in the war.

Pierre Gemayyel and Camille Chamoun reflected conventional Maronite politics. Publicly, though, their statements were always in favor of a balanced Lebanon, with proper representation of the Muslim and Christian sides. Furthermore, they were always very sensitive to the accusation of collaboration with Israel and, until the day each of them died, they always denied any connection with the Zionist state, although it was later revealed that these connections had in fact existed.

(5)

At this point I should like to address the still unresolved question as to whether or not the war between the Palestinians and some segments of the Lebanese, particularly the Phalange, had been avoidable.

Phalange–PLO relations had a fraught history, but there was always contact between their respective officials and I can go so far as to say that some relationships even developed into solid friendships. My own relationship with Sheikh Pierre himself dates back to the mid-1950s, during the same period in which I first met Kamal Jumblatt, his inveterate political adversary.

Whenever I met Sheikh Pierre, he would stress my Lebanese origins and play down my Palestinian identity. Once, when a discussion between us got into full swing, he said half-jokingly: "You are a Lebanese of well-known and noble descent. You are the descendant of Sheikh Mohammad al-Hout and Sheikh Abdul Rahman al-Hout ... So why are you carrying the burden of Palestine on your shoulders?" I answered: "Sheikh Pierre, because I am a noble Lebanese from a decent family, as you said, I cannot be disloyal to the country and people that hosted my grandfather and treated him as if he were a native Palestinian."

I also had a good relationship with Sheikh Amin, Pierre's eldest son, from the day he became a member of parliament in 1969, until he became president, in 1982. These facts give the answer to the question I posed above, derived from my own experience and from the incidents I myself have witnessed.

Since the mid-1960s, the Palestinian national movement in

general, and Fatah in particular, had always rejected the conventional division of the Arab states into either progressive or reactionary regimes. Instead, they classified them on the basis of their position towards Palestine and the Palestinian revolution. Through its envoys and offices, the PLO reached out to a number of states, seeking new friendships, ties, and support. Lebanon was one of the first states to recognize the PLO and, as I said earlier, the Lebanese government also agreed in 1964 to allow the PLO to open an office and granted it immunity, as with any other diplomatic mission. The PLO Office staff worked openly from the very beginning with all political forces and parties, with special attention to the non-leftist or non-pan-Arab groups, particularly the Phalange and al-Ahrar parties. We were aware of their sensitivities on several issues, especially our relations with their political opponents.

In addition, to claim that "Christian Lebanon" was isolationist or uninterested in the overall revolutionary climate is a distortion of the truth. The best proof of this is that we managed to find plenty of room in that constituency to discuss our cause, our affairs, and our newly born *fedayeen* movement in the Occupied Territories. This "revolutionary consciousness" was probably one of the early signs that alarmed the conventional leaderships in Lebanon, whether Muslim or Christian.

On the international scene, a massive wave of student movements in support of the communist revolution in Vietnam further intensified the fears of right-wingers. The PLO had good relations with the

Photo 4 Going with Arafat to a closed meeting (Beirut, mid-1970s). Al-Hout drives his car while the bodyguard is in the back seat.

international movements, but was at the same time keen on avoiding internal tensions in Lebanon. Yet tension did arise, and it developed first into a crisis, then a confrontation, and eventually a war that lasted for two years: 1975–76. Some people hold the PLO fully responsible for what happened. They believe that had the PLO been more aware of the intricacies of the Lebanese system and achieved better relations with the Christian constituency in general, and the Phalange in particular, it would have been able to avoid the war and things would not have ended in the catastrophe that came about. But is this true?

An immediate answer, whether yes or no, would be more emotional than objective. It is not that easy to arrive at the correct response.

The ideology of the Palestinian resistance is, by definition, in opposition to any non-revolutionary ideology; the Phalange, as a predominantly conservative, Christian party, follows an ideology that opposes any revolutionary agenda. Nevertheless, the Phalange could have been kept uninvolved, or could have even contributed positively on occasions, had the Palestinian revolution remained outside of Lebanese territory. But the moment Lebanon became the "host country" of the revolution, this was no longer possible, regardless of how hard the revolution tried to impose limits on its undisciplined members. Undoubtedly, Israel and other enemies of the Palestinians discovered this weak spot and knew how to exploit it and how to plan a succession of conspiracies, until they were finally able to ignite the conflict. I am one of those who believes that, in the immediate pre-war period, between 1973 and 1975, there really was a third party which used to deliberately stoked up the situation whenever it cooled down. That third party was Israel and Israel alone. This belief was substantiated by later events, when the Israeli alliance with a sub-group of the Phalange and al-Ahrar came to light.

To this day, the Phalange has continued to justify what it did to the Palestinian revolution. Its supporters have presented good arguments, but none of them was true. Its real motivation was fear of a change in the Lebanese political map, though that was something which was desired by many Lebanese, even to the extent of risking to a division of the country. Various bloody inter-Lebanese battles that later took place prove this. A good example is the long battle in the late 1980s between the Lebanese army under General Michel Aoun and Lebanese Forces units commanded by Samir Geagea. The ferocity of this fighting was worse than that of the 1975–76 war, although the PLO had by then departed and no longer had any impact on the Lebanese arena.

(6)

A major ordeal occurred on January 31, 1976, when I went, as usual, to my office at *al-Muharrer* newspaper to write my daily column.

In the lobby of the building I met one of the secretaries, who told me that Walid Abu Dhahr, proprietor of the newspaper, wished to invite me to have a cup of coffee with him. I took the lift to the fifth floor and entered Walid's office. He received me warmly and, just as we began to chat, we heard the sound of shooting at a very close distance, from light and heavy machine guns as well as rocket-propelled grenades. Before we could ascertain what was happening, we heard a voice calling for us to surrender and leave the building. A minute later, a second voice called me by name and demanded that I surrender my weapon and give myself up. I was certainly able to comply with the first command. I picked up a pen from the desk, went to the window and threw it out onto the street.

The attack sparked panic in the building. Some people tried to go downstairs and surrender. But when they got to the first floor, they discovered that the entrance was on fire. Black smoke filled the halls and blew upwards through the stairs and lift shafts. They rushed up the stairs again. I remember hearing coughing and spluttering as they gasped for oxygen in the smoky stairwell. So we all ran up to the roof, but just as we arrived, a hail of bullets came from the roofs of neighboring buildings, where the assailants had taken up positions.

We had no choice but to jump to the roof of a building next door, which was still under construction. I can't say where we got the necessary strength and courage to leap the two-meter gap between the two structures, but we just flew through the air like deer. Thank God we made it, but, unfortunately for me, I landed in a pool of wet concrete and found myself up to my knees in it. When I realized what had happened, I could not help laughing, almost hysterically, until the others came and helped pull me out of the concrete.

As soon as we had come under attack, I phoned Abu Ammar and told him what was happening. He immediately dispatched some of his men to check out the situation. As they approached the *al-Muharrer* office in the Shayyah district, they were intercepted at a checkpoint set up by al-Saiqa, a pro-Syrian Palestinian organization, whose men told them that the attacks and clashes had ended and that the situation had returned to normal. Abu Ammar's men believed them: they turned around, and left. Fortunately, my driver, who had been unable to get to the car, ran to Abu Ammar's office and asked to see him. The guards there tried to prevent him, as Abu Ammar was in a meeting with leaders of the Lebanese National Movement and a high-level Syrian delegation. But my driver did not give up and began shouting to attract the attention of Abu Ammar. The tactic succeeded and he was allowed to enter. The story was told and the reasons behind the attack were obvious to all those in the meeting. *Al-Muharrer* had been targeted for having supported Baghdad and the Iraqi Ba'th party against the Syrians. The assailants were a group consisting of members of al-Saiqa and a little known local Lebanese faction. Two colleagues were killed during this incident, God rest their souls: Nayef Shiblaq, a Palestinian, and Ibrahim Amer from Egypt. More than seven people were wounded.

Another rescue team was dispatched and, when they reached the area, the assailants fled. The rescuers delivered me quickly to Abu Ammar. I entered his office, which was full of senior officials and personalities, including the Syrian Minister of Foreign Affairs, Abdul Halim Khaddam, and Brigadier Naji Jamil of the Syrian army. Arafat rushed to embrace me. My first words were: "Abu Ammar, those were comrades, not enemies!" He put his hand over my mouth and told me to stay calm. I went to wash my face and lay down as a doctor gave me a quick checkup. When I walked back to the hall, Abu Ammar's guests were on their way out, but Khaddam came up to me, patted my shoulder and told me in so many words that they had not been after me and that he was glad I was safe.

On the way home, my driver said: "That was the fifth attempt .... May God keep on protecting you." I replied: "But this time they were our brothers ... brothers-in-arms!"

(7)

A few months later, in June 1976, I chaired the PLO delegation at a housing conference in Vancouver, Canada – a conference that had almost been canceled by the Canadian government under pressure from a Zionist campaign protesting against the PLO's participation and demanding that we be denied visas.

There were three of us: Nabila Breir, the poet Mahmoud Darwish, and myself. It was a bad day to set off, as artillery shells were being continuously exchanged between the two sides in Beirut. Just before takeoff, artillery fire rained down on the airport. We were ordered to evacuate the plane, and sought refuge in one of the maintenance hangers. The bombardment continued intensively for half an hour. After the shelling stopped, we heard on the public address system that our plane was ready to fly to Paris, as planned. We did not know what to do: proceed or go home. But an airport employee made the decision a bit easier by telling us that all the roads from the airport were still being shelled and so it was probably less risky to fly than to return home. With a few other daring people, we boarded the plane again. The captain, Adel Qawwas, was perspiring profusely as he welcomed us back onto the aircraft, and off we went.

None of us realized that this trip might be one without a return journey, as only a few days later it was announced that Beirut International Airport was closed until further notice. At that time, the battles between supposed comrades – Syrians, Lebanese, and Palestinians – were at their peak throughout the city and all the way up to Zahleh in the Beqaa, Akkar in the north, and Jizzine in the south, not to mention the daily battles between the Israeli occupation forces and the Palestinian revolutionary forces in the south.

The Vancouver Conference ended, and Mahmoud and I headed to New York to participate in the UN Security Council meetings. There, the PLO Representative at the UN, Zuhdi al-Tarazi, handed me a telex from my wife, informing me that she had left Lebanon with our three children and gone to Cairo. Beirut airport had briefly re-opened for three days during the last week of June. The plane my family had boarded was the last for many months.

When my mission in the United States ended I caught up with my family, who had left Cairo for East Germany. The Syrian military had decided to intervene in the civil war, as a result of a meeting between al-Assad, Franjieh, and other leaders of the Lebanese Front bloc. It was obvious that Americans had given the green light for this move. The Lebanese Front had welcomed it, although the Arab states had registered mildly worded objections.

We maintained communication with Beirut through the PLO Office in East Berlin. We watched on TV the painful daily news broadcasting the battles of Tel al-Za'tar camp, which had been under siege and continuous bombardment by the Lebanese Phalange with

Syrian support. After three months of brave resistance, the camp fell in August 1976. There were thousands of casualties, most of them shot as they tried to escape.

I am not particularly interested here in enumerating all the Arab conferences that were held or the decisions that were taken, as none of them managed to retrieve the situation or stop the killing in Lebanon. Even worse, the Arab interventions actually deepened the conflict between Syria and the Palestinian–Lebanese alliance, known as the Joint Forces. A fierce war started in Mount Lebanon between the Syrians and the Joint Forces, who had started to retreat from Bhamdoun and Saufar. The Syrians advanced onto Mount Lebanon and continued to score further victories, and the situation became increasingly dangerous.

(8)

In September 1976, Suleiman Franjieh's term as President of Lebanon ended and Elias Sarkis took office. Some people hoped that this change would allow a return to normality. What happened, however, was that rather than resolving the situation, Sarkis merely presided over the continuing crisis. A joint Arab security force was sent into Lebanon, but these troops were predominantly Syrian. Other participants included Saudi Arabia, Sudan, Yemen, and the United Arab Emirates. The name of the Arab security forces was changed from Quwwat al-Amn (Security Forces) to Quwwat al-Rad' (Deterrent Forces). In the end, all but the Syrians withdrew from Lebanon. These troops were theoretically under Lebanese command, led first by Brigadier Ahmad al-Hajj and later Brigadier Sami al-Khatib. The latter held this position until the Taif Conference in 1989, which included most Lebanese politicians and warlords and which, under Saudi auspices, resulted in a temporary end of the war. In the meantime however, and despite the Syrian presence, the situation in Lebanon remained unchanged, with battles, followed by conferences, followed by ceasefire decisions, followed by violations of these decisions.

On March 16, 1977, we held the Thirteenth Session of the Palestine National Council in Cairo. It was during this conference that the first hint was given that a Palestinian state might be established over only a part of Palestinian soil. On that same day, we heard shocking news: Kamal Jumblatt, together with his driver and aide, had been assassinated as they drove to his residence at al-Mukhtara in the Chouf mountain range. Jumblatt's assassination was catastrophic and led to some of his followers spontaneously killing dozens of Lebanese Maronites. But the overall outcome still tilted the scales in favor of the Syrian forces, which had completed their takeover of most of Mount Lebanon.

Just over a year later, on June 13, 1978, the son of Suleiman Franjieh, Toni Franjieh, together with his wife Vera and daughter Jihan, were murdered in their own house in Ehden, in northern Lebanon. In reaction, Franjieh withdrew from the Lebanese Front and launched an attack on the Phalange in Zgharta, which led to their eviction from northern Lebanon. At the end of August in the same year, Imam Moussa al-Sadr, head of the Higher Islamic Shia Council in Lebanon, and two of his aides disappeared while on an official trip to Tripoli, Libya. This caused consternation among the Shia Muslim community, and particularly the Amal Movement which the Imam had founded. After Imam Moussa al Sadr's disappearance, first Hussein al-Husseini, then Nabih Berri, took over the leadership of Amal.

On January 22, 1979, Ali Salameh (Abu Hassan), a PLO leader, was assassinated in Beirut. Six months later, on July 28, Zuheir Mohsen, Secretary General of al-Saiqa, was assassinated in Cannes. On February 24, 1980, Salim al-Lawzi, my ex-director at *al-Hawadeth*, was kidnapped while on his way to the airport in Beirut. A few days later, his brutally mutilated body was found. I grieved over Salim immensely, but my grief did not lessen my anger towards him. He had been careless, and had not heeded the advice of his friends, who had always urged him to be more cautious in his movements.

Five months after Salim al-Lawzi was killed, on July 23, Riad Taha, President of the Syndicate of Journalism, was killed, a victim of the conflicts between the Syrian Ba'th and the Iraqi Ba'th. Riad was a true friend and I grieved deeply for him.

With events like these, you have to ask yourself: Is it possible that an entire people can lose its collective sanity?

9
THE PLO AT THE UNITED NATIONS

The years between the September 1970 war in Jordan and the 1982 Israeli invasion of Lebanon were critical ones for the PLO. First we had to go through the bitter stalemate of "no war, no peace," after which we witnessed the victory of October 1973. One year later, the Arab Summit held in Rabat recognized the PLO as the sole legitimate representative of the Palestinian people. That led us to the United Nations and a new phase of diplomacy.

Palestinian political thinking also evolved during this time. Its political agenda became clearer, especially in the eyes of international public opinion, and that strengthened and expanded the base of the PLO's allies. This evolution was clearly manifested in the resolutions of the Palestine National Council (PNC), which sat ten times in Cairo, Damascus, and Algiers. The development of these resolutions reveals that they were always strongly influenced by international events, the most important of which – in my opinion – was the October War. This conflict restored Arab confidence and redressed some of the balance of power, which had been severely disrupted in the aftermath of the 1967 defeat. It also tilted the scales in favor of the Arab political struggle at the expense of military options.

Without getting too bogged down in the intricacies and intrigues of this war, let us just review these two concrete results: the first was that the balance of power was neither fixed nor eternal, but rather quite vulnerable to change; the second was that the Arab–Israeli conflict could never be resolved in the presence of the two superpowers. The instant the scales started to tilt in either direction, the superpower on the receiving end would react immediately to take matters under control and restore the balance.

Apparently, the two Arab nations that were directly involved, Egypt and Syria, recognized this reality. Consequently, they both accepted UN Resolution 338, which substantiated the earlier 242 Resolution, which had brought about the ceasefire to the 1967 war.

(1)

The Palestinian factions viewed these new developments somewhat differently. In one seminar held by *Shu'un Filistiniya* magazine, the Secretary General of the pro-Syrian faction al-Saiqa, Zuheir Mohsen, declared that the 1973 war had transformed the Palestinian revolution "from romanticism into realism." I quote Zuheir in particular because his statement reflected an unexpected position of the Syrian Ba'th Party. Fatah and the Democratic Front Movement concurred with al-Saiqa, whereas the Popular Front and all the others did not, and together they formed what was referred to as Jabhat al-Rafd (the Rejection Front).

Consequently, it was not possible to adopt a unanimous Palestinian position, especially in regard to the invitation we had received from Egypt's President Sadat to attend the Geneva Conference. Therefore a session of the PNC was convened in Cairo, in June 1974, to establish a common stand. During this Twelfth Session, the famous Ten-Point Program was issued; the most significant part of this was the second clause, which called for the "implementation of a national authority over every part of liberated or vacated Palestinian territory." This meant that a Palestinian state over only a part of Palestinian soil was accepted for the first time. Another significant clause dealt with the "adoption of all possible means, including the armed struggle, to achieve national goals," in contrast to all the previous PNC sessions which had insisted upon armed struggle alone. Each faction then started to offer its own subjective understanding of this program.

Instead of attending the Geneva Conference, the PLO headed to the UN in New York three months later in November 1974.

(2)

Ten years after the birth of the PLO, Chairman Arafat's visit to the UN in New York at the head of a Palestinian delegation consolidated his position and set him apart from the rest of his comrades. From that moment on, he was elevated to the status of an international liberation movement leader, on a par with Che Guevara, Fidel Castro, and Nelson Mandela.

Abu Ammar asked me to take charge of media relations. Before we set off for New York, my first major concern was the speech that Arafat was going to deliver to the General Assembly – in fact to the whole world. All that I had as a basis was a generic document that had been drafted by Nabil Sha'th. Abu Ammar had sent it on to me and asked me to review and amend it as necessary, in conjunction with Walid Khalidi, Salah Dabbagh, and Mahmoud Darwish. It took us three whole days to accomplish this task.

After we had obtained Abu Ammar's approval of the revised text, Walid Khalidi said, in his unique semi-serious style: "Abu Ammar, there is just one issue left, but no one can add it to the speech but you in person." Abu Ammar scanned through the paper looking for the missing item, but he could find nothing, so he looked at Walid and asked: "What are you talking about, Walid?" To which he answered: "Your beard, sir ... do you promise us to shave it before you deliver the speech?" The notoriously stubbly Abu Ammar laughed and promised he would do so. He also asked Mahmoud Darwish and me to include all the vowel marks in the text clearly in bright red ink. We did so, but despite our best efforts, he still managed to ride roughshod over the complexities of Arabic grammar as he read out the speech.

The travel arrangements were kept secret, a necessary measure bearing in mind the fact that our delegation included men and women from various places, including Lebanon, Syria, Jordan, and Egypt. Most of us used code names and carried diplomatic passports issued by the People's Democratic Republic of Yemen.

We left Lebanon discreetly, the government having put a private lounge at our disposal at Beirut International Airport, so that we would not mingle with other passengers awaiting the Air France jet to Paris. Before we got on board, the plane and its passengers were searched. When we landed in Paris, the plane used a separate runway and we got off before all the other passengers. Ten police cars and a bus were laid on for us and we were taken straight to the airport hotel. As we left the plane, I couldn't help noticing the agitation of the other passengers, including a group which had changed flight in Beirut from Hong Kong. It seemed word had spread through the aircraft that "those Palestinians" were on board and the passengers had spent the entire trip in a state of fear. Security at the Paris hotel was very tight. Each room had two men outside equipped with walkie-talkies which kept them in constant contact with their command center. A few hours later, we headed back to the airport and boarded a jumbo jet to New York, again sitting in our own group apart from the other passengers. The cabin crew paid special attention to us, as did a group of French secret agents who escorted us all the way, just in case.

Just prior our landing, a member of the crew told me that the pilot had received a signal from New York saying that a "special reception" was awaiting us there, and we were to prepare to be the first passengers off the plane. A few minutes later, the pilot announced that the plane was going to make two stops and "the passengers from Beirut" should get off at the first.

The plane came to a halt and through the windows we could see a huge number of vehicles on the tarmac, including dozens of police cars with their lights flashing. Two helicopters were hovering overhead. Several police officers then boarded the plane and verified our code names against our real names. Then they took us off the plane in pairs and put us into black limousines. The motorcade moved off as one, or at least I thought so at the time. In fact, I learnt later that three separate convoys departed: two decoys and a real convoy containing our party.

The police had reserved three floors for us at the Waldorf Astoria Hotel. The middle floor was for us, while the upper and lower ones were for our security detail. Don't even ask about the number of guards armed with submachine guns that were there. Guards all over the place, at each doorway, staircase, and exit. We were there for two weeks and every day it was the same routine. We were ferried from our hotel to the UN building and back, each day taking a different route and always under continuous surveillance.

(3)

The highlight of the trip was the night when an exhausted Yasser Arafat arrived in New York and delivered his speech. Afterwards we got into the car, part of a convoy that also carried, among others, some of his bodyguards under the command of Abu Hasan Salameh and an American security detail. Before Abu Ammar could give the order to move off, the officer in charge told us that we were going to make a stop during the trip and another car would meet us. "This car is part of our convoy," he said. "Chairman Arafat will be quickly transferred to it and Mr Hout will sit instead of him in this car. This way we will neutralize any possible ambush or assassination attempt." And so it was. It only took a few seconds for the convoy to stop and allow the switch to take place. The new convoy headed to the hotel as if Abu Ammar were still on board, and we were greeted by a crowd of reporters at the hotel, waiting to catch a glimpse of him as he went in. It had been assumed that he would go to the following day's UN session to hear the speech of Lebanese President Suleiman Franjieh. But the secret plans dictated otherwise and Abu Ammar boarded a plane to Cuba in the early hours, arriving in Havana at 8 o'clock in the morning. Even Castro was taken by surprise, having expected Abu Ammar to arrive that afternoon. The Cuban ambassador in New York had to wake Castro up to tell him that Abu Ammar was on the way.

There were memorable moments during this trip. My eyes twice welled up with tears. The first time was when I saw some members of the Arab Palestinian community in New York marching towards the United Nations building, carrying Palestinian flags and singing patriotic anthems, in a direct challenge to the groups of Zionist protesters who had taken up positions around the building. The Zionists melted away as soon as they saw the Palestinians approaching. The second time was when I saw the world standing up to salute Arafat while on his way to the General Assembly podium, while Israel's representative, Yosef Tekoa, slunk out of the hall ignored by everyone. The whole of the UN, from diplomats to clerical staff and janitors, rushed to the hall of the General Assembly just to see this newcomer from the Middle East with their own eyes, a man who had defied Israel and laid down a challenge to the whole world to recognize the rights of Palestinians. It was an unforgettable sight. Arafat entered the hall to a prolonged standing ovation. As the applause continued, he leant against the chair usually reserved for kings and presidents, as if he was saying: "Soon, I shall be sitting on this chair too." We had waited a quarter of a century for this moment and we had paid very dearly for it.

Abu Ammar's arrival in New York had been highly secretive. The Algerian plane that had delivered him had not identified itself before reaching American shores. Even the NYPD itself had not known about the plan until about two hours prior to its arrival. One of the officers in charge, Jim Ziadeh, who was of Lebanese extraction, told me that in his 20 years in the police he had never seen such security measures being laid on for any other international personality. I have to admit that Abu Ammar had caused them all sorts of difficulties. According to the records, three planes had been heading for New York, but it was not known which flight carried him. No one knew. They came to us for some kind of indication, but our guess was as good as theirs. Then they told us that they had orders to shoot down any plane that had not identified itself at least three hours before reaching the US coast, so we urgently relayed this information to Arafat's team. In the end his plane only identified itself to the Americans two hours before reaching US airspace, barely enough time for the security forces to call off their air defense plan and proceed with the reception at the airport. The idea was that Abu Ammar's plane would taxi to a distant part of the runway where two helicopters would immediately whisk him and his entourage to the UN headquarters. And so it was. The plane landed in the early morning at 6 a.m., and within half an hour the helicopters had landed safely at the UN helipad.

He arrived just four hours before he was due to make his speech. Despite the long journey and jet lag, this incredibly dynamic individual delivered his speech without any sign of fatigue.

In fact, Abu Ammar showed up, stood on the podium, and was at his most energetic. The only refreshment he had taken was some coffee and he had not rested at all, mainly because of the commotion around him. But he remained calm and confident, answering everyone's questions with a smile on his face.

Photo 5 Al-Hout, head of the Palestinian media delegation to the UN at a press conference (New York, 1974). To his left Nabil Sha'th, Abdul Jawad Saleh, Clovis Maqsoud and Randa Khalidi; to his right Abdum Karim al-Shaikhali, Fouad Yassin.

There was one detail that he had time to take care of, a detail that he had completely overlooked despite his promise to Walid Khalidi in the preceding weeks. But Walid reminded him: "Sir, you promised to shave." Arafat smiled and admitted that Walid Khalidi had won that round. He left the room and returned clean shaven with a neat black moustache.

For the first time, the United Nations was transformed into a festival of Palestine. Immediately following the speech, the Soviet ambassador rushed over to Abu Ammar and embraced him warmly. In the end it took him an hour and a quarter to receive the congratulations of everyone in the hall that day.

(4)

When Abu Ammar had finished, I held a press conference in which we distributed an English copy of the speech, which had been translated by Edward Said and Randa Khalidi.

Somebody made the memorable comment that "You came here as terrorists and you are leaving as freedom fighters." Another French commentator said: "Thank God I am neither Israeli nor Zionist. This is really not their day." A third asked me: "There is a massive rally of Jewish New Yorkers just outside the UN building carrying a banner saying 'Palestinians, go home.' What is your response?" I replied: "That is exactly what we are here for. We are here so that we can go home, back to Palestine, which is occupied by the Zionists." I was also asked if Arafat had been carrying his gun at the General Assembly session. "I was very close to Abu Ammar while he was on his way to the podium, and I even recall being in accidental contact with him, and I didn't feel any solid object at his side." Another reporter said: "But we saw he was armed in the photo!" I answered: "What you saw was his holster. Who said that a gun was inside it?" Actually, it was the *New York Times* that started this debate, when it published the picture of a gun on its front page the day Arafat arrived in New York. It said a Zionist extremist was going to use it to assassinate Arafat. It did not appear that the US government reacted in any way to this statement.

US television programs were generally extremely antagonistic towards us. I was invited to the popular Barbara Walters show, watched every day by 20 million viewers. Barbara gave me a cool reception and then she addressed the audience: "Today we welcome

Sharif al-Hout, so that he can talk to us about what he and his terrorist comrades think of what happened yesterday in the Israeli town of Beit Shean." She then looked at me and said: "Yesterday, you confirmed that you were not uncomfortable as a result of this terrorist act, so what do you say now?"

I answered calmly: "Allow me first to correct my name, as it is not as you mentioned or as it appeared on the screen," and I spelled out my full name and my job description. Then I continued: "The Zionists were the ones who invented terrorism in the Middle East and it is true that we managed to learn some of it from them." And I added: "But no, I am not uncomfortable, because the question that you should raise is, what were the Israelis doing in Bissan?"

Barbara commented in surprise: "I am talking about Beit Shean, not this Bissan."

I said: "See, that's the problem, Beit Shean used to be a Palestinian town called Bissan."

She became embarrassed and she said defensively: "Don't change the subject. I'm not asking you about the Israelis."

I struck again, this time in cold blood: "I give the answers my way, not yours. You should also appreciate that your insistence on calling our struggle terrorism will incite us to arm ourselves more vigorously. Maybe you'll be happier on the day we acquire Phantoms or Skyhawk jets to drop napalm bombs from the sky, so that we can wipe out Israeli towns and villages the same way they do to our camps. Then these operations will earn the term acts of war rather than terrorism."

(5)

Amidst all the bitter suffering that the Palestinians had tasted up to that moment, our decision to present ourselves at the United Nations remains one of the most outstanding initiatives the PLO has ever undertaken. It followed tremendous political upheavals in Palestinian diplomacy, at both the Arab and international levels, and its impact was manifested in various ways: invitations to the PLO to participate in several international and regional gatherings, positive resolutions in the Arab summit in Algiers and the Organization of Islamic Conference summit in Lahore, and finally the Arab summit in Rabat, where the historic resolution was finally put in force recognizing that the PLO was the sole and legitimate representative of the Palestinian people. According to Henry Kissinger, this resolution subverted American conceptions and he said he was going to work on its abolition. President Tito reported that to Yasser Arafat and warned him of the possibility of an American conspiracy, just prior to the 1975 war in Lebanon.

It was President Tito who first advised us to go to the United Nations back in July 1969 in Belgrade. That year, we had received for the first time an invitation to participate in a conference of foreign ministers of the Non-Aligned Movement (NAM), in preparation for later acceptance of our NAM membership in the capacity of observers. At the gala reception, where 51 states applauded the PLO, Tito took us aside and opened the subject of engaging with the UN. A member of our delegation said: "But that would be an implicit recognition of the partition of Palestine." The old revolutionary answered: "If you manage to get the part that was entitled to you by the international resolutions, then that would be better than nothing. For my part, I promise you that I won't interfere to prevent you from regaining the remainder of your land."

But things were not that simple. Going to the UN was not an easy decision to make. Some considered it to be a betrayal of the cause and carried banners condemning those that had approved it. It was a decision born of years of bitter struggle and sacrifice by the people of Palestine, especially during the preceding nine years.

In addition, we should not overlook another reality that also paved the way for the PLO to reach the UN: the changes that the world had undergone since 1947. Dozens of newly liberated nations had joined the UN. Consequently, these young nations, which still harbored painful and vivid memories of colonialism and oppression, were fully conscious of the importance of international solidarity with other peoples still struggling against injustice. In this regard, we acknowledge the efforts of Algeria which were crucial in making it happen. At that time, the UN General Assembly was under the presidency of Algeria, whose leader was Ahmad Ben Bella, a revolutionary figure. Abdul Aziz Boutaflika, then foreign minister and now president himself, chaired the General Assembly session.

The leader of one country's mission, Senegal, said the invitation to the PLO was as much of a victory for the UN as it was for Palestine and its people. Throwing off the yoke of colonial oppression brought about an upgrading of the UN as an international institution and allowed it to better exercise the role for which it had been created.

The halls of the UN became a new alternative to the battlefield and paved the way for oppressed peoples' aspirations to be realized without massive sacrifice or tragedy. That was the situation of the UN in the 1970s. It is not like that today, when the United States has acquired almost complete control over the UN and rendered it practically ineffective.

Some people believe that the UN resolutions are merely ink on paper and they carry only moral weight. This is true and it will remain so until the balance of power is changed. But this is another issue and it can be only achieved through different kinds of struggle. However, the year 1974 was Palestine's year at the UN and it established a good foundation for the years to follow, which were of no less importance. In 1975, the General Assembly condemned Zionism as a form of racial discrimination. Later on, more and more states recognized the PLO, especially after the latter had become an observer member at the international body. Japan agreed to set up an office for the PLO in Tokyo. France lifted a ban on publicity about its secret relations with the PLO and allowed us to establish a public relations office in Paris. Next came West Germany, Austria, Italy, Belgium, Sweden, and others. The PLO evolved and became a significant player in Euro-Arab political dialogue. As for the Soviet Bloc, the Non-Aligned Movement, the Organization of African Unity, and Organization of Islamic Conferences, the PLO's status was significantly reinforced and it was promoted to the level of a "state," enjoying full privileges.

It has to be re-emphasized that none of those political victories and gains would have been achieved had the PLO not made this giant step into the United Nations. Furthermore, we should proudly acknowledge that the PLO managed to acquire this international acceptance and support in the face of continuous Zionist blackmail and claims that the Arabs and the Palestinians were determined to "throw the Jews into the sea." This lie is unfounded. When President Tito asked his friend President Nasser about it, the latter requested that Mohammad Hasanein Haykal investigate the issue. *Al-Ahram* carried out the research and found no evidence that we had ever called for this.

For the first time in history, the whole world heard the leadership of the Palestinian people bring forward an alternative solution to the lie of "throwing the Jews into the sea." The PLO presented a democratic solution in the shape of a single, democratic, and secular state for Arabs and Jews, where all citizens would live with equal rights and duties. It was a blow to the Zionists and their allies, as who could possibly refuse coexistence rather than adhering to the option of war? What could be more magnanimous than this position, where the victims, the dispossessed owners of the land, called for coexistence with the aggressors, forgetting all the tragedies of the past and looking forward to a new future? Israel was cornered, especially as it used to claim, when its presence was uncontested in the international arena, that it had always been the promoter of peace while the Palestinians had rejected its offers.

The language of Arafat's speech was up to date and its contents were realistic. At the same time, the speech promoted international revolution and stayed faithful to all resistance movements. It was sophisticated, it reflected self-confidence in the justice of the Palestinian cause and revolution. What attests to that is the strong applause that followed when Abu Ammar said: "When they speak

Photo 6 The author on one of his regular trips to the United Nations, talking to Palestinians and supporters coming from different parts of the USA (New York, 1981).

out, our people look forward to the future rather than being bound with the tragedies of the past or the chains of the present. If we talk of the present or refer back to the past, it is only because we want to shed more light on the beginnings of this new path, aimed towards a brighter future which we want to build with all peoples of the world." Perhaps the most exhilarating thing about this speech was that it managed to address literally everyone in a single language. It was quite something that the chairman of the PLO could talk like this and receive equally positive responses at the United Nations, in the refugee camps, and among Palestinian audiences all over the globe.

His assertion that "the war starts in Palestine, and the peace starts in Palestine" has become a piece of everyday wisdom.

The transition from al-Fakhani to the United Nations was immense.

10

PALESTINE, AROUND THE GLOBE

It was a major political victory that we scored at the United Nations. Palestine was returned to the international community and Resolution 3236 was issued defining the legitimate rights of its people to self-determination without foreign intervention and to regain homes and properties they were driven out of in 1948. After this triumph, we went back to our places of exile, to continue the struggle and to translate the resolutions into tangible results. But little did we know that Israel's Mossad was already preparing a surprise for us, on the same scale as its recent defeat.

(1)

On the morning of December 14, 1974, I was awakened by the sound of a massive explosion. The PLO office, less than 200 meters from my house had been the target. As soon as I arrived there, I learned the PLO-affiliated Palestine Research Center as well as one of Abu Jihad's units had been hit by similar attacks. The Israelis had rented cars and fitted portable missile launchers to their roofs, fired by remote control or pre-programmed timers.

While I was still standing on the pavement opposite my office, next to the car from where the missiles had been launched, someone told me a similar car was parked nearby. The building was evacuated and I and a number of explosives experts ran towards the suspect car. Just before we reached it, we heard a noise and saw the mobile launcher rise up and point towards its target. The missiles took off and slammed into the PLO office. The delayed timing showed that they meant to kill rescue workers as well as PLO senior commanders as they arrived to inspect the site.

This was the fourth attempt on my life but not the last, although I was not to know that at the time.

Once again we buried our dead, repaired our offices and went back to work, steadfast and determined to continue our journey at the start of the eleventh year with the PLO.

(2)

1975 was a bad year. So many unfortunate things happened. Kissinger's plan to ignite a war in Lebanon succeeded.

The incident which began the civil war was the shooting of Ma'rouf Sa'd, leader of the Nasserite Popular Organization, on February 26 by members of the Lebanese army. The attack sparked widespread outrage against the government, which was accused of being in a conspiracy with the former president Camille Chamoun and the Protein Company. Chamoun and the company had been trying to gain a monopoly of fishing rights, which would have put thousands of independent fishermen out of work. Ma'rouf Sa'd had led the fishermen's uprising against these moves. A few days after the shooting, Sa'd died of his wounds. This spark was enough to start the war.

At that time, the PLO had developed its relations with some local Lebanese forces. Those who had chosen to support our cause became known as the Lebanese National Movement, led by Kamal Joumblat. On the opposite side was what came to be known as the Lebanese National Front, chaired by the trio of Camille Chamoun, Pierre al-Gemayyel, and Suleiman Franjieh, each of whom already had his own armed faction.

The spark became a fire with the Ain al-Rummaneh incident when some elements from Gemayyel's Phalange party attacked a bus carrying Palestinians on their way back to Tell al-Za'tar refugee camp, killing them all. More than 20 people were killed. It was a very ugly crime indeed.

The catastrophe had started to bring enormous destruction to both Lebanese and Palestinians. It began a series of civil conflict that lasted more than 17 years.

(3)

In August 1975, the PLO received an invitation to participate in a ceremony to commemorate the 30th anniversary of the American atomic attack on Hiroshima and Nagasaki. The invitation had come from the Japanese Council against Atomic and Hydrogen Bombs, who were supported by the Japanese Communist Party. A few days later, another invitation from a similar organization arrived, but this time it was from the Socialist Party. The PLO Command decided that I should go to Tokyo, hoping to take advantage of this opportunity to develop the PLO's relations with the Liberal Democratic Party, which had ruled Japan since 1945.

Japan had voted in favor of the PLO's participation in General Assembly sessions in 1974, but it had failed to repeat the gesture a few months later when the Japanese representative to the UN abstained on Resolution 3236 so as not to antagonize the United States. But less than a year later, in December 1975, Prime Minister Takeo Miki declared publicly in the Diet Council that the Palestinian issue would never be solved as long as it was regarded merely as a refugee crisis rather than a major international concern. Minister of Foreign Affairs Kiichi Miyazawa followed suit, and even went a step further and declared that his government would seriously consider any request made by the PLO to establish an office in Tokyo.

I took a KLM flight to Haneda Airport, where I was surprised and thrilled to see a large number of people standing on the tarmac waiting for me, including some Arab ambassadors. There were also some Japanese party representatives, including of course the host party, and one MP, our friend Jamila Yamagushi.

Many reporters and cameramen had already gathered at the VIP Lounge, where I started my mission with a news conference. My 20-day trip also ended with a news conference in the same lounge, but with one difference: this time in my hand was a letter from the Japanese Ministry of Foreign Affairs inviting us to open a PLO office in Tokyo. The letter, signed by the Ministry's Undersecretary Terohiko Nakamura and dated August 19, 1975, was delivered to me at the airport, half an hour before I was due to leave.

A few months later, in April 1976, Farouq Qaddoumi, or Abu Lutf, head of foreign affairs at the PLO, received an invitation from the Japanese Ministry of Foreign Affairs to visit Tokyo. I went with him. The plane landed in the evening and, while it was still taxiing, we saw large numbers of police, several cars, and a podium. Abu Lutf commented: "Apparently there is some VIP on the plane." I said: "That would be you, and no one else." I handed him a brief speech that I had drafted in anticipation of an official reception.

We met with most senior officials, particularly the prime minister, the minister of foreign affairs and party leaders. Finally, we signed a joint agreement to open our office in Tokyo, the capital of a major industrial power.

After Tokyo, Abu Lutf headed to Beijing and I returned to Beirut, where I discovered that increasingly alarming events were taking

place. I regret to say that within weeks, there were pitched battles
breaking out between the PLO and the Lebanese National Movement
forces on one side and the Syrian army on the other.

(4)

In November 1975, Palestinian diplomacy scored another success.
We managed to get a resolution passed by the General Assembly that
declared Zionism was a form of racial discrimination.

Another historic decision during that year, but one that the Arabs
failed to use to full advantage, was the formation of a committee to
seek the implementation of these new political resolutions, so that
they would not remain mere words. It was called the Committee
for the Exercise of the Inalienable Rights of the Palestinian People.
The term inalienable carried legal significance: it made plain that
it was illegal to tamper with the national rights of the Palestinian
people, regardless of how long their exile continued. Twenty-three
states participated in the committee under the chairmanship of the
Senegalese representative, Maydun Val.

Committee 23, as it became known, held more than 30 meetings
in 1976. Its first assignment was to submit a preliminary report to
the Security Council outlining the necessary means for implementing
of the rights of the Palestinian people. This report remains one of the
most important UN documents associated with the Palestinian cause.
Even after submitting the report, the committee continued to work
hard on raising global awareness of the Palestinian cause with conferences, seminars, exhibitions, and in the media around the world. It
also sponsored the International Day of Solidarity with the People of
Palestine, on November 29 of each year. This committee suspended
its activities after the PLO signed the 1993 Oslo Agreement with
Israel and the United States, an act which unfortunately exempted
the international community from most of its moral responsibilities
vis-à-vis Palestine.

(5)

The United Nations was a gateway through which Palestinian
diplomacy was able to gain entry to the countries of North and
South America and the Caribbean. At that time, people in the United
States were still living with the aftermath of the popular demonstra-

tions against the Vietnam War, and that allowed several unresolved issues to resurface, including Palestine and South Africa, among others.

Despite all the restrictions and limitations imposed on us, our presence in New York did bear some fruit. We were also able to make inroads into Israel's previous monopoly of media coverage. A number of politicians and important public intellectuals came on board, including Professor Noam Chomsky, former Attorney General Ramsey Clark, Senator James Abourezk, and Edward Said, and we had an energizing effect on various Palestinian and Arab organizations and communities, such as the Arab American University Graduates (AAUG). This all happened despite laws forbidding any contact with any representative of the PLO, which was still branded a terrorist organization by Washington.

In June 1976, the poet Mahmoud Darwish and I were assigned to attend an extraordinary meeting of the Security Council in New York. We also received an invitation from Senator Abourezk to visit Washington. The senator managed to process all the necessary permits to allow us to leave New York, and we became the first members of the PLO to set foot on Capitol Hill. Not only that but we also had lunch with ten members of Congress, including Senator, and former presidential candidate, George McGovern. The Arab League representative in Washington, Clovis Maqsoud, was also there. Senator McGovern made a brief welcoming speech calling on his government to reconsider its position towards the PLO and to initiate a formal dialogue. On the following day, the newspapers launched vicious attacks against us, reflecting the anxiety that had struck the pro-Israel lobby, which demanded our immediate deportation.

I had been through a similar experience six months earlier on a visit to Canada. I had been invited by the president of the Arab Canadian Community, Khaled Mo'ammar, and my arrival coincided with the UN resolution condemning Zionism as a form of racism. Supporters of Israel chased me all over the country, starting at the airport in Ottawa, where I was met by more than 200 Zionists shouting slogans and carrying banners demanding my expulsion for having been a "terrorist" and a "racist." A few hours later, they blocked the entrance of the Public Library, where I had been scheduled to deliver a speech. Inside the hall, a group of hard-line ultra-Orthodox Jews in their black outfits and long beards and side ringlets, had already occupied the front seats.

There was an intense discussion after my speech, with one rabbi asking: "You have talked about the Palestinian people's right to self-determination, but don't the people of Israel also have the right to live by themselves in their own state?" I answered: "Yes, they do – as long as it is on land that legitimately belongs to them, and not over land that they have annexed." He then metaphorically cut his own throat by saying: "But that means less than 10 percent of the land." I smiled, as I fine-tuned his answer: "Yes, 6.4 percent, to be precise."

News of my exchanges in Ottawa reached Toronto before I arrived there on the following day. I was scheduled to give a speech at the University of Toronto, but the Zionists were prepared to do whatever they must to prevent me. They packed the hall, and the instant I arrived started screaming and whistling and making all kinds of noise. No one could quell the cacophony, including the professor who was supposed to introduce me. He did his best but got nowhere and had to withdraw.

This provocation was intolerable to the Arab students present in the hall and physical confrontations broke out. I stood on the stage giving the V-for-Victory sign as the press and TV cameras looked on. The headline in the *Toronto Star* the next day was: "Freedom of Speech Diminished amid Skirmishes between the PLO and Zionists." Some commentators warned of the potential repercussions of such an incident on life in Canada, a cosmopolitan country where freedom of speech and of expression must be granted to all parties with no prejudice.

But just as there were some Canadians who attacked us and agitated against us, there were also some who expressed solidarity and support for our cause, including our right to an independent state. I passed through various cities, including London, Windsor, and Waterloo, meeting many Lebanese expatriates who welcomed me graciously.

(6)

In November 1978, while I was in New York with the Palestinian Delegation to the UN, Columbia University hosted a seminar by Israeli Professor Aharon Yariv on the Arab–Israeli conflict in the Middle East, in which he was allowed to present his case unopposed. Edward Said, a Palestinian-American professor at Columbia and a member of the Palestine National Council, asked the university to invite someone representing the Arab side for the next seminar.

I received the invitation from Columbia in March 1979. Edward sent me a telegram and mentioned that several other major universities had also expressed an interest in inviting me to speak, including Harvard, Princeton, the University of Chicago, and the Foreign Policy Institute in Washington, DC.

I applied for a tourist visa at the US Embassy in Beirut. The approval process dragged on for what seemed to be an eternity, and the date of the first lecture was getting closer and closer. I contacted Edward and informed him that the embassy was holding up the paperwork. He got in touch with the universities, which in turn contacted the State Department, including the Secretary of State Cyrus Vance in person. (Vance told me these details later himself, during a private meeting in his office in New York, after he had resigned from the Carter Administration.) I finally received my visa on April 3, just two days before the date of the first lecture. The visa was conditional: I was not allowed to participate in any public gatherings or make any statements to the press, otherwise I would be subject to deportation and would be banned from reapplying for a visa in the future. I did not know what to do: what about the numerous invitations to speak at universities and colleges? I consulted the PLO's lawyer, who advised that my hosts had to ask the State Department for special permission to hold the meetings. And so it was.

The program started at Columbia University in New York. The meeting was heated, and it included a large number of students on both sides of the dispute, so there was some sort of a balance. The second encounter was in Harvard, under the auspices of Professor Stanley Hoffmann, Dean of the Political Science Department, and a distinguished personality in the United States. Despite all the security measures, the Zionist students were able to stage demonstrations intended to prevent me from entering the auditorium. They almost succeeded by completely blocking the front of the building, but my escort managed to sneak me in through the back door.

After the speech, I had a private talk with Dr Hoffmann in his office. He said that he had appreciated what I had said concerning the willingness of the Palestinian people to live in peace and side by side with the Jews. But then, he asked me whether or not I was serious about what I had said! I assured him I was. But he carried on to my increasing astonishment by asking what kind of reassurances the PLO were ready to give to the Jews. I replied: "I'm not sure who should be asking for reassurance from whom, us or the Israelis. Who was it who annexed the whole of Palestine, dispossessed its people, and now pride themselves on being the fifth strongest power in the world, with more than 200 nuclear warheads?" Then, I added: "However, we are ready to comply with whatever the United Nations decides, along with the two superpowers, if that's what it will take to reassure the Jews." He shook his head in denial and indicated that it was not enough, as the Jews needed even more reassurance than that. I said: "So you are saying that Israel feels insecure, even though it is a firm ally of the United States, which has a permanent commitment towards it, including safeguarding its existence and ensuring it always remains stronger than all the Arab states?" He replied, to my utter disbelief: "There are some Jews who fear that the United States might not stay the way it is today. It may change. What would happen then?" At that point, all I could say was: "Mr Hoffmann ... I am a politician not a psychiatrist. I think we should hand this case over to a team of doctors, and I hope they will prescribe the proper treatment." And I bade him farewell.

At Princeton, the meetings were confined to a few professors and some graduate students. Professor Richard Falk, a well-known activist and one of the people who had personally intervened to help me get the visa, was the mediator. The discussion was calm and objective, and there was no provocation. There were several questions related to the PLO's position on the Camp David Agreement, at that time a year old.

Apparently, there were many more protests against my visit than I had been aware of. The Committee of Presidents of Jewish American Organizations sent a memo to the State Department asking for my immediate deportation; the memo emphasized how surprised they had been to learn that the government was granting entry to people who killed Jewish babies, jeopardized American interests in the Middle East, and threatened to chop off the hands of those who signed the Camp David Agreement. The State Department was forced to issue an official response. Spokesman Hooding Carter appeared in public and made it unequivocally clear that I had had no involvement whatsoever in any terrorist activities, and there was no Jewish blood on my hands! He also said that the State Department had granted me the right to conduct this visit because I had a right to speak.

Under this new pressure, the University of Chicago decided to cancel my invitation, and my visit to the windy city was called off. But that was not such a big deal, as there was one more major engagement on my schedule. A group of newspapers and magazines, including the well-known and influential *Foreign Affairs*, had invited me to a meeting at the Institute of Foreign Policy. Morris Draper, then Assistant Secretary of State, could not but allow this meeting, fearing that calling it off would incite a negative reaction from my hosts. I surprised the audience by telling them, right from the start, that under the conditions of my stay in their country, I was not allowed to appear in public or speak to the press and, consequently, I cautioned them that quoting anything I said was entirely at their own risk.

But *The Washington Post* could not resist publishing an article under the headline "The Little Secret," which read:

Did you know that Shafik Hout, director of the Palestine Liberation Organization office in Beirut, is paying a visit to Washington? No, you didn't, unless you were among the handful of people who, under the terms of the visa granted to him by the State Department, were forced to turn up the collars of their coats, sneak into privately arranged meetings and promise not to divulge anything they might hear inside. The US State Department, you see, granted him entry only on the condition that Mr Hout address no public gatherings and avoid all publicity. Otherwise he risks being thrown out and denied entry next time.

The *Post* continued:

It is shameful. It is shameful that Mr Hout is not allowed to say what he has to say on a burning public issue. It's even more shameful that his listeners, American citizens, must enter into a conspiracy of silence to gain the privilege of talking with him. Take our word for it: You feel shabby, a bit dirty, for having to accept a distinct infringement of your normal liberties. It happens, of course, because the PLO is a political hot potato.

And it concluded:

The question of admitting foreigners to meet openly with private citizens and to offer their views to the American public is not, strictly speaking, political at all. It is, or at least it ought to be, a matter of fundamental American values and rights.

Anyone aware of the influence of this paper, which had put paid to President Nixon, will realize the importance of this article, which caused shockwaves in both the United States and the Arab World.

(7)

I was not such a fool as to think that we could change American policy through the media. That was impossible, and it was a lost battle from the start because of the power of Jewish influence in the West in general, and the United States in particular. What we could achieve, however, was to have an impact on American policy through changes in our own policies, through local lobbying, and every other possible means. Cyrus Vance confirmed this to us when we met him following his resignation. There were four of us at the meeting: Edward Said, Ibrahim Abu Lughod, Ahmad Sidki al-Dajani, and myself. He said: "What I don't understand is why you always focus on principles and values, and you constantly remind us of the Statue of Liberty, War of Independence, and so on. All of that makes no difference to the decision makers, who only understand their own interests."

Nevertheless, we should always make a distinction between the US administration and other American institutions, especially the academic ones. Administrations were never, and did not want to be, convinced of the justice of our cause, because they failed to see any advantage in modifying their current policies. As one senator put it to me: "Why are you asking me to change my position and jeopardize my electoral interests when my country's global interests are secure and unthreatened in the Middle East."

(8)

After the UN decision, the PLO arrived in Latin America: Mexico, Venezuela, Argentina, Chile, and other places. As for Cuba, we had already had solid ties with this young socialist state, which was often closer to our thinking than many Arab and Islamic nations.

The first time I set foot in Cuba was in July 1964, for the sixth anniversary celebrations of Castro's revolution, four months prior to my resignation from *al-Hawadeth* and the start of my new mission as the PLO representative in Lebanon. The delegation comprised only three people, invited because of their sympathetic positions towards Cuba: Farid Gubran, a Lebanese MP, Fadlo Abu Haydar of the Progressive Socialist Party, and myself. Because of the American siege of this revolutionary island, there were only two available routes to it. The first went to Havana via Moscow, the second via Prague, Shannon Airport in Ireland, and Gander in Canada. We chose the second route.

The welcome was quite gracious, although Cuba's resources were still quite limited. At that time, the people were going through the early stages of their transition, building the base of the new communist regime under Fidel Castro's leadership. We saw and learned a lot during that single week on the island, which had been nothing more than a backyard for the United States, where all of its people and properties were practically enslaved by a bunch of gangsters, pimps, and money launderers.

The Cuban people were elated after the victory of their revolution, and they had serious ambitions for a better future, despite all the problems they were experiencing as a result of the siege. The quality of service of electric power, water, and other public utilities was seriously compromised, but nevertheless the people were still smiling, singing, and dancing, as if all those hardships would soon be over. This proved to be true, but only after a long struggle.

During the visit, we received an invitation from the Egyptian Embassy to participate in the twelfth anniversary of their July Revolution. Che Guevara attended on Castro's behalf, and we all celebrated this occasion together. I was struck that Guevara was even more handsome in person than in the photographs which had been plastered on walls all over the world in the 1960s. Though we did not speak his language, we nevertheless enjoyed listening to him talking. We had a similar experience later, in a football stadium, hearing Castro speak for three continuous hours.

(9)

My second visit to Cuba was just before the end of 1970, in response to an invitation from the International Organization of Journalists to participate in an international conference for progressive journalists and writers that was to demonstrate public support for the Cuban people and all other peoples who were rebelling against imperialism and colonialism.

This time, we picked the other route to Cuba. We arrived in Moscow on December 30, 1970, on a freezing night. But it was a quite interesting experience in its own right, especially as the hotel we stayed in was full of journalists from all over the world.

On the following morning, the Aeroflot representative called and told us that, due to the large number of passengers to Havana, the airline had decided to schedule another flight the following day, the first day of the New Year. He gave us a choice between the two flights, and so we had the luxury of choosing between New Year's Eve in Moscow or Havana. It was a tough call, as both cities had their own charm and temptations. In the end, I chose Havana and carried on with my journey. The President of the Syndicate of Egyptian Journalists, Kamel Zuhairy, was also on board. Had we known what destiny had in store, we would have picked the later trip.

The plane was a jet-engined Antonov, considered the cream of Soviet airliners. Fortunately, Kamel and I were seated at the very front, near the cockpit, where we could see and hear all the action. After a couple of hours, it seemed that the plane had started to fly at a reduced speed. We asked the stewardess, who confirmed that that was because we were flying into a headwind. But she reassured us that we were still on schedule, and were not going to miss the New Year's celebrations in Havana.

Bear in mind the worrying fact that we flying over the infamous Bermuda Triangle at the very moment when we became aware of frantic sounding Russian voices coming from the cockpit. Not being able to understand what they were saying made it all the more terrifying. After a few long minutes, there was an announcement on the address system, including something in English about the plane experiencing some difficulties and the need to make an emergency landing.

The sound and number of voices coming from the cockpit and the crackle of more radio messages grew in intensity, so we called the stewardess back and questioned her more urgently. She explained that the pilot had used up a lot of his fuel reserves and there was some doubt whether we would be able to make it to Cuba without refueling. We wondered how the pilot would be able to refuel when it was the height of the Cold War and we were thousands of miles away from any of Moscow's allies, the nearest friendly airport being Havana itself. However, the stewardess told us that the pilot was trying to get permission from the Americans to let us use their military base in Bermuda. In the end, it took the intervention of Anatoly Dobrynin himself, the Soviet ambassador in Washington, to get us clearance to land there.

The plane landed safely and was immediately surrounded by military vehicles. An American officer walked up the stairs of the plane, where he was met by the Russian pilot. The American then greeted the passengers and asked if we needed food, water, or even ice cream. The Russian pilot interrupted: "No, thank you. This is a Soviet plane and it is equipped with everything it needs." Soon the plane was being refueled and we were ready to take off again. But, wait! We did not have clearance to take off, and once again the passengers started panicking.

We heard more wireless conferences from the cockpit, and this time we actually heard Ambassador Dobrynin himself, apparently reassuring the pilot that it would only be a matter of minutes before we could take off, but there would be a delay for some reason. We later found out that the US Air Force had demanded a last-minute inspection of the aircraft, to check that there were no secret espionage cameras on the underside of the plane. Finally, we got off the ground, and applause and patriotic songs rose up from all parts of the plane.

When we landed in Havana, we immediately headed to a beautiful park where hundreds of young Cubans were waiting to welcome guests. No people on earth even come close to the people of Latin America where fun and vivacity are concerned. Actually, we Orientals are on the opposite side of the spectrum, with our conservatism and strict social rules about segregating the sexes. As we mingled in the party, we noticed a lot of people crowding around one area. As we approached it we realized that Fidel Castro himself was in the middle of the crowd, with a jug of rum on his shoulder, challenging another Cuban fellow to a drinking contest. Castro won and there was applause from everyone. The dancing continued.

The following day, we began our work. The journalists started to tell their stories. I was shocked to hear the story of a Vietnamese village wiped off the map by the American military. I could almost hear the moans and cries of the women and children. I was shocked to hear a white South African reporter who had spent almost half of his life in colleges and academic institutions in search of a decent education. When he decided to integrate and share his knowledge with the blacks, he was sentenced to prison and hard labor. I was shocked to hear about the criminal invasion attempt on Cuba, hoping to return it to pre-revolution times as a playground for wealthy Americans. I was shocked to hear stories from Mozambique, Angola, and last but not least, Guinea, then under Communist President Ahmed Sékou Touré, which had been subjected to a brutal invasion by Portuguese forces just a few weeks earlier. At the same time, others were shocked to hear of my people's endless ordeals and struggle against the British mandate and the Zionists before 1948, and against international Zionism and neo-colonialism afterwards.

Although progressive and socialist reporters know more than the average person about freedom fighters, their knowledge remains basic. That was why an international journalists' organization had been established. This was its seventh international conference and the reason for our presence in Havana. This organization bestowed upon me its medal of honor in December 1971.

In May 1978, I paid another visit to Havana, to participate in preparations for the conference of the Non-Aligned Movement, scheduled to take place in 1979. This time, I had the privilege of getting closer to Castro. Our PLO representative in Havana, Issam Kamel, had made all the necessary arrangements. Castro was a charismatic person who approached you as if he had known you for ages.

The main topic of the meeting was the war between Eritrea and Ethiopia, then under communist ruler Mengistu Haile Mariam. Supported by the Soviet Union, Cuba had been playing an influential role in Africa. One of its activities was to support the Ethiopians with arms and training. The Eritreans, on the other hand, had asked Abu Ammar to persuade Castro to stop his support for the Ethiopians. Their reasoning was that they were also a national freedom movement that had the right to self-determination and independence. Needless to say, Abu Ammar delegated this mediation mission to me.

Castro seemed already to be aware of the real reasons behind my visit and gave me little time for any formalities, especially as he was quite busy with what was happening in Angola at that time. The phone rang several times during our meeting, and it was almost always the Swiss ambassador on the line who was looking after American interests in Cuba. Castro told me that he was complaining about Cuba's actions in Angola.

He then sighed and said: "It is quite difficult to deal with our

African comrades. You can never tell whether they are committed to socialism, or will revert to tribalism. ... I can't understand them any more."

He then returned to our subject and said: "Tell Arafat to reassure the Eritreans that our forces in Ethiopia will not engage in any fighting against them. In return, they have to accept the proposals that are being put forward and which are intended to put an end to the battles. They are in everyone's interest."

The meeting ended, and he actually kissed me goodbye. In fact, kissing was one of the things he had in common with Arafat.

(10)

My visits to Cuba continued, whether on the bilateral or the international level. I will only tell of one other visit, which I made as part of my duties with Committee 23. Several groups attended this seminar, including representatives of various non-governmental organizations as well as international public figures, such as writers, reporters, and peace activists in the Palestine/Israel conflict.

The PLO representative, Imad Jadaa, held a reception before the beginning of the seminar. The retired Israeli General Matti Peled, one of the chief advocates of reconciliation between Israelis and Palestinians, was there. Personally, I was not too thrilled about the idea of meeting him, but I could ill afford to go against the current, especially in the presence of senior allies and sympathizers. I said to him: "It won't be easy for you to convince me of the genuineness of your intentions for permanent and just peace with the Palestinians, knowing that you have killed dozens of Arabs, especially on the Egyptian front."

As if he had expected such an antagonistic question, he replied: "Actually I may have killed hundreds of Arabs and not just dozens. But that is the reason why I support the peace process. I have come to realize that there is no solution in wars, as they only lead to further war and hatred. I have fought and I have killed, and I could have been killed myself. Being fortunate enough not to be among the dead, I sure as Hell don't want my grandchildren to be." He paused for a moment and continued: "Had I realized the nature of the Palestinian people earlier, I might have called for the abandonment of the idea of the declaration of the state of Israel. You are a stubborn people, and we were quite unlucky to run into you, just like you were with us. We must draw a line under this conflict. We must come up with a solution that leads to peace."

That was back in 1987 and still no "peace" has been established. Many more Israelis and Palestinians have been killed in the years that followed the 1993 Oslo Agreement than in the years that preceded it. Who could have imagined that peace would be more costly than war?

(11)

I visited North Korea in 1969, accompanied by Palestinian poet Abdul Karim al-Karmi (Abi Salma), to represent the PLO in a solidarity conference with North Korea and its people. Compared with Cuba, socialist North Korea was stiff and dry. The authorities had almost completely eliminated individuality. Everyone in Korea is a "Kim," and Kim Il-sung embodied all of them in his uniquely dignified personality as leader of 40 million Koreans (that was their number in the North and South in 1969).

Pyongyang was large and spacious, with modest construction and almost deserted roads. The hotel where we stayed had no signs of luxury whatsoever. There was a picture of Kim Il-Sung on the wall of every guestroom. You did not need to tune your radio, because that would change nothing: there were no radio stations except the government's.

But I was impressed with the Korean people themselves, who were working very hard on building their nation and looking forward to a better future. Korean children were enjoying a good life; we visited nurseries and day-care centers and found them run very professionally. Factories also seemed to have high standards: clean, well maintained, and properly managed.

Strongly influenced by various religions, cultures, and philosophies that had prevailed in the region throughout history, the cultural background of the Far Eastern people is very different from ours. As a matter of fact, worship of leaders in that part of the world had preceded socialism: the emperors of Japan were considered gods, and so were those of China before Mao Zedong's time.

Now, 40 years later, I wish to confirm that I hold utmost respect and appreciation for the North Korean people, who have managed to maintain their independence and sovereignty. Together with their fun-loving Cuban partners, they remain among the few who have kept up their defiance of the United States.

(12)

In early 1990, the UN Geneva International Conference came up with a peace proposal that had some chance of being acceptable to both sides. I was asked to make some trips to promote this proposal. I visited seven cities: London, Oslo, Tokyo, Manila, Bangkok, Singapore, and Delhi. An Israeli journalist represented the other side. The third member of the party was a UN official called Mahmoud Said, who was in charge of all the logistics.

London was our first stop, where we met only formally at the negotiation table. In Oslo, though, I unintentionally antagonized my Israeli so-called colleague. I made a distinction between Judaism and Zionism, thinking that by doing so I would free the conflict from any religious aspects and find a common interest. But apparently that was a red line that most Jews would not cross then, especially after the 1967 War and the consequent reinforcement of the Zionist entity.

Tokyo was the third city on the list, and that was where journalists put us to the real test, trying to find out whether we were really able to coexist. For example, one of them asked me if I was capable of forgetting about Jaffa, the town where I was born and raised. I admitted that I could not, but I added: "Actually, I would be just as interested to learn from my colleague about his nostalgia for his hometown in Poland, and the feelings of millions of others like him, who have no connection with Palestine." Mahmoud Said intervened here and started to moderate the dialogue.

Manila was not very interested in us or our seminar, where the audience was restricted to UN employees and a few journalists. The Bangkok and Singapore experiences were also of little value.

Our last stop was Delhi, a city where I had some friends and acquaintances. Thanks to India's solid relations with the Arabs at that time, our seminar was crowded and well received. You could sense the sympathy with the Palestinian Cause.

Today's India is a very different place. What have we done to our friends around the globe? The truth is they started to desert us after we began to give up our rights and accepted the humiliating Oslo Agreement.

11

THE ISRAELI INVASION OF LEBANON

The Israeli invasion of Lebanon in 1982 was an important milestone in the history of the Palestinian national struggle and the Arab–Israeli conflict. It was a major strategic development that had a lasting impact and wide repercussions, and inevitably resulted in retaliation of a comparable magnitude. In fact, the retaliation that came was twofold: firstly the *Intifada*, or uprising, in occupied Palestine at the end of 1987, and secondly the victory of the Islamic and Lebanese national resistance forces which liberated south Lebanon in 2000 – the first time Israel had been forced to surrender any occupied Arab territory unconditionally since 1948.

(1)

There did not seem anything particularly out of the ordinary in the Israeli aggression that was unleashed on June 4, 1982, with air raids hitting Palestinian targets in Beirut and southern Lebanon. It was not the first time Israel had launched such attacks and it surely was not going to be the last. They had become routine from the moment the Palestinian military presence appeared on Lebanese soil.

That said, fearful rumors had been doing the rounds in Lebanon to the effect that Israel was intending to wipe out the Palestinian armed forces there and impose a unilateral peace treaty with the Lebanese government. Newspapers and radio stations had been talking about this possibility, and the Israeli media had even gone so far as to commission an opinion poll to test the public appetite for a war. It was said that Prime Minister Menachem Begin was ready to use any pretext to trigger the aggression. In the event, it was the shooting of Shlomo Argov, the Israeli ambassador in London, on June 3, 1982. That attack by members of the Abu Nidal splinter group, which Argov survived, set the ball rolling; what we didn't know was how far Israel's aggression would extend.

Almost immediately, the Israeli army started its bombardment from land, sea, and air. All the critical locations were shelled: Beirut, the south, and the mountainous Chouf region. Within five days, the Zionist forces had occupied the southern cities of Tyre, Nabatiyeh, and Hasbaya, along with the whole of the Chouf. On June 9, Sidon fell after a fierce confrontation. The Israelis kept pressing north-wards and they managed to occupy the coastal towns of Dammour and Dowha, before reaching the outskirts of Khaldeh, less than seven miles south of Beirut. The enemy, however, had underestimated the strength of the resistance's rear guard defenses in Khaldeh and their advance was held up for a few days.

The enemy's main concern was to finish the job as quickly as possible, before a serious international or Arab response could be mounted. In Khaldeh, particularly near the airport, fierce battles erupted and hundreds of young men from all parts of the Arab world fell as martyrs. But although the Israeli advance had been checked, on June 13 the southern suburb of Baabda fell to the invaders and with it the Baabda Palace, the official residence of the President of the Lebanese republic. On that day, Alexander Haig, then US Secretary of State, made a statement calling all foreign forces to leave Lebanon. In parallel, the Christian Phalange leader Bashir al-Gemayyel stated: "These are the last eight days of an eight-year war." But the air raids on Beirut did not stop, although their intensity waxed and waned.

(2)

On June 8, Abu Ammar sent one of his bodyguards to me with a message asking me to stay home that evening. At about 7 o'clock, he arrived with Brigadier General Saad Sayel. Despite the times we were living through, Abu Ammar never lost his sense of courtesy and started the conversation off by asking about my wife and children. He then told me that he had arranged to meet a Lebanese official and wanted the meeting to take place at my house. I asked General Sayel who it was and he replied: "Colonel Johnny Abdo," the highest official in the Lebanese military intelligence unit, the Deuxième Bureau.

While we were waiting for the colonel, I replayed in my memory all the bitter episodes of suffering and injustice the Palestinians had gone through at the hands of the Deuxieme Bureau. Surely we weren't going back to square one, after all the gains and improvements that we had won.

Finally, Colonel Abdo arrived. With him were Hani al-Hassan, a Fatah official, and Nouhad al-Mashnouq, a reporter who had acted as a go-between for the PLO leaders and Colonel Abdo.

The latter was extremely polite and courteous, and he accorded Abu Ammar exactly the same respect and deference that he would have given a head of state.

"Colonel, is it true what we heard about the fall of Baabda, that the Lebanese army surrendered the palace without firing a single bullet?"

It was a critical question, but the colonel was able to see the lighter side in one respect: "We were at headquarters when we heard something was happening at Baabda, so we called up and the officer, Rafiq al-Hassan, answered the phone and said: 'The Minister of Defense is right here!' And so I asked: "Joseph Beik is there?' [meaning Lebanese Minister of Defense Joseph Skaf]. The answer came, abruptly: 'No, sir ... not the Lebanese minister of defense, the Israeli one, Ariel Sharon.'"

So, what had Johnny Abdo come to talk about?

After he had summarized the military situation and the fall of south Lebanon, the Chouf, and some other towns, including East Beirut and Jounieh to the north, he addressed the situation in West Beirut and focused on what would happen if the Israelis attempted to invade it. He suggested that the Palestinian–Lebanese alliance ought to allow the Lebanese army to enter West Beirut to assume responsibility for its defense. He also proposed setting up a meeting with Sheikh Bashir al-Gemayyel, "a man worthy of serious attention," to settle all outstanding issues concerning the Palestinian military and civilian presence in Lebanon. He was able to assure us that Sheikh Bashir was willing to have this meeting and reach an agreement.

Abu Ammar did not utter a single word; he was just taking notes, leaving all comments and questions to General Sayel and Hani al-Hassan. Although he managed to maintain a smile throughout the whole meeting, it was obvious that he was quite tense as his leg kept bouncing up and down under the table.

Saad Sayel did not agree with Abdo's first proposal and said he would by no means recommend that the Lebanese army take over Beirut. There were two reasons for this: the first was the army's loss of credibility over the fall of the presidential palace, which had been taken by Israeli troops right under its nose; and the second was the absence of any guarantees regarding Israel, even if the Palestinian and Lebanese positions were guaranteed. A move like that would put the Lebanese army between the jaws of a vice. One false move might result in its complete annihilation.

Colonel Abdo did not disagree with this analysis, but he still wondered about the best solution.

At that point, Abu Ammar interrupted, meaning that it was time to wrap up the meeting, and he commented that the whole of Lebanon, not just the PLO and its supporters, was the target of the Israeli invasion. Abdo, therefore, should concentrate on the position of the Lebanese national forces and forget about West Beirut.

While bidding farewell, Abu Ammar added: "Sharon will not find Beirut easy to swallow in one mouthful. Lebanon's sovereignty is just as precious to us as our own."

Before he left, Abu Ammar said to me: "You need to prepare a list that outlines the requirements of the Palestinian people in Lebanon." He then provided me with a list of names of contacts who could form a delegation for negotiations with the Lebanese authorities. And, he added: "I only have time for military affairs now. I must reinforce Beirut sufficiently to allow it to hold firm." I realized from that moment that the PLO's departure from Lebanon had become inevitable.

(3)

Before midnight, on Saturday July 3, Abu Ammar paid me a surprise visit at my new place of residence in West Beirut. Hani al-Hassan was with him. Abu Ammar started to talk about his personal suffering during the past few days, and added: "The enemy had estimated that it would take four hours to finish us off. They then played it a bit more modestly and asked for four days. And here we are, it's the fourth week, the beginning of the second month, and Beirut is still solid as a rock. All their assaults have been repulsed."

He began to speak lyrically about Beirut, as if he were some romantic poet, improvising simple and slightly awkward verses about the city. His words were punctuated with the bright lights of Israeli flares in the night sky and the incessant sound of the artillery.

"Speaking of love," I interrupted. "I remember a line from a film I saw as a teenager; the hero says to his lover: 'I love you enough to leave you, if doing so makes you happy.'"

Abu Ammar answered sadly: "Beirut has given Palestine what no other Arab capital has. It has given and given, without asking for anything in return. And it never would ask. Nor should we make it ask. We should pay it back of our own free will."

Then he handed me a letter addressed to the Lebanese Prime Minister, Shafiq al-Wazzan, to read and comment on. It was composed of only a few lines, which confirmed that the PLO agreed to leave Lebanon, in return for guarantees for the security of the Palestinian civilians and their Lebanese supporters.

"Did the leaders of all the factions agree to this?" I asked, and he replied: "Without exception."

He got up and we went out together. We drove along deserted roads ravaged by the siege. It was past midnight when Shafiq al-Wazzan opened the door. The prime minister was in his pajamas, but it was obvious that he had not slept for days.

He was not surprised to see us, as all kinds of unexpected things were taking place at that time.

Abu Ammar handed him the letter. Al-Wazzan did not open it or even ask about its contents. He put it on a small side table and then walked to a closet, removed a large book, and handed it to Abu Ammar. "I can't think of anything more precious to offer you than the Holy Qu'ran. Allow me to present it to you, so it can support you in your long journey, our journey, to Jerusalem."

I kept silent. My eyes were trained towards Abu Ammar at this touching moment, the man who was to carry the responsibility of leading his stubborn, unfortunate people for the next 22 years.

He kissed the Qu'ran and said to the prime minister: "Now that you have our pledge in your hands, I wish you to recognize that neither Israel nor the United States have yet achieved their goals. They will continue with their maneuvers and ruses, in order to gain extra time to carry out more killings and destruction, and to occupy Beirut. Their main goal is to cause the heroic Lebanese people to believe that they are suffering this ordeal because of us."

Al-Wazzan answered: "The letter is in my custody and no one shall see it before I make sure of everything, including written guarantees and a ceasefire declaration."

(4)

The days that followed the delivery of the letter witnessed the worst raids since the beginning of the invasion. The United States was claiming to be working hard at mediating a ceasefire, but President Ronald Reagan's special envoy, Philip Habib, was in fact completely biased towards the Israeli side, despite his Lebanese ancestry.

Two months into the invasion, at the beginning of August 1982, the Palestinian and Lebanese masses were thanking God that their fighters had been able to withstand an army that prided itself on being the fourth strongest military power in the world. On August 4, 1982, Beirut was still as steadfast as a mountain, indifferent to all the shelling and bombardment, the electricity and water being cut off, and leaflets dropped by Israeli aircraft calling on the residents to flee.

Morale in the capital was lifted by news of resistance in the south, and people were preparing themselves for the possibility of a long war. We heard about the heroic "RPG children" and ambushes of senior Israeli officers.

On August 4, in the Alexander Hotel in Ashrafieh in East Beirut, the Israeli staff officers were not hiding what was planned for the following day, Yasser Arafat's birthday.

I heard later from an American reporter that he had told one of the loose-talking Israeli officers at the hotel: "You're revealing classified information, you know. Don't you worry it might leak out to the enemy?"

Arrogantly, the officer replied: "It won't matter how ready the enemy is. We're going to hit them so hard they won't be able to take it, and if you don't believe me now, let's have this conversation again tomorrow night, in the Commodore Hotel in so-called West Beirut."

As it was, the Palestinian–Lebanese Allied Forces did not need any inside information about the enemy's intentions: tanks and armored vehicles were plainly in view at all the entrances to the city: the port, downtown, Ras al-Nab', the Museum, al-Ouza'i, and the Kuwaiti embassy.

The advance started early in the morning on all fronts, following an exhausting night in which there was continuous bombardment from the air, sea, and land. The only unexpected element was the Israeli paratroop landing at the Bain Militaire beach. If they had succeeded in taking the beach, Beirut would have been besieged from all four sides, not to mention from above, where Israeli fighter pilots had grow used to roaming in the skies over the city without fear of being hit. It was futile to keep firing into the air with our limited resources.

The Israeli plan was to split West Beirut along an axis from the Museum, along Fouad al-Awwal St and Corniche al-Mazraa all the way to the Bain Militaire. Consequently, the ferocity of the fighting escalated at the two extremities of this axis. There were bloody and heroic fights at both the Museum and the Bain Militaire. Although much has already been said about that day, a lot remains yet to be told about those young people who fought until the last bullet, making sure that the enemy would not break through.

From the first moment, it was obvious the Israelis intended systematically to wipe out any obstruction, barricades, residential buildings, and hospitals that stood in the way.

Consequently, the defenders had no choice but to resist this aggression in a fierce face-to-face confrontation. The frontlines drew in fighters from the whole of West Beirut who had no heavy weaponry except anti-tank grenades.

The enemy gave it up its airborne assault on the Bain Militaire after four failed attempts and not a single paratrooper managed to gain a foothold on Lebanese soil. The Israelis evacuated their casualties and withdrew to the sea.

But the Israelis' worst setback was at the Museum, in a battle which seriously tarnished their reputation and punctured their arrogance. Israeli tanks made six attempts to break through during that day, but they only managed to advance 100 meters. They renewed their onslaught after dark, under the illusion that the night would afford them more success.

In the final analysis, the enemy tasted defeat and they pulled back. Their diplomats sought to justify the failure by claiming what had happened was not an attempt to enter West Beirut, but rather a response to a "ceasefire violation by the terrorists."

Beirut was in flames, dying, but she refused to raise a white flag. Abu Ammar saluted the Allied Forces for their brave stand to safeguard what was left of Arab honor. Meanwhile, we heard on the news that Arab League foreign ministers were going to meet two days later, to prepare for an Arab Summit. Who in Beirut that night thought they could survive for another two days? But those who stayed and witnessed the events of August 12 and still managed to get out alive would never forget those days, even though many of the horrors were almost too terrible to remember.

That night, people stayed in their homes or shelters. As time passed, the intensity of the shelling began to escalate and we prepared for another bloody night.

As dear as life might be, where humans instinctively strive for survival many learned that night that there are times when the fear of death is worse than death itself and they wished for nothing more than to die. I passed through that experience myself for a few seconds, when I found myself and my wife snatching up our children as we ran down the stairs. Just as we made it to the shelter, a bomb landed close by. We were engulfed by clouds of thick smoke and my wife almost lost consciousness. I was coughing like a bull in a slaughterhouse.

We hurled ourselves towards the entrance of the building in search of oxygen. I could not see anything beyond the door. Everything had become dark again, although some early morning light had started to appear on the horizon.

Soon afterwards, in my dazed and confused state, I was suddenly aware of a motorcycle making a stop outside the entrance of our building. The rider got off, came up to the doorway, and chucked something inside. Instinctively, I threw myself to the floor, expecting an explosion. But the object was not a grenade. I raised my head and I crawled over to see what it was. Curiosity kills the cat, they say, but not in this instance. I got closer and saw a plastic bag on the ground. I knew what it was even before I had read what was written on the bag: "Revolution Bakeries – Fatah."

I grabbed the bag and scurried back into the shelter, where the other residents of the building were all sitting.

One of our neighbors went into his apartment and got us some thyme and olive oil. The sandwiches we made were probably the best I ever tasted. Behind each loaf stood dozens of noble fighters, who had provided the flour, kneaded the dough and baked it, and distributed the bread. That is the essence of popular resistance.

I don't think that there was a single person in Beirut on the night of August 12 who did not confront death, in some way or another. It was an unforgettable night, followed by an equally unforgettable day. The living hell did not come to an end until 5 o'clock in the evening, when a ceasefire began, and this time it was a "serious" ceasefire.

On August 14, my wife and I, together with some friends, went on a tour of the damage. We did not stop for long at our homes, as there was no time for personal grief. Instead, we headed to al-Fakhani, the PLO quarter. What we saw was indescribable. Everyone was dead, or at least that is how it appeared at first glance. Gradually, the picture started to change, and the steadfast fighters and residents started to emerge from their hiding places.

We ran into the artist Abdul Hayy Musallam, who later made an exhibition out of the remnants of the conflict. A group of journalists had assembled a collection of shell casings and pieces of shrapnel which the Israelis had used against us. There was one item that they were unable to carry, however, so you had to go to where it had landed in order to see it.

We did. I am not a military expert who can describe the make or brand of this bomb, so I will merely repeat what was written on it in English: "Weight 1,000 Pounds – Good for all Targets – Made in the United States." I don't know if this gift came from the air or from the sea, but I saw that it had penetrated four floors of the concrete building and come to rest in a child's bedroom, where it had failed to explode. Thank goodness for that, as the family were in their home when the bomb hit.

Despite all the death and destruction, Washington and Tel Aviv were still describing the Palestinians as "terrorists." What hypocrisy! What double standards!

Shafiq al-Wazzan put up a good stand at the Presidential Palace, threatening to resign after he had established what America and Israel's intentions were (although these were intentions that Abu Ammar had flagged up on July 3, when he had handed over the famous letter). Israel claimed it had received no offer regarding the withdrawal of the Palestinian fighters from Beirut. I am still not sure who was lying, Begin's official spokesperson or Reagan's (that is, Philip Habib). It was probably both.

Things calmed down, relatively speaking. There was no more hell, but the volcano was still silently seething. It was then that preparations for the departure from Beirut started.

Zero hour was going to be on August 21, when the first Palestinian convoy was due to leave. The people of Beirut had a genuine, boundless love for the Palestinians and they threw rice and sang patriotic songs for them as they departed. But it was evident that the local residents were relieved to have the pressure lifted from them.

When the day for Abu Ammar's departure came, I could not escort him to the port. It was beyond my emotional capability. I bade him farewell at the front of his Command Center, known as Command 17, in al-Fakhani. He said: "Are you sure you want to stay?" I nodded my head in the affirmative and he continued: "May God support you. You need to know that I have received a letter from Sheikh Bashir, promising that the Palestinians residing here will be safe under his auspices. I've already sent him a message saying that, as he has become president of the country, he must act accordingly. In light of that, we will do our part and define our strategy with him."

Abu Ammar's car moved towards the port, from where he would board a ship and start a new journey. Hundreds of thousands of Lebanese and Palestinians, including party leaders and officials, were there to say goodbye. Prime Minister al-Wazzan represented the government and René Mouawad represented President Elias Sarkis. In addition, all the Lebanese National Movement leaders were present there. Walid Jumblatt was unable to keep his emotions in check and he lifted his machine gun into the air and started firing.

Victory and defeat are two extremities in which genuine leaders are put to the test. Throughout history, many leaders have managed to turn defeat into victory, as Nasser did, while others have managed to do the opposite, like Sadat.

Assessments differed in regards to Abu Ammar: whether on the day of his departure he was victorious or vanquished. But there was unanimity that he departed with honor, and the farewell was more of a celebration than a wake. He was equal to that day: upright, proud, unusually elegant, aware of the cameras. He even found time to stop and play with some children who were in the crowd.

I started to walk away from al-Fakhani. I kept on walking with no fixed destination, until I found myself at the PLO office, with its bullet-scarred walls and steel reinforcements hanging down.

I don't remember how long I stood in front of the building, in an almost catatonic state. A friend came up to me and took my arm and escorted me to my house. That too was in need of some rehabilitation, hit by waves of shrapnel that had shattered all windows.

I sat down amidst the rubble and thought about the tests that still lay ahead of us. I was now the only PLO official in Lebanon, representing 350,000 Palestinians living in the country. Every single one of those people had been affected in one way or another by the invasion and they all were in need of support, be it a roof over their heads, a loaf of bread for their family, or a word of reassurance to alleviate the feeling of peril in their minds.

12

THE SABRA AND SHATILA MASSACRE

On August 21, 1982, the first convoy of Palestinian fighters left Beirut. Abu Ammar departed on August 30. During those nine days, Beirut went through a state of disequilibrium. The Palestinians were not the only ones who were fearful of the unknown; all Lebanese nationalists had the same feeling.

(1)

Of particular significance was August 23, the day when Sheikh Bashir al-Gemayyel was elected as President of the Lebanese Republic. All Lebanese felt the election like an electric shock; Bashir's own supporters were almost driven mad with elation. It seemed Bashir al-Gemayyel's acquisition of power had decisively settled the outcome of the war: for once there was a winner and there was a loser.

While the supporters of the nationalist and Islamic masses were still recovering from the shock, their leaders started to reconsider their positions. Some were a little hasty in making a 180-degree turn from their original positions, and they rushed to congratulate the new president-elect.

I did not know Bashir al-Gemayyel very well, unlike his father, Sheikh Pierre, and his older brother Amin.

I had met him only once, with his father at the Kuwaiti embassy in 1977. Eight years before that, I had helped secure his release after he was captured by Palestinian guerillas in al-Dekwaneh, near Tall al-Za'tar Camp, in revenge for the Kahhaleh massacre in which 14 Palestinians were shot in cold blood.

The instant I heard about his election, I wondered whether my efforts to save his life back then would be repaid now. But I did not get my hopes up too high: Sheikh Bashir had become a symbol of extremism and boundless defiance in those intervening years.

As for Sheikh Pierre, whom I had known since pre-PLO times, he had been completely eclipsed by his son and was no longer the decision maker. My only hope was Bashir's brother, Sheikh Amin.

Sheikh Amin had always nurtured a good reputation among Palestinian circles and leftwing parties. He was regarded as a moderate and a tireless proponent of dialogue. He also had close relations with several PLO officials, Abu Iyad in particular. And most recently, during the invasion, he had made some positive gestures, such as visiting West Beirut and condemning the Israeli siege.

Over and above all that, I knew the man quite well. We had met several times, mostly in the context of our efforts to reduce tensions between the Revolution and the Phalange.

I recall one of our encounters in Tunisia, back in 1970. He was a member of the Lebanese delegation presided over by Prime Minister Dr Amin al-Hafez, which had been attending the Conference of the Union of Arab Parliamentarians. All the delegations were staying in the same hotel, including the Palestinian delegation, of which I was a member, and we found ample opportunity to get together and discuss matters of mutual interest. We agreed then that both Lebanon and the Palestinian cause would suffer massively should the Phalange and the Palestinian fighters ever come into armed conflict. We also agreed to work on setting up a meeting between his father, Sheikh Pierre, and Abu Ammar when we returned to Beirut.

When we returned, Sheikh Amin requested that I arrange for a meeting between himself and Abu Ammar first, in preparation for the latter meeting. And so it was decided. Unescorted, Sheikh Amin drove his own car to Abu Ammar's headquarters in al-Fakhani. After an extremely warm and positive talk, Abu Ammar concluded: "I know that Sheikh Bashir is still upset with us, after our people captured him. I know they confiscated his machine gun. Therefore, I would like you to deliver a gift on my behalf, so that we all start a new chapter in our relationship."

Abu Ammar then called for one of his comrades and told him: "Go and get me a Dikteriov [a medium-duty machine gun]." He then turned to Sheikh Amin and said: "I offer him this gift in my military capacity. After all, the weapon is the soldier's most priceless property."

One of the men escorted Sheikh Amin to his car carrying the machine gun and put it in the boot of the car.

I bade him farewell and wished him luck.

We did not lose touch. A few months later, a delegation of European parliamentarians came to Lebanon, wanting to make contact with the PLO and visit the refugee camps. Coincidentally, at the time they arrived, Israel had just launched an air raid on the camp in Nabatiyeh, completely wiping it out.

I accompanied this delegation on their field trip to south Lebanon. I was happy to see Sheikh Amin was with them also, as representative of the Lebanese parliament, to explain Lebanon's dilemma over the Palestinians and underline the need to find a quick and just solution.

The day after Sheikh Bashir was elected, I went to my office with some of my staff to start getting the place back into some kind of order. As far as we were concerned we were returning to the normal routine, particularly as there had been nothing in the agreement governing the PLO's departure that indicated its Beirut office was to be closed down. But, this proved later to be a misapprehension.

I called Sheikh Amin, who was very courteous and asked me about my family, before continuing: "I heard that you are staying here to represent the PLO. Therefore I'd like you to cooperate with us so that we put the past behind us. You are well aware, just as I am, of Sheikh Bashir's image among the Palestinians. That's why I hope we can work together to rectify matters and push things forward in a manner that will guarantee everyone's well-being."

I admit this call was a relief to me, and I had some hope of being able to overcome all difficulties and heal the wounds between the Phalange and the PLO. As a first step, I decided to leave my temporary place of residence, to which I had relocated at the beginning of the invasion, and to return home. The next two weeks I spent working hard to rehabilitate the office, as well as my own residence. In parallel, I also had to act swiftly on the political level, in the light of the new developments.

One evening, Bayan and I received a visit from a German diplomat and his wife, and we started talking about Sheikh Bashir and our expectations of what his relationship with the Palestinians would be like. We were interrupted by a news bulletin on the radio which reported an as-yet unconfirmed explosion at the Phalange head-quarters in Ashrafieh during a meeting between Sheikh Bashir and a number of his aides.

The date was September 14, 1982, and it was the night when Sheikh Bashir al-Gemayyel was assassinated.

(2)

I don't think anyone in Lebanon that night, particularly in Beirut, managed to get much sleep, especially after it was confirmed that Sheikh Bashir had died.

Whoever is closely acquainted with the situation in Lebanon knows that the assassination of one of the "big players" is considered unforgivable: a scapegoat had to be found to settle the account.

Sheikh Bashir had become one of the biggest of the big players. For many Christians, he had been regarded almost as a saint or a superhero. I started to wonder: Who was going to be the scapegoat on the following morning?

I was sure that the angry mob would not wait for the outcome of any investigation before seeking vengeance. Also, I knew for sure that Ariel Sharon, who had failed to break into West Beirut, would not waste an opportunity like this to make his dream come true: to invade West Beirut and have his photograph taken in front of each and every office of the PLO and the Lebanese National Movement.

I felt petrified as I started to remember how the recent history of the Palestinian people been punctuated by massacres and mass murders: Deir Yassine, Qibiya, Kafr Kassem, al-Samou in Palestine ... then Kahhaleh, Ain al-Remmaneh, Tall al-Za'tar in Lebanon ...

As I was lost in these dark thoughts, the phone suddenly rang and Bayan answered. The caller was a female friend of ours, who had close connections in the media. With minimal explanation and the most abrupt language, she made it clear that our lives were in danger and we had better leave the house straight away.

But where could we go? On a night like that, any movement in the street would arouse suspicion. We could not just go around knocking at people's doors at such a late hour.

Thank goodness our children had made it out of Lebanon a few days earlier. We looked at each other spellbound. Surely, we were both thinking, this night was going to be our last on earth. In the end, we stayed put and hoped for the best.

Just as light broke in on the morning of September 15, the Israeli occupation forces started to shell Beirut and advance from Ouza'i, less than 2 kilometers south of my house, and just couple of hundred meters from the Sabra and Shatila camps, the greatest concentration of Palestinians in Beirut. I didn't need anyone to confirm the news for me this time, as I could see the Israeli tanks and vehicles from my bedroom window, approaching Cola Square. Within seconds, Bayan and I found ourselves in the car, driving without knowing where we were headed.

(3)

Nothing can be worse than the experience of displacement that is felt by a refugee! I have sampled it from one country to another, and from one house to another. A few days earlier we could not have been happier, as we went back home and started to re-shelve our cherished library. These books were our only fortune and we had lugged them around endlessly to ensure their safety. And here we were now, leaving them behind without knowing where we were going.

The first door we knocked on belonged to some dear friends of ours who were our close companions throughout the period of the invasion. A friend in need is always a friend indeed. It is during the hardest times that a person's true mettle is laid bare.

On that day, Bashir was buried and his brother gave a speech. Like everyone else in Lebanon we were glued to the TV and saw how badly injured he was and heard the deep sense of responsibility in his words. "That's a campaign speech," I commented. "Sheikh Amin is the next candidate." The day also witnessed the first Israeli infiltration into West Beirut. Sharon's aspirations had finally been realized, but only after the Lebanese capital had given up her weapons, removed her mines, and dismantled her barricades, and that was only because she had believed Philip Habib's word of honor, on behalf of the United States, that Beirut was not going to be invaded and none of her residents were going to be touched.

On the evening of that day, at around 9 o'clock, someone told me that the Israeli tanks had reached the Soviet embassy at Corniche al-Mazra'a, less than half a kilometer from the PLO Office. What was occupying my mind was how on earth could we get to the building to prevent our most confidential documents falling into enemy hands.

In fact, my sister Salwa and her friend Basman, who were with us in our hiding place, sneaked out on the pretext that they had to make a private visit. But I knew exactly where they were going. As the minutes passed, I said to my companions: "If they do not show up soon, you can hold me responsible for their deaths."

But our anxiety did not last long; Salwa and Basman showed up, carrying all the papers that they had been able to retrieve, and we spent the remainder of the night burning them, as Salwa and Basman reported to us what they had seen. There were Israeli tanks and soldiers all over the place, yet some valiant young men and women had been scuttling around between the alleyways like ghosts, carrying RPGs.

On the morning of September 16, which was a Thursday, the newspapers reported sickening news that the PLO office had fallen into the Zionists' hands and was being turned into their headquarters. Their trespass had reached all around West Beirut. They had also started to search every street and every residence, looking for "wanted" Palestinians.

(4)

On that morning, I had to plan a way to protect myself from an assault by Mossad. I was also becoming all too aware that my presence had started to endanger my hosts, which was a burden no one could tolerate and I would never ask anyone to.

Bayan had made up her mind that she wanted to go back and stay at home, irrespective of the consequences. She said: "I deserted our house in Jerusalem and I have spent the rest of my life regretting it. They stole my father's library in 1948 and I don't want to let them repeat that with our library."

As dangerous as her decision was, it came as a relief as it was still less dangerous than the possibly endless undercover journey which I had to make.

We bade each other farewell. Bayan did not ask me what I was about to do, either because she knew that I did not know, or because she knew I would not tell her, or because she did not want to know, fearing what the enemy might do to elicit a confession from her. And so, we parted company.

She went back home and I headed to the house of Prime Minister Shafiq al-Wazzan. The following days were eventful for both Bayan and myself, but we remained incommunicado. Neither of us was aware of the terrible events that were going on that day in Sabra and Shatila.

My reception by Shafiq al-Wazzan was very gracious; something which encouraged me to consider seeking refuge at his house until the smoke cleared. The problem was, though, that the prime minister's house was like a beehive, with all kinds of ministers, senior officials, and press people milling around.

So I decided to head to a friend who lived in Ras Beirut. You know, people sometimes do really stupid things during cruel times. I mean, how could Ras Beirut be any safer than any other place? Hadn't the entire city come under occupation? Actually, until that very moment I wasn't sure that it had. However, I came upon a militiaman who said: "Don't you know that the Israelis have reached Bliss Street? Their vehicles are stationed right across from Hbeish Police Station." Then he approached the car in which I was sitting and asked: "Aren't you Shafiq al-Hout?" I said I was, and he replied angrily: "What the hell are you doing out on the roads? Don't you know that you'd be good prey for them?"

So, I saw no alternative but to return to the prime minister's house. Beirut had become too small for me.

The PM invited me to lunch and then he went back to entertain his guests. I stayed on the balcony, which had a beautiful sea view, now besmirched by the sight of Israel's navy moored offshore. After what seemed like a short time, I felt a hand patting my shoulder and the prime minister's voice saying: "You know, I've been watching you for the past 15 minutes. I didn't want to interrupt your thoughts."

I answered: "Mr Prime Minister, I thank you for your kindness. Actually, I was in another world. I was thinking about the day we left Jaffa, April 24, 1948. I was 17 and, as we were sailing to Beirut, I kept on dreaming about going back and I was sure that I would. All of my friends lived through the same experience and the same dream, and we have devoted our lives to realizing it. Here we are today, in Beirut, and the tragedy is repeating itself. The dream is fading and there is very little hope left. Who would have thought that, after 34 years of struggle for the restoration of Palestine and Jerusalem, we would end up losing Lebanon and Beirut?"

I got up and excused myself, and went back on the road.

(5)

As a 50-year-old man with no place to go, I found myself wondering: Why can't I be 17 again? Isn't it time to let the young people take over the cause? Like anything else, surely it needs new blood, the steadfastness of youth and its willingness to join the struggle.

Had the streets of Beirut got so narrow that they could only allow the passage of a single person? Where was everybody else? Where were my 200 relatives, my friends? Their doors had been wide open to me for more than 30 years. Who had closed them now? No, Beirut had not changed, but I had. More than once I stood at the door of a friend or relative, but I just could not knock and go in, for fear that I would embarrass my host. Why should I experience such a feeling? Perhaps it was not that surprising, as I had even started to feel ill at ease with myself. If only my features and appearance could change. Why not, if there was a fake ID card in my pocket? How could I blame anyone else for not wanting to know me, when even I was denying my own existence?

Darkness fell and I had become quite exhausted. I went back to the friends with whom I had been in the morning. Their warm welcome helped me regain some of my confidence in people and in myself.

We went to sleep without knowing that human beings were then being slaughtered like cattle in Sabra and Shatila, and that something horrendous was taking place in Beirut.

We were awakened by the sound of an Israeli patrol walking right past my friends' house. It was the first time I had caught a direct glimpse of Israeli soldiers outside their tanks or war planes.

I did not think of myself, but rather of my hosts. I left their house as soon as possible and I found myself opposite the patrol on the other side of the street. I was carrying a small briefcase, inside which there was a gun, a passport, and $1,000. I had decided to use the gun on myself rather than fall into enemy hands. I had already told Bayan of this plan. "If I am taken prisoner and you see me being paraded on TV, be certain that I must have been drugged in some way or another," I had said. Just then, a car pulled up next to me and a familiar voice told me to get in quickly. That was my dear friend, who was then minister of social affairs, Dr Abdul Rahman al-Labban.

"Where are you going?" he asked.

"X," I replied.

We headed towards X and passed an Israeli vehicle along the way.

"Stop right here," I said and Abdul Rahman stopped the car. I thanked him and we agreed that he would forget the name of the place I was heading towards and where he had dropped me, and to say nothing to anyone, even Bayan.

Henceforth, I was cut off from the world. I entered a new secret existence and that story must remain secret, out of respect to the two friends from abroad who granted me protection. Even if it meant putting their careers on the line, they opened their door without a second thought, for friendship and for their belief in human rights and Palestinian self-determination. I shall remain indebted to them for the rest of my life.

I woke up on the morning of September 18, a Saturday, still worn out, and now isolated and lonely as well. There was no transistor radio or newspaper as my friends had promised.

I felt like calling Bayan, but I didn't. I had promised her and my friends not to make any calls, as everyone was under surveillance. It's a good job I didn't call home, because if I had I would have found myself talking to an Israeli intelligence officer or one of his men. It was then that the Israelis chose to search my house and interrogate my wife, as I learned later.

I stayed where I was, biding my time until my two friends arrived with the newspapers. I read about Sabra and Shatila. The news was not very clear, with many caveats and contradictions. On the following day, Sunday September 19, 1982, the newspapers were able to publish all the details of the massacre, the latest in the chain of massacres perpetrated against the Palestinian people in recent history. Although much has been written about the massacre already, we still await the testimony of those children, now grown-up, who watched as their families and loved ones were cut down in front of them.

As Mahmoud Darwish, the great poet of Palestine once described it, the Sabra and Shatila massacre constitutes the core of our collective identity, past, present, and future.

(6)

The massacre stunned the world. In Beirut, it caused anger and defiance. From my hiding place, I would try to get as much news as possible. As strange as it may sound, the whole world was receiving more up-to-date information than I was, despite how close I was to the action. Even more strangely, Palestinians started to hear cries of protests and condemnation from Tel Aviv, rather than from any Arab capital.

Incidentally, while scanning through the newspapers, I came across a few remarkable photos on the front page of *al-Safir*: One showed Israeli soldiers posing and laughing in front of the PLO Office, and in another they were hanging out in a café. I then realized that the Israelis and their collaborators had fallen in the trap of arrogance and self-conceit. I knew then that they were doomed to be defeated.

Having remained steadfast for more than 80 days, in the midst of fire and siege, absorbing thousands of tonnes of all kinds of bombs and missiles, Beirut would never surrender to occupation. This was not a daydream or wishful thinking, but an actual fact. Very soon the papers were publishing news about attacks carried out by brave Beirutis against the Occupation Forces.

The Israeli death toll escalated steeply, at least in terms of what they had expected. Within a day or two, a few Israeli soldiers had been gunned down in various locations. Most significantly, one of their officers was assassinated at Wimpy Café on Hamra Street, while their temporary headquarters at the PLO office, which used to be mine, was subjected to a missile attack. The enemy started to reassess the situation. Not only did they withdraw, but they did so quickly, announcing it through loudspeakers on their vehicles as they left.

(7)

On September 21, 1982, Sheikh Amin al-Gemayyel was elected President of the Republic. He managed to get more votes in the Parliament than his late brother Bashir had, and his election was received more positively in the Arab world and among Palestinians in exile. There was a sigh of relief in West Beirut, unlike East Beirut where most of the residents were still in deep sorrow for the loss of Sheikh Bashir.

I remained in hiding, but I could hardly have been more frustrated. I had had no access to information about what was happening to my people. More particularly, I had no knowledge about what had happened to my wife, who had remained steadfast on her own, with no power or strength except her belief in God, her Arab identity, and the justice of the cause to which she has always been devoted.

I was still unaware that the Israelis had started to withdraw and had reached the southern side of Beirut, near the airport. But I did receive a hint through my radio, which suddenly started receiving the Station of Arab Lebanon again, which was associated with the Nasserite Murabitoon forces. They were playing patriotic music and reporting on the brave resistance, which had been successful in liquidating several collaborators. Enough was enough. I turned off the radio and told my two friends that I was going out, irrespective of the consequences. This time, I asked them not to try to persuade me to change my mind. In the end, they gave up and I left. It was Sunday, September 26, 1982.

I saw Bayan less than an hour later, but not at home. It was still too risky to go back there. We had been married for almost 20 years, but I had never felt the thumping of my heart as strongly as I did that day when we were reunited. We both felt like crying, but we did not, as we had to uphold the "role" that we had chosen: refusal to bow to oppression or defeat.

She told me about the Israelis' trespass into our house, looking for me on Friday, September 17. Bayan knew they were coming, as she could hear them moving from one floor to another in the building. Umm Ghassan (my brother Ziad's wife) and their three children were there as well, and Bayan begged her to take the kids and leave, but she refused and insisted upon staying.

The soldiers knocked violently on the door, she said. There were four of them, including their commanding officer, in full battle dress. "I can't describe how I managed to lose all fear the instant I opened the door," Bayan told me.

"Is this the residence of Shafiq al-Hout?" the officer asked. When my wife said "yes," all four of them barged inside the house. The officer continued: "Where is he?"

"He's not here. He left a few days ago."

"Are all your men like that? They run away, leaving their women behind?"

"Our men don't run. You know that very well, and so does the whole world, who saw them leaving with their heads held high."

"Where did your husband go?"

"I don't know exactly, but he said that he was going to the United States."

"The United States?

"I mean New York, home of the United Nations."

"Do you think that we can get together with him in New York?

"With such an outfit and weapons, I doubt it."

"So, he doesn't like war?"

"Do you?"

"If he's a peace lover, then why doesn't he convince Arafat?"

"And who told you that Arafat doesn't love peace? I think it's your prime minister who has a concept of peace that is unacceptable to Arafat: peace by coercion and surrender."

During the questioning, the three other soldiers were searching all over the house, looking for me and any documents of possible value. Then, one of the soldiers came, enthusiastically carrying a file in his hand. The officer went through it, and then he asked: "What are these lists? Are they the names of terrorists?"

"You seem to know Arabic, so why don't you just read what's written there. Anyway, what you have is a list of people you may consider terrorists, but I don't think any of them are still alive. They are the members of the Palestine Conference that was held in 1927."

"Do you mind if we search the flat?" (As if his men had just been standing around doing nothing until then!)

"Am I in a position to stop you?"

He got up and went straight to the library and started to look through all the shelves. The first book he pulled out was a study of the *Protocols of the Elders of Zion*, and as soon as he saw what it was, he said angrily: "That's a bad book, and I shall confiscate it."

"I am a professor of political science at the Lebanese University. In our academic world, we don't label books bad or good. It is my duty to read all books of value to my field of expertise. If you think this is a bad book, then allow me to show you some books that *I* consider to be bad," and Bayan pulled out a few books written by Israeli authors.

"Nevertheless, I am going to confiscate it!"

"This book was a gift from my father – you can even read the dedication, if you like. It means a lot to me."

He checked the title page and put the book back. He had probably not realized that Bayan's father was actually the author of the book as well. He then continued his search till he found my passport, and he said immediately: "You allege that your husband has gone abroad. Then how did he manage to leave without a passport?"

"That's an old passport. Take a closer look and you'll see that it expired some time ago."

"That's a Lebanese passport, how did your husband obtain it?"

"My husband is like thousands of other Lebanese whose fathers or grandfathers emigrated. He is of Lebanese origins, and he and his family retrieved their citizenship when they came back from Palestine."

"So, what you're saying is that this passport is not fake and your husband can renew it in a routine fashion?"

"Of course; he is Lebanese, and this is his homeland, just like Palestine is."

"So he can return to Lebanon?"

"He can, unless you were to enforce new rules that would also prevent the Lebanese from returning to their homeland."

"Now what do we have here?" the officer cried out when he found my Palestinian passport. The three soldiers handed the passport around and looked at its pages in amazement.

"Your reaction is no surprise to me. I am sure you have never seen such a document. This is a Palestinian passport from the time of the British Mandate. As you can see, the text is written in all three languages: Arabic, English, and Hebrew. It comes from the time when Palestine had enough room for everyone, regardless of his religion or sect."

"We shall take this passport!"

"You are in a position to confiscate whatever you want, and you have done so already, but I wish you would not. This document in particular means a lot to my husband and I can't see how it would benefit you. There's nothing in there that you don't already know."

"Sorry. We must take it."

When Bayan reached this point in the story she could not stop her tears, as she knew how attached I was to this passport. Number 212023, six digits I could never forget.

"I tried hard to get the passport back," she told me. "I asked if any of them was born in Jerusalem. One came forward timidly and admitted that he was. I said to him, although I was actually addressing his officer: 'So how come you get to carry a passport that proves that, whereas I don't, even though I was born there before you were?' But, I couldn't convince them."

Of course she couldn't. Anything that recalls the situation of pre-1948 Palestine instills tremendous fear in Israeli hearts. That is why they want to wipe out our history, all of it.

The officer continued his search, until he came across her book *Palestinian Leaderships and Institutions 1917–1948*. He actually asked if he could take it. He was not confiscating the book this time, he just wanted to read it and send us money for it later by mail!

Bayan told him: "Once again, I must remind you that you are in a position to take whatever you choose. But what puzzles me is that you are asking me for a copy of this book, even though you have already taken possession of more than 200 copies of it that my husband had been storing at the PLO office. In any case, I don't sell books from my own home. I don't want any money for it." And he took it.

When the ordeal was almost over, the officer said to Bayan: "We may well come back, after we have verified whether your husband has gone to New York or not. But, before we leave, can you confirm that we have treated you in a civilized manner."

"Up until now, as far as I am concerned, my answer is yes. But I cannot speak for what you have done with others, elsewhere."

Again, Bayan burst into tears in front of me as she spoke. She struggled to continue the story.

"At that point, I did not yet know about what was taking place in Sabra and Shatila. It was already the second day of slaughter there. The soldier then left me, only to surprise me with a second visit three days later. That was on Monday, September 20, 1982, and they repeated the same questions about your whereabouts, because they had discovered that you were not in New York."

I shall not continue this story, because I think the message has already been spelled out clearly enough. It is that the Zionists' perpetual objective is the elimination of Palestinian national identity. Why else would they insist on continuing to eradicate all physical, spiritual, and cultural traces of our presence in Palestine? But as long as something remains, even if it is just a painting, a poem, or a sculpture, Israel will never rest assured of its subsistence or survival.

13

AFTER THE DEPARTURE

Although they withdrew from West Beirut on September 26, 1982, the Zionist Occupation Forces left behind many collaborators, hoping to drive the remaining members of the PLO and its institutions from Lebanon. As for the PLO office, it was now under the custody of the Lebanese army.

Prime Minister al-Wazzan recommended that I leave Lebanon, if only for a while. Thanks to his help, Bayan and I managed to make it to the airport. We boarded the first Middle East Airlines plane that departed after the war, on October 4, 1982. Where to? It didn't really matter. What mattered was to get as far away as possible from the Israeli checkpoint at the end of the Eastern Runway, less than half a mile away from the plane.

I only felt relief after the plane had made it into the air.

(1)

At the last minute we had chosen Germany as our refuge, and we were exceptionally lucky with this choice. I had called up a friend in Bonn, the ambassador of Sudan in West Germany, none other than my good friend Mustafa Madani. The man practically ordered me to get on the first plane to Germany. As incredible as it may sound, nothing was planned. But if, before leaving Lebanon, Bayan or I had had the luxury of choosing one family to stay with, we would have picked Mustafa and his wife, Aida.

To remind the reader, I had met Mustafa back in the early 1950s, when we were both attending the American University of Beirut. We were both politically active and we even did some jail time together, after the AUB had expelled both of us for causing "political unrest." Then our paths separated until the mid-1960s when he returned to Beirut as Sudanese ambassador and I had become the PLO representative. We spent wonderful times in Beirut and our families got along very well together.

We arrived at the Madanis, where we were reunited with our children. For the past month they had been in Bremen, northern Germany, where they had been staying at the house of their school's head teacher. Strange as it may sound we spent a charming vacation in Bonn. We can really never repay Mustafa and Aida for their generosity. Also, we remain indebted to Dr Otto Suhling and his wife, Helga, for having graciously hosted our children during these harsh times.

Once, at dinnertime, Hanine, the youngest of Mustafa's children, who was named after my eldest daughter, came to tell me that Abu Ammar was on the phone. That was my first conversation with him since his departure from Beirut. Everyone in the house wanted a chance to speak with the man directly. We had all been concerned about his safety. After catching up on each other's news, he asked me to go to Montreal to attend the annual conference of the Arab American University Graduates.

I knew several AAUG members very well, so I could hardly refuse, but I was well aware that that was going to be an exceptionally difficult assignment, taking place in the wake of a painful setback, an earthquake even.

Having participated in many of these conferences, I had learned many lessons about them. One was that the audience often managed to impose its will on the speaker, rather than the other way around. Speakers frequently fell into this trap as it is remarkably easy to say over and over again what people enjoy hearing. It is usually the truth that most people do not wish to hear.

But I decided to go and speak the truth, even if it was going to be a shock to some people.

(2)

Unlike most other Canadian cities, Montreal had always been extremely gracious towards the Palestinians and the Quebec government had repeatedly expressed its sympathy for the PLO.

The hotel where the conference was being held was filled with hundreds of young Arab men and women who had come from all over the North American continent. I could sense their sorrow through their eyes, and not only that but I could sense they were being overly hospitable and handling me with kid gloves – as though I was a living witness who had just survived a fresh Holocaust.

When my turn came to speak, I was touched when everyone stood up and gave me a long round of applause. At that point, I was still somewhat apprehensive about divulging the truth, admitting that what had taken place in Lebanon was a severe blow that had brought a whole phase of our history to an end. It was going to be hard to tell those people that, despite all the heroism, we should not confuse wishful thinking with reality, or try to avoid self-criticism.

But I said what I had to say. The audience went completely silent for long periods. Sometimes they cried, sometimes they let out angry murmurs. I left the podium leaving a challenging question behind me: What now after the departure from Lebanon? How would our intellectuals, professors, and students address this question, in their seminars and studies, to prepare us for a new beginning?

After the conference, I received half a dozen invitations to meet up with Palestinian communities in various provinces in Canada. Ottawa was to be my first stop and Toronto the second. While I was getting ready for the first trip, Zuhdi al-Tarazi, the PLO representative at the United Nations, called me. He conveyed new orders from the leadership. I was to go immediately to Beirut, in response to a proposal that had come from the Lebanese president himself, Sheikh Amin al-Gemayyel.

"Beirut?" I asked with astonishment.

"Yes," Zuhdi said. "And, if you can leave to Paris tonight, you might catch Sheikh Amin there. He actually asked about you when I met him at the reception for him at the United Nations. He told me he wanted you in Beirut to coordinate the channels of communication between the Lebanese government and the PLO leadership."

I managed to get a flight to Paris. But I was not so fortunate as to meet up with Sheikh Amin, who was occupied with endless meetings that continued late into the night. On the following morning, he flew to Rome to meet the Pope. Lebanon's ambassador in France at that time, Dr Butros Deeb, was very courteous and gracious. He promised me that he would call the president and inform him I was going to Beirut to carry out his wishes.

On the following day I flew to Athens, from where I was supposed to continue to Beirut. From Athens, I rang the Lebanese ambassador in Greece, Suheil Shammas, who was an old friend of mine, and asked him to check again with the president's office that I really was expected. He called Baabda and rang back to inform me that everything was in place, and "the president welcomes your return and wants to see good results from your work in getting broken relations back to normal."

Within an hour and a half, I was back home, with friends and relatives, and my distraught fellow countrymen. The Palestinians were happy to see me back, as a symbol of the return of the PLO, a reference point, a Wailing Wall if you like.

From that day on, my house was converted into an office. I hoped at least that some things could be straightened out as soon as I got together with the president, but I had to wait a long time for that.

(3)

The year 1983 was no less terrifying for the Palestinians residing in Lebanon than 1982. In fact, it was worse in many respects, as a result of the departure of the Palestinian fighters, leaving the remaining civilians feeling that they no longer had any protection.

Although the French and Italian multinational forces had returned and stationed themselves at the borders of the Palestinian camps in Beirut and the suburbs, the specter of Sabra and Shatila continued to haunt the refugees. Some were still sleeping in public shelters at night and only returned home in the morning. There were three sources for their fear:

- The first was Israel and its intelligence services. After its official forces had withdrawn, Israel pursued a terrorist intelligence war, hoping to uproot resistance at all levels, even its social, humanitarian, and cultural elements.
- The second was Bashir's Lebanese Forces (LF), or that part of the LF which still felt an unquenched thirst for revenge.
- The third was the official authorities, represented by the Army Intelligence Unit, which had again resorted to oppressive policies and, consequently, antagonized large numbers of Palestinians who sought nothing but security and livelihood.

When we finally established that straightening things out with the official government was getting us nowhere, we had no choice but to get into direct contact with the officials at the Military Intelligence or the General Security. There were a lot of matters pending, the most significant of which were:

- The daily raids and mass arrests.
- The daily direct and indirect threats to the PLO or its members, some of which were published in the papers. Some of these threats went beyond words, and attacks were carried out against houses and businesses belonging to individual Palestinians. There were also assassinations and kidnappings.
- The failure to facilitate administrative transactions, such as renewal of travel documents, which resulted in major problems to the thousands of Palestinian families who had members working abroad.
- The suspension of all compensation, whereby humanitarian organizations such as Community of Martyrs' Families were banned from paying out compensation to the needy, including those who had lost a breadwinner or their whole house.
- The PLO office itself, whose status remained unclear.

We got in touch with all the people in charge and proposed many initiatives, in a sincere attempt to get things back to normal. The principle was that the Palestinians would abide by all of Lebanon's laws and respect its sovereignty in return for security and a right to decent living conditions, in line with previous commitments from all previous Lebanese governments.

Things started to improve slowly. But always the enemies of peace would intervene and mess things up again. One day, the prime minister said to me on my way out of his office after a meeting: "Please keep this [knowledge of the meeting] between us." At that point, I realized there were many more people with influence in Lebanon than one could see on the surface. Why else would the PM want our meetings to be kept secret? What about meeting the president, after he had sent for me personally when I was in Canada? There was no choice but to be patient.

Days continued slowly and miserably, until the middle of February 1983, when the Sixteenth Session of the Palestine National Council had been scheduled, this time in Algiers. It would be the first session after the Zionist invasion of Lebanon.

(4)

The officials in Algiers were sensitive to our needs, and they were extremely gracious and hospitable. Those who know the Algerians, a people not known for either their flexibility or their adherence to conventions, realized how hard those officials must have worked to keep the smiles on their faces.

The Algerian capital played host to all kinds of guests from all over the globe who had come to spend a few days with us. On the first two days, the guests spoke, and their speeches were very sympathetic and supportive. They reminded us of the overwhelming support we still had all over the world. Speakers emphasized that what had happened in Lebanon was nothing but one link in a long chain of struggle, and that the PLO must try to capitalize on this new reality and convert military defeat into political triumph.

Gradually, the conference became transformed into a kind of popular festival, with speakers talking endlessly about the heroic operations that Palestinian and Arab fighters had staged during the war, which was the longest Arab–Israeli war ever. It helped raise the morale of the people and the Resistance, but that was not the objective of the conference. We were there to assess, fearlessly and objectively, some crucial issues.

While the "festival" went on in the main hall, officials behind the scenes were busy with their closed meetings and debates. Some argued against holding clandestine talks and wanted things out in the open with everyone's participation. Many wanted the people to be involved rather than to keep things between the various factions. But that was just more wishful thinking. Whether we liked it or not, the Council was always under the factions' control. Nothing, whether major or minor, would ever go public or be adopted officially without the consent of all the factions.

On the positive side, there was no one at the PNC who did not want the leaders of the factions to come to an agreement. We all did our best to reduce tensions and play down rumors that were flowing back and forth. We pleaded with the press corps to release only good news.

As if we didn't already have enough on our plates, new reports started to leak out about conflicts within Fatah itself. This time, even in the main hall, the speakers could not hide their differences with sugar-coated speeches.

I was careful to listen to all of the speeches, in order to compare what the speakers had been saying eight months earlier during the siege and what they were saying now. I concluded that the secret behind successful political work was self-control.

The speeches finally came to an end and everyone was sure that the conference had, relatively speaking, been a success. No alliances were broken, and every group got what they had come for. That was an important achievement in itself.

But what about the central question on which the meeting had been convened in the first place: What now after the departure from Beirut?

I was not alone in believing that we had not "won" the war in Lebanon. People like me were not too thrilled with the "festival of resistance" in Algiers. For goodness' sake, would no one utter a single word of self-criticism!

That's why this session was not up to the standard I had expected. It was not commensurate with the huge blow which the Palestinian movement had just received. We needed a response that was of the same magnitude.

But this did not happen. The conference was hollow, celebratory.

(5)

Although I fully appreciate the importance of moral encouragement and the refusal to surrender, I also believe that revolutionary slogans alone cannot lead to the fulfillment of national goals. We need to supplement our words with actions. Actions are precious, and they require planning, which in turn depends on in-depth study and analysis of past experiences.

From this perspective, international observers were stunned at the proceedings at the conference, which failed to produce a single Palestinian official, including Abu Ammar himself, who tried to analyze the Palestinian experience in Lebanon. Satisfaction was derived from merely praising victory, with no reference to the shortcomings of any official. There was only the conventional discourse about "the conspiracy," "imperialism," "Zionism," "reactionary regimes," and so on; it was as if the speakers were satisfied that they had invented gunpowder in the Atomic Age.

Several of the members wanted truthful and accurate answers to many important and crucial questions. In my speech, I tried to provide such answers.

People wanted to know whether Lebanon, with its heterogeneous social and political systems, was in fact a suitable hub for the Palestinian revolution. They also wanted to know whether the Palestinian presence had resulted from *force majeure*, or from a political decision which had envisaged Lebanon as the best place from which to confront Israel.

No one would deny Lebanon's contribution to the Palestinian cause. We would always remain indebted to the noble position that Lebanon chose to adopt. But weren't there also some Lebanese citizens who had been on the diametrically opposite side of the table? Hadn't some Lebanese not only fought the Palestinians but allied themselves with Israel? In Lebanon, there were some Lebanese who had supported the Palestine Revolution and had died trying to defend it. But there were others who had died fighting the Revolution and trying to drive it from Lebanese soil.

There were people in the audience who wanted to know all the intricacies related to the alliances of the Revolution, at the Arab and international levels, and particularly those that used to be described as "strategic alliances." Some leaders had repeatedly talked about alliances they had established with this or that Arab or non-Arab state, and the public would take their words at face value. But we had learned through bitter experience, the Lebanese experience being the most striking, that no such alliance could be relied upon. So where was the truth?

"Even if we were to skirt round this issue and strike it from our agenda, can we possibly eradicate it completely?" I asked. "Can we just ignore the fact that there is not a single Arab state bordering Israel with which we have not clashed? Even if our leadership suppresses this fact, will the leaders of the Arab world do the same?"

People wanted to know exactly what we, the PLO officials, wanted to achieve. Even after 18 years, and so many events, people were confused about this question.

In essence, people wanted to know whether "liberation of the whole of Palestine" was still our goal. If yes, then how were we supposed to achieve it, and through which strategy? Did we need Arab support or could we do it alone? Could the PLO, with its current organizational structure, alliances, and relations, carry out this mission? If not, then how could it be developed or upgraded to make that objective possible?

People wanted to know if the "political option" was feasible, and whether or not the proposals that were being put forth might lead to an acceptable solution. They also wanted to know the outcome of eight years of political engagement with the United Nations and other international decision-making bodies. They wanted to know the price that had to be paid for recognition of the political option, and, consequently, whether or not it was acceptable. Some were also interested in discussing the dialectical relation between the military and the political options, and how we could employ one in support of the other.

On the factional level, the prevailing question was about the truth behind "Palestinian national unity." Never had the military forces been truly united. There were no national elections or national media outlets. On the contrary, divisions and splits had always dominated the relationship between separate factions. The overall setup had started to resemble a kind of loose confederation, if not worse. "Each Palestinian faction has its own flag, its own spokesman, its own military forces and annual celebrations," I told the conference. "All that's missing is an exchange of ambassadors!"

But public investigation of this issue was taboo. Any person calling boldly for it to be addressed was likely to get into trouble. Why? Because he was seen to be tampering with "national unity."

The Lebanon earthquake had seen the fighters doing their duty without even receiving orders. They had all fought bravely together, with no regard to faction or ideology. The detainees in the prison which the Israelis constructed at Ansar in south Lebanon during the invasion were as united as they could be. They could not have cared less about the splits which might have been going on outside the prison fence. Detainees in the prison camps in the Occupied Territories had always acted in the same positive manner.

After more than 15 years of common struggle, no Palestinian could find any good reason to accept this illusion of a phony national unity. For example, how many times did the Palestine National Council pass a resolution to unite the military forces of the factions? This resolution was passed almost at every session of the PNC, but it was never implemented. In Algiers, people wanted to know the reasons behind that paralysis, and which officials were responsible. And how could it be achieved now?

All of these questions remain unanswered at the PNC.

That is why I said this session did not come up to either expectations or the necessary standard. Instead, the resolutions were cheap carbon copies of their predecessors. We could have let it slide had we only been interested in questioning the past. But the real problem was greater than that: it was the future we had to start planning for.

The conference was over, and the final communiqué was released.

It was like one of those crossword puzzles where you can read from right to -left or left to right, and from top to bottom or vice versa. Every person could interpret it his own way and find nothing offensive in it. This was supposed to preserve the glue of so-called national unity. Even the Executive Committee of the PLO was allowed to renew its term with no change to its membership whatsoever except for the resignation of the Treasurer, Salah al-Dabbagh, who was not replaced. The PNC members had feared disagreement, so they just delegated Salah's missions unofficially to another Executive Committee member.

The point that the Palestinian leaderships had missed was that this was not just another session. Papering over the cracks was no longer good enough. "After Lebanon" demanded more radical approaches.

(6)

No doubt the Algerian officials were relieved when it was announced that the PNC session was over. They were happy to see everyone pack their bags and head off to the airport. Their main concern had been that the PNC would fragment on Algerian soil, the soil on which the Algerian Revolution had been born and marched to victory. That meant they tried not to miss a single opportunity to make things better and improve the chances of success, but without interfering with internal Palestinian affairs. They were also very assiduous about security: from the land, air, and sea. I cannot forget the sight of the warship which remained anchored across from the Conference Palace until the very last minute. They must have breathed a sigh of relief when the conference was concluded without any drastic changes or developments.

What no one knew was that drastic changes were afoot, and unfortunately changes of an extremely undemocratic nature. Less than 60 days later, a split took place within Fatah. That then led to new fighting, fresh tragedies, and more journeys across the sea.

14

THE MYSTERIOUS TRIANGLE

Having devoted almost my whole life to the Palestinian cause, I know that its political laws share the mathematical properties of the triangle. We all know that triangles have three sides and three angles whose values are governed by the immutable laws of geometry. Similarly, Palestine has three sides: the internal (or Palestinian) side, the regional (or Arab) side, and the international side. If you were to remove any of these three sides or negate the relationship between them, it would result in a collapse of the legal structure of the cause and consequently would eliminate any chance of finding a solution. The priorities may fluctuate according to political circumstances – for example, internal affairs may occasionally take precedence over regional ones, or the international dimension over the internal – but always in a manner that maintains the overall equilibrium, just as the sum of the angles of a triangle always remains equal to 180 degrees. For now, let us depart momentarily from the Palestinian and regional sides of this triangle and focus on the international one.

(1)

We left Algeria, our historic friend, and everyone headed back to his or her enforced exile. I decided to return to Beirut and I made a quick stop-off in Tunis on my way. There, I received a message from Abu Ammar asking me to fly to Delhi, to participate in the conference of the Movement of Non-Aligned Nations. I tried to bail out, but Abu Ammar insisted, saying: "You've spent all this time in Beirut and you haven't been able to see Sheikh Amin al-Gemayyel once. But we will certainly meet him in Delhi and I want you to be there."

Within hours, I was heading east towards a nation that I had always wanted to visit but never had the chance: India, the largest democracy in the world, which despite its immense size, density of population, and diversity, has always managed to maintain a liberal and democratic system of government.

This summit was going to be the first of such a broad international scope since the Zionist invasion of Lebanon and the PLO's forced departure from that country. Abu Ammar wasted no opportunity to convene meetings with as many leaders as he could. People joked that he would be the first person to arrive at any session and the last person to leave, apart from the security guards. This man's dynamism was his most valuable asset. I once commented that his brain only worked properly when he was on the move.

The Palestinian delegation had three urgent matters to resolve, or at least put onto the table: the PLO's relations with Syria, those with Lebanon, and those with Egypt.

(2)

In its most recent session, in February 1983, the PNC had issued the following statement regarding ties between the PLO and Damascus:

> Relations with our brothers in Syria are based on the previous PNC resolutions, which emphasized the importance of the strategic relations between the two sides and which will continue to serve patriotic goals and to stand up to the Zionist and imperialist enemies, given that both the PLO and Syria are on the front line against this common danger.

Through these words, everyone saw an opportunity for healing the rift between the PLO and Syria. In parallel, we invested extra efforts in preparing for a meeting between President Hafez al-Assad and Yasser Arafat. We almost made it, but unfortunately, our plans were aborted owing to counter-efforts from other groups of Syrians and Palestinians who opposed the reconciliation.

With regard to Lebanon, the PLO leadership was mainly concerned with finding the most suitable way to back the Lebanese National Resistance against Israel's occupation of south Lebanon, and to ensure the security of Palestinian civilians in the country. We had to discuss these matters with our Lebanese counterparts. The Lebanese delegation was presided over by President Amin al-Gemayyel, who had his own worries and troubles. At the time, Lebanese–Israeli negotiations had begun. Gemayyel was very optimistic and confident about the "American role" in bringing the Lebanese crisis to an end. This optimism soon faded, however, built as it was on nothing but self-deception.

Meanwhile, Syrian–Lebanese ties had not been cut completely, but they were in a far from healthy condition. Consequently, the Palestinian delegation was happy to hear about a meeting between Presidents Assad and Gemayyel, considering it a good precedent for a Palestinian–Lebanese meeting. Abu Ammar asked me to go to President Gemayyel and propose the launch of bilateral talks. I did, and that was the first time I had seen the man since his elevation to the presidency.

At first, President Gemayyel showed no enthusiasm about holding talks with Abu Ammar. Perhaps this was because he feared negative reactions from the Phalange and the Lebanese Forces elements in his delegation. To justify his negative attitude, he asked:

"What can Abu Ammar offer me? Isn't it just going to be a formality?

"I know what you can offer Abu Ammar, and you can ask him what you want in return," I replied.

"I suggest you talk to Ghassan Tuwaini (editor of the Lebanese newspaper *an-Nahar*), as you are friends and understand one another. He will tell you what we want and, if you reach an agreement, I'll be ready for a meeting."

I saw Ghassan, who approached me in his usual brusque yet amicable manner.

"Is it going to be action or just words?" he asked.

"It is action that we are after."

"What is it you want from Lebanon?"

"The safety and security of the Palestinian citizens living there."

"And in return, we want the withdrawal of all armed Palestinian factions from the Bekaa valley and the north."

I told him that he knew as well as I did that Abu Ammar had put his forces at Lebanon's disposal as leverage against the Israelis. But he interrupted and said: "We want everything in writing and we want a fixed schedule for the withdrawal of Palestinian forces. We can no longer afford to waste time, as we have an American commitment that Israel's withdrawal will not drag out beyond the end of this month."

Ghassan Tuwaini then drafted a document called "A Lebanese–Palestinian agreement" and I conveyed it to Abu Lutf to review and make comments. After some further discussions we reached an agreement, and both Abu Ammar and Gemayyel accepted it. Finally, the two men met.

(3)

In regards to Egypt, the PNC had called for the following:

The PNC confirms its rejection of the Camp David accords, including all items related to self-rule and civil administration. Based on its firm belief in the role of Egypt and its great people in global Arab struggle, the PNC also confirms its support for the struggle of the Egyptian popular and nationalist parties which express a determination to put an end to the Camp David policies and allow Egypt to go back to its original position in our Arab world. Along those lines, the PNC calls on the Executive Committee to further develop relations between the PLO and nationalist and popular parties in Egypt. The PNC calls upon the Executive Committee to define its relations with the Egyptian regime on the basis of the latter's ultimate abandonment of Camp David.

This resolution came after a very long and sustained effort in the presence of Egyptian observers. An official response came from the Egyptian Ministry of Foreign Affairs. It was measured, not provocative, and sounded optimistic. Everyone thought that things had been settled at that point. But we were wrong, as we later received news that President Hosni Mubarak had issued some harsh statements and warnings to the PLO, as well as to Palestinians in Egypt.

In Delhi, some of us became quite anxious about the Egyptian position and wondered what could be done to alleviate the situation. There were others who were delighted at the rift, paying no heed to the plight of hundreds of thousands of Palestinian refugees and students in Egypt, or the fact that Egypt remained the only free route between the Palestinians in the Gaza Strip and the outside world.

I took the initiative and I asked my friend Ahmad Sidki al-Dajani to introduce me to the Egyptian deputy prime minister and minister of foreign affairs, Kamal Hassan Ali, who was heading the Egyptian delegation in India. At the meeting, the minister greeted me with excessive courtesy and consideration, as is customary in Egyptian diplomacy, but we quickly got to the matter in hand. This is an outline of what he said:

Firstly, there is no reason for panic or fear. What President Mubarak had said has been misinterpreted or misquoted. When he referred to the presence of the Palestinian masses in Egypt, the president intended to remind people of Egypt's support and aid, and by no means did he intend to threaten them. As for the press campaign against the PLO, it has been suspended.

"Secondly, I wish my Palestinian brothers would enlighten me and tell me the reason that they want to dig up problems from the past. We have declared our acceptance of the Fez Summit resolutions and believe that they are a good basis for us to turn a new page in Arab–Egyptian relations."

I asked him what "secret" causes lay behind this surprising new crisis, and he said: "There are people on your side who do not seem to want relations between Egypt and the PLO to be rectified, or between Egypt and the rest of the Arab world for that matter. I have dozens of statements testifying to that fact, right here in my briefcase, if you wish to take a look."

"But aren't there some people in Egypt who hate to the idea of a reconciliation, just as much?"

He answered without hesitation: "Of course there are – but why don't you come and see them for yourself, or has visiting Egypt become a taboo?" I gave him my word that I would, and I lived up to this promise on the morning of Sunday, April 3, 1983.

(4)

Going back to my discussion of geometry, it was apparent in Delhi that the international side of the triangle had grown considerably, compared with its importance at other previous conferences. The other two sides, meanwhile, had been substantially foreshortened. The Palestinians were weakened as a result of the bloody developments in Lebanon and the Arab nation was suffering from an ongoing deterioration of inter-Arab and Arab–PLO relations.

What could be done at the international level to keep the cause on the front-burner? This was particularly important because the PLO had benefited immensely from the international support it had received since joining the United Nations, after having being absent for more than a decade during which this international forum had been the exclusive preserve of Israel.

There was already a UN resolution to convene an International Conference on the Question of Palestine at UNESCO Headquarters in Paris in late summer 1983. In preparation for this conference, the commission in charge decided to hold five intercontinental conferences, each of which would raise a number of issues related to the Palestinian cause.

The locations for these conferences were:

- Africa: Arusha, Tanzania.
- Latin America: Managua, Nicaragua.
- Western Asia: Sharjah, United Arab Emirates.
- East Asia and the Pacific: Kuala Lumpur, Malaysia.
- Europe: Geneva, Switzerland.

I represented the PLO at all except the Managua conference, which was impossible to attend due to Nicaragua's security situation and travel restrictions which were imposed during that period.

(5)

On the evening of March 26, 1983, while waiting at Vienna Airport for a Scandinavian plane en route to Dar as-Salam in Tanzania, I was surprised to see Zuhdi al-Tarazi, our representative at the United Nations, waiting to board the same plane. It was a good opportunity for us to coordinate our work for the upcoming meetings. Actually, Zuhdi and I stayed together throughout the conferences which I attended, and I came to appreciate his qualifications, diligence, good sense of humor, and wide knowledge of international forums.

On the following morning, the plane was flying over one of the most beautiful mountain landscapes in the world, Kilimanjaro. It was only a matter of minutes before we landed in Arusha, the origin of whose name allegedly comes from the Arabic *arusa* (bride), probably due to its superb natural beauty.

The Arusha Conference was quite successful. In it, we managed to produce more resolutions than in any subsequent conference. First and foremost, the credit goes to those brave African nations which had suffered under colonialism even more than we had, and who had gone through long struggles until they managed to reclaim their freedom and independence. In addition, we should acknowledge the efforts of that great friend of the Palestinian people in Tanzania, Minister of Foreign Affairs Salim Ahmad Salim, one of the most exceptional African diplomats at the United Nations. Had it not been for the US veto, this man would have become secretary general.

Ironically, the conference could have scored even better results had the Arabs themselves been more interested in its success. I recall Salim Ahmad Salim telling me: "We have given up on Arab aid and we are no longer building up our hopes for it, but aren't we entitled to complain when we observe Arab aid going to other African nations that are against you? Do you want us to behave like these nations, so that we too become eligible for aid?" I did not have an answer. All that I was able to do was to nod my head and share his grief.

This conference also allowed me to come to an appreciation of Egypt's weight in Africa. Headed by Taha Farnawani, President of the Palestine Department at the Egyptian Ministry of Foreign Affairs, the Egyptian delegation had fortunately assisted in tilting the scales in favor of Palestinian demands. Farnawani told me: "Egypt's political impact in Africa is as old and diverse as the Nile, whose branches reach deep into the continent." In turn, the Africans were also keen to maintain good relations with Egypt. They might have occasional disagreements, but these have always remained marginal. In light of all of that, we managed to formulate our resolutions in such a way so as not to provoke objections from any party.

My impression of Farnawani's decency and his calm personality encouraged me to tell him of the invitation that I had received from Kamal Hassan Ali to visit Cairo. When I spoke of this, he insisted that I go to Cairo with him when the conference adjourned.

On the next day, I left Arusha for Dar al-Salam, from where I would board the plane for Cairo. While I was waiting for the plane, someone came and told me that a group of Palestinians who lived there wanted to see me. Frankly, I had not been aware that our diaspora had reached all the way to the heartland of Africa. The meeting was an emotional one and just before we bade farewell one person came forward and said: "We have a favor to ask of you." He then handed me an open envelope and added: "In this envelope there is $1,000, which we have raised; there is also a list of names and we have allocated a share next to each name." I asked him whether the addresses would be easy to find and he answered, with tears in his eyes: "Those are the names of our families and relatives at Sabra and Shatila, or whoever is left of them."

I took the envelope and we embraced one another, hoping to see one another again, without knowing where that might be.

A little while later, Egypt's consul in Dar al-Salam came in person and stamped my passport with the visa, after the Foreign Ministry had sent its official approval, as arranged by Taha Farnawani.

(6)

During the flight, I kept asking myself, what would I be capable of doing in Egypt? Would it be possible to rebuild the circle of trust between Egypt and the PLO? Would it be possible to restore relations to what they had been to be prior to November 19, 1977, when Anwar Sadat went to Occupied Jerusalem? On that day, a vital connection that had bound Egypt to the rest of the Arab world was severed. Hundreds of thousands of Arab citizens, who used to frequent Egypt, a country they had loved, respected, and considered their mentor, refused to set foot on its soil. I was one of them. I could never forget the day Sadat delivered his infamous speech in the Egyptian parliament, declaring his readiness to visit Jerusalem.

Despite its apparent seriousness, most observers did not believe Sadat's statement at the time, and some thought it had been a slip of a tongue. Their analysis appeared to be substantiated when Sadat himself ordered Egyptian newspapers to omit that part of the speech. Had Sadat really meant it, they argued, he would not have insisted that Yasser Arafat interrupt his visit to Libya and attend the parliamentary session. Surely Sadat would not make such a move in the presence of the leader of the Palestinian freedom movement?

Although Sadat had reiterated his intention to visit Occupied Jerusalem in the following days, the Egyptian Foreign Minister, Ismail Fahmi, had still not believed that he was serious. He said as much to the PLO members attending the Ministerial Conference in Tunis on November 14, 1977. Two days later, when his president's intentions were confirmed, however, Fahmi submitted his resignation. Sadat also tried to get Syrian President Hafez al-Assad's endorsement of his mission, but the latter delivered a blunt refusal.

At our end, as the PLO delegation, we had to go back to New York, hoping that the Egyptian president would abandon his plans. A few hours after our arrival, however, we watched Sadat's arrival at al-Lidd Airport on TV. All the key officials and military commanders of the Zionist movement, who had participated in six wars against Egypt and the Arab World, were there to receive him. Millions of Arabs watched that moment with tears in their eyes. Although their tears had flowed often before, this time it was worse, as it was not only military defeat that they were witnessing but subjugation, humiliation.

We did not have much to say at the General Assembly, apart

from condemning the visit and telling people that Sadat had lost his eligibility to speak on our behalf or for the Arabs.

Some Arabs preferred not to say anything, leaving it to history to deliver the justification of their silence. Some of them hoped Sadat would come to his senses when he discovered that Israel had nothing to offer but everything to gain. Others saw some positive aspects to Sadat's speech in the Knesset, and consoled themselves that he had not completely overlooked Arab rights.

As Sadat pursued his plan, ramping up his concessions to Israel and his attacks on fellow Arabs, the Arab governments also fell silent and did nothing. To make matters worse, Israel escalated its aggression in southern Lebanon. The only glimmer of light was the establishment of the *Jabhat al-Soumoud wa l-Tasseddi* (Front of Steadfastness and Defense), but this initiative remained limited to Syria, Libya, South Yemen, and the PLO. Iraq played no active role in it.

By the time Sadat signed the Camp David accords on September 17, 1978, more than ten months after his initial visit to Jerusalem, the Arabs had still not agreed on either of the two alternatives – to get Egypt back into the Arab camp before it fell into Israel's trap or to formulate an alternative policy that would make up for the strategic imbalance resulting from Egypt's unilateral peace treaty with Israel.

An Arab summit was not convened to discuss this new crisis until October 5, 1978, in other words three whole weeks after Sadat had signed the accords. The meetings took place in Baghdad and I was part of the Palestinian delegation. The whole conference was a disaster, but the worst thing was its conclusion, in which the attendees decided merely to dispatch a delegation to Cairo, headed by Lebanese Prime Minister Salim al-Hoss, to meet Sadat and ask him to reconsider his position, with the offer of a $5 billion aid package. Sadat refused. He signed the final peace treaty on behalf of Egypt in on March 27, 1979. Menachem Begin signed on behalf of Israel and Jimmy Carter signed on behalf of the United States. The Arab response, decided on at a Ministerial Conference in Baghdad, was to sever all relations with Egypt.

(7)

I arrived in Cairo at dawn on April 3, 1983, in the sixth year after Sadat's visit to Jerusalem. They were only six years, but the impact they had had was more like six centuries.

I confess I was very excited to be back in Cairo. I roamed the streets admiring all the recently constructed roads and bridges and the new buildings. But my heart sank when the taxi driver pointed proudly at a half-built skyscraper which was being erected on the site of the demolished Semiramis Hotel, for two generations a political meeting place for intellectuals from Egypt and across the Arab world.

I could have tolerated it, had the changes in Cairo been restricted merely to its infrastructure. But there was something more than that, something bigger and more dangerous: the regime and the course that it was following had changed. The Egyptian state – the most ancient state in human history – had always held a special position. When we talk of a "state" or a "nation" or a "country," the narrowness of the terms cannot do justice to a place like Egypt. She is the eternal geography of the mighty River Nile, she is at the hub of two great continents, she is steeped in millennia of history. These factors have endowed her with firm and unchangeable values which have anchored her to her soil. They also mean change comes slowly and gradually, but when it does it is overwhelming, like a tsunami.

I said to the driver: "On the surface, a lot of things have changed. Even Midan al-Tahreer (Liberation Square) now looks different, thanks to all the new buildings and overpasses."

The driver commented, ironically: "Many things have changed, both on the surface and behind the scenes. Many people have gone up in the world, while many others have been screwed. Conditions for the poor have gone from bad to worse; all we've got is traffic jams, crumbling houses, inflation."

When I went back to the hotel, I found a message from Taha Farnawani. I called him and we discussed the agenda for the coming days. I was frank and explained that I would prefer to stay away from the press, but I would like to meet as many people as possible, at both the official and unofficial levels, loyalists and opponents. And so it was.

I met with senior officials as well as several opposition leaders. In each meeting, I made it clear from the beginning that I had not come to Cairo to judge anyone for their beliefs, or to be judged for mine. The main aim of the visit was to appraise the facts on the ground and to answer some simple questions: What to do now? Is there any chance that the Arabs can regain some semblance of solidarity or collaboration? How long can we survive with such negativity dominating inter-Arab relations and Egyptian–Arab relations? Are we supposed to keep waiting, either for Egypt's abandonment of Camp David or for the Arabs to succeed in demolishing it? Neither seemed a likely prospect. So what was the alternative to this boycott of Egypt?

The officials I met were: Prime Minister Dr Fouad Muhieddine, Deputy Prime Minister and Minister of Foreign Affairs Kamal Hassan Ali, Minister of State for Foreign Affairs Dr Boutros Boutros Ghali, and presidential political adviser Dr Osama al-Baz.

Among the opponents of Camp David that I met were a number of intellectuals and nationalists, including: Mourad Ghaleb, Mohammad Hassanein Haykal, Amin Huwaidi, Yehya al-Jamal, Ahmad Hamrouche, Lutfi al-Khouli, Fouad Mursi, Saadeddin Ibrahim, Mahdi Hafez, Mohammed Fayeq, Milad Hanna, and Abdul Azim Anis.

I also met dozens of members of the Palestinian community in Egypt and I listened to their complaints and grievances. In addition, the Union of Palestinian Women in Cairo invited me to a large convention, which was attended by over 100 Palestinian and Egyptian men and women. It was the first Palestinian public meeting on this scale since Sadat had gone to Israel. The authorities pretended to ignore it, although there were more than enough intelligence officers mingling among the crowd and the venue was kept under continuous surveillance.

Overall, my visit resulted in several impressions, which I will summarize here.

Firstly, two years on from Sadat's assassination, he still had enough supporters who were passionately determined to preserve his legacy. However, I did not think their enthusiasm stemmed particularly from a desire to safeguard the peace treaty he had signed with Israel. Rather, it was a reaction by anti-Nasserite factions who had opposed the July 1952 Revolution.

Secondly, I noticed that most government institutions remained strongly anti-Zionist. Indeed, despite Sadat's oppressive rule, there were enough people in the Ministry of Foreign Affairs, the armed forces and the Intelligence Service who still regarded Israel with suspicion.

Thirdly, despite their unanimous rejection and condemnation of Sadatism, opposition parties had not yet agreed on a strategy to stand up to the new regime. One of their leaders even said to me: "We have no strategy. The Egyptian masses are miles ahead of us."

Fourthly, it was indisputable that the Palestinian community in

Cairo had an urgent need to mend fences with the Egyptian authorities. Some thought that the closure of the PLO Office in Cairo had been a mistake, especially as it had impacted on our people in the Gaza Strip, whose only route out was via Egypt.

I quote this statement from Mohammad Hassanien Haykal to illustrate my fifth conclusion: "We have been hearing a lot of talk about the military option and the strategic balance of power. This is fine, but is it achievable without an Egyptian–Syrian–Palestinian and, if possible, Jordanian alliance?"

I conveyed all of my impressions to the PLO command and flew from Egypt to the Gulf, where the next Palestine conference was to be held.

(8)

I was happy to visit Sharjah and participate in the second Preparatory Conference for Western Asian Nations. Except for Kuwait, where I had worked as a schoolteacher in 1956–58, I had never had an opportunity to visit any nation in the Gulf or the Arabian Peninsula, including the Kingdom of Saudi Arabia itself. I landed in the United Arab Emirates in April 22, 1983, and was looking forward to this new experience.

The future of the "Gulf Arab" identity was my primary concern. The second point of interest was oil and the role it was playing in developing the peninsula, and its dangerous demographic impact. After witnessing destitution and emigration for thousands of years, this Arab desert had now become a center of attraction for hundreds of thousands of Arabs and non-Arabs alike, seeking the riches that it now produced.

What kind of society had now taken shape in those countries and how could one best characterize it? They had undoubtedly made a drastic transition, although their evolution still had a way to go. It was important to make sure they did not lose their way in the future and squander their two most valuable assets: Islam and the oil.

The principal questions remain to this day: How do Gulf nations stand up to the challenges they face? How prepared are they for future challenges, with the Palestinian cause, a highly sensitive Arab and Islamic cause, at the forefront? This cause has never been at greater risk than when power in the Arab world has shifted from its traditional centers towards the Gulf. I was also curious to assess what impact

Palestine had had on that society. It had repeatedly been said that the
Palestinian cause and the petroleum cause were two sides of the same
coin. The two are naturally, and often deliberately, interconnected.

When I arrived it was clear that these issues were already the subject
of widespread debate among the population, as well as in official circles,
albeit more narrowly. One of the Emirati sheikhs received me in his
office overlooking the Gulf, where dozens of container ships and oil
tankers lay at anchor. I expressed my admiration at the development
and evolution his nation had achieved: new airports, harbors, infrastructure. He said: "Of what use is it if we were to going to lose it all?
After the experience of Lebanon, what guarantee does anyone have
that Israel will not come and do the same to us?"

And so, there were concerns about a renewed aggression. But
what I could be certain of, based on my understanding of Arab
history, was that, in the absence of a minimum level of Arab unity,
even nominally, the concerns would remain.

(9)

I left the UAE for Kuala Lumpur to catch up with Abu Lutf and
participate in the next Preparatory Conference, which encompassed
East Asia and the Pacific countries. That experience opened my eyes
further to the importance of the Islamic dimension of the Palestinian
cause. I shall never forget the massive gathering of people that
greeted our delegation at one of Kuala Lumpur's sports stadiums.
There were thousands of Malays who had not been in the least put
off by the terrible weather. The instant our representative appeared
on the podium everyone shouted: *Allah Akbar.*

In Kuala Lumpur, we managed to obtain a series of major resolutions, in the presence of two tough representatives for the two
superpowers, the United States and the Soviet Union, which were
particularly jumpy about this volatile area, not to forget the People's
Republic of China, whose weight was almost as critical here.

We then went back to Western Asia, specifically to Kuwait. There,
I spent one week in which I kept track of the negotiations that were
going on between Lebanon and Israel. Within a few days, I learned
of two major setbacks: the agreement between Lebanon and Israel
and the eruption of internecine fighting within Fatah.

I did what I could: I wrote and warned people about the dangers.
I wrote in the *al-Anbaa* newspaper, whose chief editor was my

friend and colleague Samir Atallah. I published several articles and warned the Lebanese government against getting into this agreement. I reminded it of all the anticipated implications of such a step. On the Palestinian side, I called on our brothers in Fatah to give up their fight and refrain from breaching a code of ethics that had been respected throughout the past years, when democracy and tolerance had always been respected.

On May 17, 1983, the Lebanese government signed a treaty with Israel. But the Fatah wars did not end that May, as mediations had reached nowhere. Even worse, the conflict had widened to include a Palestinian–Syrian dimension after Syria demanded that Abu Ammar leave Syrian-controlled territory, which included a large part of Lebanon. Internal fighting continued. Members of Fatah could no longer brag about how their organization had always remained intact and immune to local divisions.

(10)

On July 4, 1983, the next Preparatory Conference took place in Geneva. That was the fourth of this series and this time it comprised European countries. With the exception of Cyprus, Malta, and Yugoslavia, the member states at this conference were almost entirely against the Palestinians. In fact, we almost lost the Maltese too, because the Arab League boycott office had chosen that moment to uncover the presence of a Maltese company working with Israel, which it consequently placed on the blacklist. The representative of Malta approached us frankly, saying: "Either you persuade the Arab League to lift its sanctions against our company or you'd better start looking for a new ally!"

The representative of Yugoslavia was Isaac Dyazdrevich, a comrade of President Tito, a friend of President Nasser and the Arabs, and the man who had first introduced the PLO delegation to Tito in Belgrade in 1969. When we met he asked me in a genuinely concerned tone: "What's going on in the Bekaa in Lebanon? What the hell is Fatah doing to itself? And what's this conflict with Syria all about? How will you live with the gloating of the Arab countries, should they decide to raise these issues?"

We had to work fast, so we coordinated with the representatives of the Syrian mission in Geneva to avoid clashes and prevent the conference from being diverted from its main purpose. In the end, we succeeded and the spirit remained mostly intact.

The overall conclusion was positive, relatively speaking. No doubt the socialist bloc had played a central role in making that happen, not to downplay the role that some Western nations had also played, specifically Austria, Spain, and Sweden, who distinguished themselves at this time by demonstrating objectivity and respect for human rights and international law.

We left Geneva, intending to return on August 27 as it had been selected to host the International Conference for Palestine, instead of the UNESCO Headquarters in Paris, as originally planned.

(11)

We headed to Tunis to start preparations for the major conference, which was going to be attended by representatives from all over the globe. It was going to be a unique event, the first gathering of such caliber in the history of the Palestinian cause.

Just as in Damascus, our Palestinian comrades in Tunis were preoccupied with internal affairs and the tensions with Syria. I felt then that the Arab and international efforts to relieve the situation were about to come to an end, after failing to achieve a settlement. There was no alternative but to call for an emergency session of the PLO Central Council, which had always acted as a bridge between the Palestine National Council and the Executive Committee. This Central Council reflects the balances of the PNC itself, thanks to its internal structure and the diversity of its members.

The Central Council convened in Tunis on a Thursday evening, August 4, 1983. There was a general feeling of frustration. But nevertheless, the Council managed to recommend the formation of a core commission of 17 PNC members who would be mandated to go to Damascus and mend our split with the Syrian government. Healthy relations had to be restored between these two sides, whose strategic alliance is of vital importance.

Abu Lutf presided over the Palestinian Delegation at the International Conference in Geneva. With him were Yasser Abed Rabbo, Head of the Public Relations Unit; Abdul Latif Abu Hijleh, Director of the Foreign Affairs Unit; Issam Kamel, the PLO Representative in East Germany; Nabil Rimlawi, the PLO Representative at the United Nations Mission in Geneva; and myself. Had the internal situation of the PLO been normal at the time, there would have been more than 20 Palestinian delegates at this exceptionally important occasion. But the delegation was nevertheless supplemented with a few prominent Palestinian intellectuals who had come from the United States, including Edward Said, Ibrahim Abu Lughod, and Zuhdi Tarazi.

At the international level, the representatives of 137 nations and 104 non-governmental organizations participated, in addition to dozens of internationally recognized advocates of liberation.

Because it was held under the auspices of the United Nations, the conference was also attended by some Arabs and Jews who lived in Israel, although Israel itself was boycotting the process. With the exception of retired General Matti Peled, well-known journalist Uri Avnery, and an Israeli army ex-soldier who had participated in the Lebanon War, all Israeli participants were from the Israeli Left, the Communist Party, and the Peace Now Movement. Toufic Tobi and Felicia Langer were the two most outstanding speakers. Progressive lawyer Langer made this unforgettable statement: "This Palestinian generation is the third to suffer under oppression and persecution, while Zionism and imperialism prevent them from regaining their national rights." When Abu Lutf spoke, the audience gave him a standing ovation.

We then received an urgent message from Tunis that Abu Ammar was on his way to Geneva and that he would address the audience on the following day. The audience was jubilant, as there were hundreds who had always wished to see this extraordinary man in person. But Abu Lutf and all of the other Palestinian delegates became worried in case Abu Ammar went off on a tangent during his speech and highlighted divisions within the Arab World, thereby putting at risk all the work we had done to patch things up with Syria. Thinking again of the triangle theory, it was obvious how the different sides were behaving at this time: the deterioration of the Palestinian and Arab sides was taking place as the international one flourished.

When Abu Ammar arrived at the hotel, he was absolutely livid – no one had been there to receive him at the airport. His fury persisted until he was assured that it was nobody's fault: the Swiss security authorities had informed no one of his time of arrival.

I asked Abu Ammar about the speech that he was going to deliver, and cheekily suggested checking the language and marking all the vowel sounds on his script, so that at least the minimum standards of formal Arabic could be preserved. He laughed and handed me a copy of the speech. In fact, I was interested in its contents rather than in its grammar. On the one hand, I was concerned that Abu Ammar might bring up uncalled-for thorny issues; on the other, I wanted to make sure that he would not contradict Abu Lutf's speech, which had been delivered on the opening day. I needn't have worried.

The audience received Abu Ammar enthusiastically. Everyone in the General Assembly Hall stood up and applauded for a long time, both at the beginning and at the end of the speech. The first hurdle of this critical day was over. We had two major ones left: the news conference and the reception.

Some of us would have preferred not to hold the news conference, in order not to get into sensitive Arab issues. Others disagreed and wanted it to happen, and I was among this group. After all, the conference was being held for the sake of Palestine and we had to face the media and enlighten them about what was taking place. At any rate, Abu Ammar needed little encouragement to meet the representatives of the media, and he went without hesitation from the podium to the news conference room. I had anticipated that, and accordingly I had prepared a list of queries that we expected the reporters would ask and handed it to Abu Ammar, so he could prepare himself. I cannot say for sure that he read it, as he put it straight in his pocket. He held the news conference and gave brilliant answers to some of the questions, although he mangled some others. But the overall result was acceptable and did not cause any more problems.

What did cause some tension, though, was the press conference that Abu Lutf held. Uri Avnery was agitated when he learned that he had not been invited and he threatened to hold his own news conference in which he would denounce the PLO as a racist organization, which had been lying when it said recently that it wanted Jewish–Arab coexistence and that sort of thing.

Our delegation could have avoided this embarrassing situation had we issued a general and open invitation to attend Abu Lutf's news conference. But it was too late. Things got even worse when the Israeli Jews found out that the invitation had been extended to the Arab citizens of Israel. Particularly angry was Amnon Kapeliouk, the author of a seminal work about the Sabra and Shatila massacre.

A solution was found: our delegation distributed open invitations to all the people who had been passed over. In parallel, Abu Ammar met Avnery and Kapeliouk and placated them.

Abu Ammar returned to Tunis and we resumed our conference-related activities and follow-up meetings with the various representatives, including the Arab delegation led by Adib Dawoodi, the Syrian Head of Mission in Geneva. Both Dawoodi and his Austrian counterpart did a splendid job in finalizing all pending resolutions in a manner acceptable to all parties. The Geneva Declaration and a supplementary work program were produced. To this day, I believe that this declaration forms the main basis for any international effort geared towards the resolution of the Palestine question.

The declaration stated that the United Nations had a key role in the establishment of a just peace, confirmed the resolutions of the UN Charter, abided by international laws, recognized the Arab Peace Plan adopted by the Arab Summit in Fez in September 1982, and emphasized the use of all of its principles in a manner that would support any international effort aiming to settle the Palestine question. Out of those principles, I highlight the following:

- Firstly: The acquisition by the Palestinian people of their legitimate and inalienable rights, including the right of return of refugees to their former homes, the right to self-determination and the right to an independent state in Palestine.
- Secondly: The right of the PLO, as representative of the Palestinian people, to participate on an equal footing with all other parties in all activities, deliberations, and conferences related to the Middle East.
- Thirdly: The urgency of ending the Israeli occupation of Arab territories, in accordance with the principle of inadmissibility of annexation; and, consequently, the assurance of Israeli withdrawal from lands occupied since 1967.
- Fourthly: The urgency of resisting and rejected all Israeli policies and practices in the Occupied Territories and Jerusalem. It was also important to identify and expose facts on the ground that were in violation of international law and UN resolutions, and that had been imposed by Israel, especially in relation to the construction of Jewish settlements.
- Fifthly: The confirmation that all legislative and administrative processes adopted by the Israeli Occupation Forces with the intent of modifying the holy character of Jerusalem were null and void. Israel had modified many of those laws to reflect its own interests, had continued to expropriate land, and unilaterally declared Jerusalem as the capital of Israel.
- Sixthly: The right of all nations in the region to exist in peace,

justice, and security, within internationally recognized borders, something which would not materialize until the legitimate and inalienable rights of the Palestinian people were recognized.

After these principles were set down, the Geneva Conference decided, in line with a proposal by Chairman of the PLO Executive Committee Yasser Arafat, to call for a further international peace conference focused on the Middle East and based on the principles of the UN Charter and relevant resolutions. The aim was to come up with a comprehensive, just, and lasting solution to the Arab–Israeli conflict, which would include the establishment of an independent state in Palestine. This conference would be convened under the auspices of the United Nations and it should include all concerned parties, including the PLO, United States, Soviet Union, and other states, on an equal footing. The Security Council would be the main coordinator and assume the responsibility for compiling the relevant past resolutions, to assure that they would be confirmed by the International Conference and, more importantly, implemented.

In its conclusion, the Geneva Declaration highlighted the importance of the time element. It emphasized that partial solutions were not adequate: any delay in a comprehensive solution would perpetuate the tensions. As for the roadmap associated with it, that is long and detailed. The reader may refer to the documents that were produced from the conference. In any case, I do not think that the roadmap included any debatable items.

The only debatable point in the Declaration, from both a Palestinian and an Arab point of view, was the following paragraph:

The right of all nations in the region to live within secure and internationally recognized borders, whilst guaranteeing justice and security to all peoples, which will not materialize until the legitimate and inalienable rights of the Palestinian people are recognized (and these have already been defined: the right of return, the right of self-determination, the right to establish an independent Palestinian state in Palestine).

Critics alleged that this text entails recognition of Israel and consequently they rejected the Geneva Declaration. Although there is an element of truth to this, it is not wholly true and one should respond cautiously to it. If what was meant was that the paragraph implied the recognition of the existence of Israel, then that is true. Israel is a reality and the people who are most aware of this are the Palestinians themselves. If there was any doubt about this, then which "Israel" were the Arabs always talking about in the United Nations and who was it that was being asked to withdraw from Arab territories? Furthermore, who had the Arabs been fighting for more than 30 years?

From this perspective, based on objective analysis, what was stated in the paragraph implied *de facto* recognition. But that does not imply legal or *de jure* recognition. There is no law on earth that compels any state to legally recognize another; this is an attribute of national sovereignty. The United States had always pioneered the exploitation of this right; it refrained from recognizing the People's Republic of China, one of the largest and most ancient nations in the world, for more than a quarter of a century, and it only changed that policy when a new relationship suited its interests.

That was the situation, as far as principles were concerned. Politically speaking, though, the PLO, along with all Arab nations and supporters, could not bypass the Charter and resolutions of the United Nations, the groundwork of international legitimacy. These explicitly call for the adoption of the Partition Resolution No 181, which was issued in November 1947, as the only source of "Israel's legitimacy." It stipulated the creation of Israel, which had already taken place, and of Palestine, which as yet had not.

Consequently, one could not just adopt one part of this clause and abrogate another; it had to be taken as a whole. It is a precisely worded text with no loopholes. The first part is contingent upon the second, which firmly calls for the respect and implementation of the inalienable rights of the Palestinian people, which would never expire and which form this holy trinity: return of refugees, self-determination, and establishment of a Palestinian state in Palestine.

The conference was over, and everyone went back home, except the Palestinians, who went back to their exile.

Given that Beirut International Airport had been closed after renewed skirmishes in Lebanon, I headed to Tunisia instead. The plane landed in Carthage Airport on Friday afternoon, September 9, 1983.

15

THE SECOND EXODUS
FROM LEBANON

It was clear that Abu Ammar was starting to feel claustrophobic as a result of his "exile" in Tunisia. His frequent trips abroad, and the troop inspections in Algeria, Yemen, and Sudan, did not really compensate for the life he was missing in Lebanon. He was suffering on two levels: from his position as a leader with awesome responsibilities, and as a human being unable to enjoy even the briefest fragment of private life. No wife, no family, no children – and how Abu Ammar loved children! Even his friendships were political and public in character, allowing for no intimate conversations or personal exchanges.

I remember one time in Lebanon, when we were on the road back to Beirut from Damascus, with the head of the Palestinian National Fund, Salah al-Dabbagh, I asked him: "Abu Ammar, why did you never get married?"

He seemed ready to talk, but he kept his guard up and tried to avoid the subject by saying: "Perhaps I should have got married a long time ago, but ..."

So Salah said to him: "Don't tell me there's a love story somewhere in your past, Abu Ammar!"

His smile broadened until it was almost a laugh and he said: "To be honest, there was."

"And why did you not get married?"

"No luck."

Neither of us wanted to tease Abu Ammar too much for fear of upsetting him, so we asked him: "What about now? Is there anything stopping you from getting married now?"

"Can't you see what my life is like?" he replied

So I said to him: "Nevertheless, Abu Ammar, the Prophet Muhammad managed to get married and he was carrying a message from God."

He laughed and said: "By God, I think our task might be more difficult than spreading Islam in the Time of Ignorance."

He then asked God's forgiveness for his impudence and laughed, saying: "Also, the Prophet had companions. He had Abu Bakr, Omar, Uthman, and Ali and ... and ... as for me" – and he guffawed with laughter – "I have Abu Iyad, Abu Houl, Abu Hasan, and Abu al-Said ..."

How I felt for "Abu Ammar, the man" and the acute loneliness he must have suffered in Tunisia. All this, with the new developments in Fatah, spawning differences between brothers of the same path.

(1)

Abu Ammar and I met again when I returned from Geneva. Joining us in this meeting was Abdul Latif Abu Hijleh, who shared my opinion and empathy for Abu Ammar's predicament.

We did not speak for very long about the crisis facing Fatah or the crisis in relations with Syria. It had become clear to him that Damascus did not want Abu Ammar around and that all his efforts would not come to fruition. He mentioned that "a decision had been taken" and that there was no way it could be backed down from. I am convinced he wanted reconciliation, but he was becoming disheartened.

I said to him: "While we're waiting for these two crises to die down, you have an important matter that requires action from you personally. It's the middle of September already and we have only two weeks before the opening of the new session of the General Assembly at the UN. I think this is a good opportunity for you to head to New York and give a speech inspired by the Geneva Declaration. It will be an opportunity for you to attend the world's largest gathering of foreign ministers and there will be many heads of state there as well."

Before I had the chance to finish, Abdul Latif said: "I second this proposal. We received a telegram from Indira Gandhi just an hour ago suggesting the same thing." He handed Abu Ammar the full text of Mrs Gandhi's message.

We took it in turns trying to convince Abu Ammar of the benefits of traveling to New York for the General Assembly. We spent much of the night going through the clauses of the Geneva Declaration and the schedule that went along with it, as well as the new drive to convene an international conference. We explored the possible repercussions on local, Arab and international levels if he agreed to the idea and visited the UN.

What Abdul Latif and I did not say was that we wanted to steer him away from the vortex of the twin crises and occupy him with something useful and significant, which would also lead him out of his isolation at the Salwa Hotel in Tunis.

He promised us to think about the matter. We left him at dawn as he was starting to give instructions to some of his aides about preparing a detail of soldiers for the coming *Eid al-Adha* festival which was a few days away.

It had always been Abu Ammar's custom to celebrate the Muslim *eids* with his troops in south Lebanon and on our way back to our hotel we speculated about the venue Abu Ammar would choose this year to celebrate, when his men were scattered over two continents!

We did not hear from Abu Ammar and I did not call him again until the morning of *Eid al-Adha*, when I went to his headquarters to offer my best wishes on the occasion of the feast. But I was surprised to hear, as were the other officials who had arrived there before me, that Abu Ammar had left Tunisia.

Where had he gone? It was said to Yemen, or to Algeria. Some people suggested Saudi Arabia, but no one really knew what they were talking about or if what they were hearing was true.

The next day, we received the news that Abu Ammar had traveled secretly to the northern Lebanese city of Tripoli. My heart sank, especially when I found out from one of the members of the Central Committee who was very close to him that no one had known in advance about his plan apart from Abu Jihad, who had remained in Lebanon to lead the fight against those who had split from Fatah and their allies in Ahmad Jibril's PFLP-GC and the Syrian-backed al-Saiqa forces.

This fighting had caused embarrassment among supporters of the Lebanese National Movement, who had no choice but to take a stand either with or against Fatah. They were in an invidious position, for despite their emotional connection and common history with the PLO, and particularly with the person of Abu Ammar, the balance of power was clearly in favor of the Syrians. I think one of the most important factors that led to the marginalization of the Lebanese communists and the dispersal of the Murabitoon (independent Nasserite forces) was their refusal to participate in the elimination of the "Arafatists," as the Fatah movement and those who supported it became known.

As for how Abu Ammar left Tunis and arrived in Tripoli, I never got the chance to ask him about all the details of his journey. What I discovered was that he had donned a disguise before leaving Tunis and his first stop was Larnaca airport in Cyprus. From there, he boarded a merchant ship which had been chartered for him, with a crew that was prepared to make the trip. Abu Jihad was waiting for him at Tripoli's port and they went by car to his operational headquarters. The fighting was at its most intense, with rockets and mortar shells slamming into the Biddawi and Nahr al-Bared refugee camps north of Tripoli. The city itself had been shattered, especially in the areas where there were Islamist forces that had stood by Abu Ammar.

(2)

The huge achievement that the PLO had made at the Geneva conference, on whose outcome we had placed many hopes, offered the real prospect of positive results at the UN Assembly's special session on Palestine. But it was being squandered and we were letting victory drop from our hands. The focus was now on the internecine fighting in Tripoli rather than on our triumph in Geneva.

Instead of devoting our time to investing in our successes, developing new resolutions, and implementing those that could be implemented, the PLO delegation had to spend its time trying to persuade the Secretary General to use the international organization's flag to protect Fatah's second exodus from Lebanon in less than a year.

Our troubles increased when we discovered that the virus of division and conflict had reached our people in United States. Those who we had hoped would bring pressure to bear on the Palestinian leaderships and factions, so they would reject division and factionalism, now needed someone to preach unity in the lands of exile.

US newspapers and broadcasters, who had never breathed a word about our statements at the UN General Assembly Hall on the Geneva conference and resolutions, took great pains to inform their readers and audiences, day after day, about the bloodshed in Lebanon's northern capital.

The task of extracting the Fatah forces from Tripoli and securing their passage to a new location was not an easy one. It could not be achieved by a resolution at the General Assembly or Security Council, and there was nothing that any single country could do. What was required was the implementation of practical measures, internationally recognized and respected symbols, guarantees of safety, and a fleet of friendly ships. The matter was complex and heartrending, especially given that the battle this time was between the sons of a single people, a single nation, and a single catastrophe!

I have to admit that I often felt overwhelmed by embarrassment, both mentally and physically, as I listened to the questions directed at our delegation from members of other delegations, especially those of friendly nations, most of whom did not understand how the fighting had broken out between servants of the same cause. How was it possible to help them understand something that we were unable to understand ourselves?

In a meeting with the head of the Soviet mission at the UN, we asked for Moscow's help to put pressure on Syria to stop the fighting in Tripoli and help in the evacuation of Palestinian fighters by sea. After some words of sympathy and kindness, the ambassador asked us to tell him specifically what was needed. After informing him of the need for ships, we said: "We want our Soviet comrades to monitor these ships and safeguard them."

All we could do now was wait for news about this second exodus from Lebanon. In the most difficult times, waiting is the hardest thing one can do.

The meetings of the special session on Palestine at the UN ended, and members of our delegation began to pack their bags in preparation for a return to their temporary enforced exile, whose duration no one knew.

(3)

We left New York as the city was starting to put up its decorations for Christmas and the New Year. How numerous were the occasions when we Palestinians stood there, perplexed and out of place, like beings from another planet for whom the holidays meant nothing. Each of us went to a different country. I went to London at the invitation of the General Union of Palestinian Students in the UK and Ireland to participate in the opening day of their general conference.

The sector of society that students represent is one of education and activism, and therefore it is usually characterized by anxiety and unrest. However, I was very pleased indeed to see that the atmosphere among our students in Britain and Ireland was more sober and balanced than what I had seen in the United States. There was some anger and extreme criticism as well as thoughtful analysis, but I did not feel that splits were emerging. The young people, with all their different backgrounds and points of view, were able to reach a consensus, sometimes meeting in the middle ground and at others balancing between their different opinions. On some issues there was complete unanimity, as is often the way with human nature.

Perhaps they had been influenced by the Anglo-Saxon coolness around them. This experience showed me that often we destroy what we are trying to build because of the way we choose to put across our points of view, not because of the content of those views. Adhering to the principle that the person with whom we are debating might actually be right is often the only way to affirm that we might be right ourselves. This is the basic foundation for dialogue, but more often what we practice is a monologue, speaking to ourselves in the mistaken belief that we are involved in a dialogue or a discussion.

To this day, I have not been able to reach a final conclusion about why chaos always seems to crush dialogue in our Arab world. Some put the blame on the language. Some relate it to the temperament of our people. Others put it down to the relatively short time we have had to develop a political system in which calm dialogue becomes the norm.

In sharp contrast to the flow of events, November 1983 came with some very good news indeed. During that month, the largest prisoner exchange in the history of the Arab–Israeli conflict took place. As a result, 5,900 Lebanese and Palestinian prisoners were released in exchange for six Israeli soldiers. This deal also included the return of most of the documents confiscated by Israeli troops from the PLO Research Center in West Beirut. It was a day of national celebration in Lebanon, and smiles returned for the first time since June 1982. One of the most important factors was that this exposed the sterility of the 17 May agreement between Israel and the Lebanese government – the politics of submission compared with the challenge laid down by resistance.

The countdown began for the exit of Abu Ammar and his fighters from Tripoli in December 1983. The Secretary General announced the UN's agreement to put its flags on Greek vessels that were to carry out the evacuation. Until that was achieved in January 1984, there were many attempts, political and military, to facilitate or hamper the exodus. The Israelis tried all possible kinds of blackmail, threats, and naval and aerial bombardment to prevent Fatah's escape unless Israel received its fee, paid up front. Moshe Erens did not hide the Zionist government's intentions when he vowed to shell the ships unless Arafat laid down his weapons and made an official statement to "renounce terrorism."

Once the ships had set sail from Tripoli, and we were sure that they were beyond the scope of Israeli military operations, I booked a ticket on the first flight to Tunis to be together with my brothers in the aftermath of this second exodus, and to decide how to stand up to the challenges of the new phase.

When I got to Tunisia, there was great commotion in Palestinian circles, as if the Day of Judgment had arrived. What was all the fuss about? The answer was in the headlines of all the Arab and international newspapers the following day: Yasser Arafat had met President Hosni Mubarak of Egypt.

I did not need a crystal ball to be able to predict the problems and arguments that would take place over the next year. I knew the Palestinian national movement had reached a dangerous fork in the road and only a miracle would ensure its survival.

(4)

I returned to Beirut to try, as director of the PLO office, to play my part in smoothing over potential disagreements with the various parties, Palestinians first, then the Lebanese, and then the Syrians. It was mission virtually impossible.

I tried to begin where I had left off, with the last phone call I'd had with the General Director of Lebanese Public Security, Zahi al-Bustani, who had been appointed to his post by the late president-elect Bashir al-Gemayyel. It was not a phone call that brought me any comfort. On the contrary it made me very anxious. One comment stands out from that conversation. He said that, despite his education at a Catholic school which did not like Jews, he had come to hate us (the Palestinians) more than the Jews.

My response was that despite the emotions that were overwhelming each of us at that moment, we had no choice, because of the positions we occupied, but to heal the wounds, alleviate the pain, and try to avoid falling into new mistakes and new sins. I also said to him that we had to preserve the thin thread that was between us and to try to make it stronger so that it became like a rope or a bridge over which we could cross. I concluded by giving him a piece of advice which could choose either to accept or reject. It was to foster positive and serious relationships with the Palestinians, because the Israelis were not to be trusted and their occupation, however long it lasted, was only temporary.

Despite the vehemence of our discussion, I think we could both feel its importance and understood frankly the necessity of turning over a tragic page and starting a new one. But Zahi al-Bustani did not remain in his position long, as President Amin al-Gemayyel replaced him with Jamil Nimeh, while Simone Qassis was appointed as Director of Military Intelligence. I met both of them and we discussed all the issues that concerned the Palestinians which had been left unresolved pending a clear and definite declaration of its position from the Lebanese government. That was not an easy matter – the Lebanese were not sure what their future held, and the Palestinians did not even know what tomorrow would bring.

From that moment, Palestinian–Lebanese relations went underground. I was not involved, but read about the new channels which had opened up like any ordinary citizen in the newspapers. There is little doubt that shared animosity towards Syria caused Lebanon's security apparatus to come together with Fatah's to a great degree. The island of Cyprus played host to a number of secret meetings during which mutual interests and services were exchanged.

(5)

My visits to Tunis became more frequent and sometimes I stayed there for several weeks at a time. The Tunisians are by nature a gentle, generous, and friendly people. No doubt, in a country which depends on tourism, these characteristics have added to the good service and hospitality which Tunisia offers visitors.

Tunisians also harbor a great love and respect for Palestine and its people. So it was no surprise to see their warm reception for the Palestinians who came to them from the east as a result of the longest Arab–Israeli war since the 1948 catastrophe.

Despite the fact that the Palestinians stayed in Tunisia for twelve

years, and they numbered in their thousands, there were no significant incidents of law-breaking or violence. There is no doubt that
al-Hakam Bil'awi, the head of our office in Tunis, who had close
contacts with the Tunisian authorities and who had been given full
authority by Abu Ammar, played an important role in fostering this
harmony.

The Palestinians lived almost like tourists in Tunisia for years.
They became an important economic resource for the country. They
also contributed to Tunisian public life, especially in the fields of
diplomacy and the media. Just as Beirut had been the capital and
fulcrum of revolution, so too was Tunis, with one important distinction: the complete absence of any weaponry, apart from the handgun
carried by Abu Ammar.

That man was utterly amazing in his ability to adapt and adjust.
I have to admit it took me more than three years to accept, however
grudgingly, the changes in lifestyle that the leadership of the PLO and
its cadres underwent in Tunis.

This is why I often felt depressed when I came from Beirut,
bringing with me the problems of our people in Lebanon. But I
found no one who asked me about their condition. Instead I received
dozens of invitations to lunch, dinner, and all-night parties.

(6)

The seeds of corruption had started to spread. The embezzlers set up
their stalls in the name of revolution, collecting money, issuing statements, and sometimes even daring to contradict the senior leadership
of the PLO.

As a result, a group of honorable intellectuals began to raise their
voices and started a media campaign against the organizational and
moral laxity that had grown up, especially in the United States. They
demanded that the PLO leadership work to control the situation,
fearing for the image of the Palestinian people and their struggle in
American public opinion, especially when the US media were always
lying in wait for us.

On December 5, 1985, the Executive Committee took the decision
to appoint me as its representative in the United States and Canada.
I would be responsible for the PLO offices in New York, Ottawa,
and Washington. Decision Number 69, as it was styled, would be
implemented on January 2, 1986.

When I was informed of this appointment I did not pay it much attention, for the simple reason that I was convinced that Abu Ammar, deep down, did not want it to happen even though he had signed the order himself. I said as much to Abu Ja'far, the director general of the politburo and the official in charge of following up these appointments. As far as I could see, the decision had been passed simply to let off steam and would not be implemented.

It was clear Abu Ja'far found my reaction strange, despite his experience and knowledge of the secrets and changing moods of our leaders, so I said to him: "If you receive anything that confirms to you this matter is serious, you know where I live."

It was four years before Abu Ja'far received a letter carrying the signature of the Secretary of the Executive Committee, Jamal al-Surani, confirming my appointment as the representative of the Executive Committee in the American arena, with my headquarters in New York.

As soon as Abu Ja'far received the new – old – resolution, he called me. I was in New York following up on some resolutions concerning our cause. I understood from him that this time the matter was serious. He also told me about a separate resolution taken by the Executive Committee to set up a Council for Palestinian Affairs in the United States, which would be made up of members of the Palestinian National Council living there as well as some well-known Palestinian personalities. Edward Said and Ibrahim Abu Lughod had been appointed to set it up. I also learned that $1 million per annum had been allocated for this council, which would be collected from Palestinian and Arab donors.

Even after hearing this, I told Abu Ja'far that I would not be totally confident until one of us had received a resolution signed by Abu Ammar himself. But I did agree with him to postpone my departure from New York for a few days in the hope that the matter would finally become clear. On January 5, I received a faxed copy of a letter from Abu Ammar to Zuhdi al-Tarazi (the PLO representative at the UN) confirming my appointment and asking Zuhdi to find appropriate accommodation for my mission. I was to choose my own assistant and an office secretary.

The news spread through UN circles and was published in some American newspapers. The comments even included some which were quite positive. Waiting for the necessary funds to arrive, I began to look for a suitable place to live, and set up contacts with the people I intended to work with. I also accepted invitations to several diplomatic functions that were held in my honor. I have to mention my friend Abdallah al-Ashtal, the Yemeni ambassador, specifically. He invited more than 100 people to a reception to welcome me into the Arab diplomatic family.

January passed and February began, and again I heard nothing from Tunis. My visa was about to expire and I had to clarify the status of my residency or I would have to leave the country.

I decided to travel to Tunis to find out the reasons behind this delay, or rather the deafening silence I was getting from the leadership.

First of all, I was surprised when Abu Ammar answered my requests for a meeting with postponement after postponement. In the past, he had always responded immediately whenever I had asked to see him and I would be granted some time on that very day, or if the worst came to the worst, in the early hours of the following morning. I was also surprised to receive a copy of a new letter from Abu Ammar to Abu Ja'far.

> Brother Shafiq al-Hout will continue in his position as representative of the Executive Committee in America according to the Executive Committee resolution on this matter. However, the nature and location of his work will be reviewed, especially as he may be able to work out of the Arab League office in Washington.

The letter was dated February 6, 1990.

The initial doubts that I had felt when this whole episode began were returning. I told Abu Ja'far: "This time I will resolve the matter myself, so please can you carry on trying to get me an appointment with Abu Ammar."

The next day, Abu Ja'far received orders that I was to have a meeting with Abu Ammar that evening. Abu Ja'far tried to avoid accompanying me, but I insisted on having a witness there, for the record. Our meeting was to be at 9 o'clock.

At exactly 9 o'clock, we were standing in front of the general headquarters. The guards received us as usual with smiles and words of welcome. Someone went in to tell Abu Ammar that we had arrived and he gave permission for us to enter.

When we entered Abu Ammar's office, gone was the simple and informal behavior which I had come to expect from him. He barely acknowledged our greetings and did not move his eyes from a pile of papers which he was reading and signing. We waited for him to start a conversation, but he did not.

Poor Abu Ja'far did not know what to do, especially as he knew how bitter and angry I felt. He tried to break the silence, but I immediately interrupted him, telling him to leave the chief be until he finished going through his mail – I didn't mind waiting the entire night to have our talk.

Then the phone rang. As soon as Abu Ammar lifted the receiver, he started hurling abuse at the person at the other end, threatening and rebuking them. He put down the receiver with such force that he almost broke it. Of course, this was all an act in order to establish the atmosphere before any conversation started.

A short time later, he lifted his head and asked me gently, as if he was not the same man who moments earlier had been shouting down the phone, what I wanted. I said, trying very hard to keep my composure: "I want to ask you a few questions if you will allow me."

"May it be good news with God's will. Ask."

"Have I ever asked you for a favor?" I did not wait for an answer and I continued: "Have I ever asked you to send any of my three children to university? When you left Beirut and I remained there by myself, did I ever ask you to give me even one pound for an emergency? You know how in the last few years, the Lebanese pound has gone from three to a dollar to more than a thousand? Did I ever ask you to review my salary, even though it went down to about $20 a month at one point? Finally, have I ever asked you to appoint me to any position, in the United States or anywhere else?"

He tried to calm me with an exaggerated defense. Was it his fault that I did not ask for a raise? How would he know about my circumstances? Then he started to talk about my children and how much he loved them, asking how I could doubt his love for them, when he had played with them so often in my home.

His thoughts wandered a little, before he said: "Despite that, you are right. The truth is that I don't want you to go to America or anywhere else. I want you beside me."

I pretended not to understand what he meant and I replied: "But I am always beside you ... All my life I have been beside you ..."

He interrupted, saying: "No, no, I want you to be my advisor."

My mood took a 180-degree turn and I started laughing and said to him: "Listen, Abu Ammar, my brother. I have noticed lately that you have changed in the way you deal with me, so I hope that you will answer me with honesty and frankness. Have you heard something about me saying something or doing something to injure you? The way you have dealt with my appointment to America confirms my fears that you do not hold me in the same loving concern you used to, but I did not imagine that you had come to hate me so much." I started repeating the word advisor with contempt ... as if it was a demeaning offer for him to make to someone of my capacity and standing.

At this point, he seemed to get quite angry and he began to raise his voice: "Ok, so tell me what do you want?"

I answered back in a loud voice: "I want to rest. To stay at home. Do not worry about me. I have often lived from my pen and I can still do that."

I got up and tried to leave but he got to the door before me and said some words to calm me down. But I did not understand any of it because I was so angry.

He left me in Abu Ja'far's care and we went out into the cold night.

The next morning I went to say goodbye to Abu Ja'far before returning to Beirut. He asked me for my passport and requested that I postpone my departure for two or three days. When I asked him why, he said: "I want to get you seven visas to seven countries."

"What countries? And why?"

"Count them my friend: Britain, Norway, Japan, the Philippines, Thailand, Singapore, and India. As for why, it is to participate in conferences being held in those countries to raise awareness of the Palestinian cause under the auspices of the international agency that is concerned with the Palestinian people's right to enjoy their inalienable rights."

When I tried to decline, Abu Ja'far told me that a change of scene would be good for me, especially as the situation in Lebanon where I was living remained as dire as ever. I continued to refuse, and Abu Ja'far said: "This is not a request, it is an order. Abu Ammar called me early in the morning and told me to convince you."

I picked up the phone and called Abu Ammar's office. When I heard his voice, I said: "As you wish, Abu Ammar."

For me, it was as if nothing had happened. The truth is that anyone who knew Abu Ammar well found it hard to bear a grudge against him. You might get angry with him, interrupt him, or even talk about him behind his back, but it was difficult to bear a grudge against him. There was something in him, in his spirit and soul, that made you forgive him.

That did not mean that I did not try and understand why he had behaved like this towards me. With time and more incidents, with myself and others, I became sure of some characteristics that one could identify in the man. One was jealousy. He could not bear anyone who was better or more successful than him at something, even if it was a farmer in a field or a laborer in a factory. He also used to rate loyalty more than merit, and he used to favor members of his own family. He liked being asked and being able to provide, but he did not like anything to be demanded from him in a way which made him have to commit.

This is how I saw the matter. As for how he saw it, he took that secret with him to the grave.

To compare two presidents, Arafat and al-Shuqayri, I recall the day that al-Shuqayri removed me and some colleagues from the Executive Committee because we opposed some of his policies. Then he decided, so that I would really learn my lesson, to transfer me from Beirut to our office in Delhi, even though we did not have one there. That was in February 1967. Months later I received a letter from the head of the Politburo at that time, Muhammad Nimr al-Masri,

Photo 7 The author on a tour to explain the Palestine question
(Tokyo, 1990)

telling me that the PLO chairman had told him – on June 4, 1967, when the war over the Straits of Tiran between Egypt and Israel was about to start – to inform me that my transfer was suspended until further notice and that I was to return to my position as the director of the PLO office in Beirut, with a request for immediate implementation of this decision.

There is a saying in Arabic that "you can know a man by his style." I never understood that until decades later after meeting thousands of people and experiencing countless different situations. Another saying is that "a man is made up of different elements." But whatever words you might justifiably use to describe a man, "perfect" is not one of them.

16

THE SESSION THAT CHANGED THE PATH

As I have said before, the Palestinian leadership did not fully grasp the danger of the strategic setbacks it had experienced after its exile from Lebanon. This was reflected in the 16th session of the Palestinian National Council, which was convened in Algeria at a time when many still believed that the departure from Lebanon was only temporary and that a return was possible.

In the light of this analysis, I could understand Abu Ammar's return to northern Lebanon, resulting in his second exile after pitched battles and many casualties. This is why there was a need for another session of the National Council to revise Palestinian strategy, this time with more precision and honesty.

It is my belief that Abu Ammar decided to change the strategy of the PLO as he was passing through the Suez Canal, on his way from Tripoli in Lebanon to the Yemeni capital Sanaa. It was not just the fact that he was passing through Egyptian territorial waters that motivated him to make contact with President Hosni Mubarak, as a courtesy call. Abu Ammar knew better than most the significance of this move and the repercussions it would have after more than five years of Egypt's isolation from the Arab world. Still, the Palestinian reaction to Arafat's meeting with Mubarak was overwhelmingly negative, not least in Fatah itself and at the level of the Executive Committee of the PLO.

My opinion that Abu Ammar was intending to reshuffle the pack and create new alliances was reinforced by his call to convene the next session of the Palestinian National Council in the Jordanian capital, Amman. This was despite the fact that the events of September 1970 and its aftermath were still a cause of anxiety among the Palestinians. Even those most angry with Syria and its regime had little desire to replace Damascus with Amman – which had re-established diplomatic relations with Cairo in September 1984 – and demanded that another Arab capital be chosen to host the conference.

In the midst of these fears, a public relations war now opened up between Fatah on the one side and the opposition movements allied to Syria on the other, between those enthusiastic about convening this session and those who rejected it.

Syria was the only Arab country which opposed convening the session, and its official media went as far as branding those who called for and participated in the conference "traitors." On the international front, Moscow and other members of the socialist bloc declared their wish that the Palestinian leadership should not take any action which did not enjoy broad national consensus.

The Arabic newspapers were full of statements and counterstatements from the leaders of the various tendencies, either supporting the conference or opposing it. Egyptian newspapers joined the campaign on the basis that Cairo wanted to regain its position in the Arab world and restore its role as the headquarters of the Arab League and its general secretariat, something that was back on the cards after Abu Ammar visited Hosni Mubarak.

(1)

The Palestinian refugees living in Syria and Lebanon were the ones who needed this conference most, wherever it was convened. This was because they were suffering as a result of events in Lebanon and the collapse of Palestinian–Syrian relations. But it was impossible for the National Council members who lived in Syria to participate in the conference and almost as difficult for their colleagues in Lebanon, which at the time was under Syrian control.

I was in Beirut at the time and had responsibility for sending out invitations to PNC members in Lebanon. There were some moments of hesitation before we took our decision. I personally, along with my sister Salwa, who was also a member of the council, decided to participate because that is what the membership had instructed us to do. It was the council's job to express its approval for one position or another. A boycott would mean we were negating all the various arguments and limiting them to those made by the leadership – in effect, the opinion of a single person, Abu Ammar. There were those who participated on condition that Fatah would secure them another place to live if they were prevented from re-entering Lebanon, or if they were threatened with imprisonment. There were others who preferred to remain silent and ask for God's help to alleviate the misery of this poor, long-suffering nation with its difficult and confusing choices.

Uppermost in our minds was how to guarantee the safety of the Palestinian refugees in Lebanon, to find ways to support their steadfastness and their precarious existence in the camps. We also wanted to bring an end to the Syrian–Palestinian dispute, whose casualties again were mainly in the refugee camps in Lebanon.

That year, 1983, had witnessed daily attacks on Palestinian institutions and businesses by armed men belonging to the ruling authority. Things were especially bad in the Fakhani, Tareeq al-Jadida, and Sabra areas. Queues of young Palestinian men lining up outside foreign embassies, seeking visas to enable them to travel to safety and to try to make a decent living, became a familiar sight. I learned from Lebanese security officials that 1983 saw the highest levels of emigration in the history of the Palestinian presence in Lebanon. Approximately 70,000 Palestinians had passed through Beirut International Airport on their way to another stage of exile in places like Scandinavia, Germany, and the United Kingdom.

(2)

The PNC meeting was set for November 23, 1984, more than 14 years after the September war between the Jordanian army and the soldiers of the PLO. There are no fixed points in this life, especially in the areas of politics and national struggle, but who could have imagined that a day would come when our National Council would be held in Amman under the PLO banner and under the auspices of King Hussein, with talk about alliances, solidarity, and ties of brotherhood with Jordan, while the regime in Syria was condemned?

Zero hour arrived at last, and after making sure that a legal quorum for the session was present – there were 257 members out of a possible 374, in other words 25 more than was needed – Abu Ammar declared the session open. He then called for a minute's silence for the souls of the martyrs. After that, Saleem Zaanoun, the Deputy President of the National Council, gave a short speech about the legality of the session according to the rules of the council. He was followed by the Secretary General of the Arab League, al-Shadhili al-Qulaybi, who gave a general speech in which he avoided touching on the matters in dispute between the PLO and Syria.

There was a large Arab and international presence, especially the

Egyptian delegation which numbered more than 50 people. There were also huge numbers of Jordanian intelligence officers, who knew when to remain silent and when to make lots of noise, whom to support and whom to oppose.

The Jordanians placed all their facilities at the service of the Arab and international media. Jordanian television broadcast the sessions live, reaching audiences in Palestine, Jordan, Syria, and Lebanon. This media coverage sparked new initiatives to drum up support for the conference, as well as campaigns against it and those who supervised it.

Soon, it was Abu Ammar's turn to give the keynote speech. Popular sympathy for him had grown enormously, especially after what he had risked by returning to Lebanon and what he had faced there.

The carefully drafted speech lasted for about 90 minutes. It was very defensive, and uncompromising. Abu Ammar began by trying to explain why the conference had been held in Amman:

> No matter how polarized politics may become and no matter how much circumstances may differ, with bitter experiences and harsh crises, there remain political absolutes that cannot be changed or overlooked. One of these is the link between our peoples, the Palestinians and the Jordanians. They are ties of family, of brotherhood, of Arab nationalism, ties brought about by a single destiny and united aims. These ties are much stronger than anything that extraneous circumstances can dictate.

That was his way of introducing the idea of establishing a special Jordanian–Palestinian relationship. He then revealed some more of his intentions by saying:

> After leaving Tripoli by sea, and after the extreme difficulties we have faced, we have received unwavering assistance and deep understanding from His Majesty King Hussein and our people in Jordan. From this we have gone on to consolidate our relationship, in order to put into effect the National Council resolutions on the establishment of confederal relations between us.

The signal was clear. The faces of his colleagues in Fatah betrayed surprise and confusion when they heard these words. On relations with Syria he said: "We have accepted with gratitude and continue to do so the mediation of our brothers and friends in order to restore the relationship." In my opinion, based on what I had heard directly from the man himself and from his words here, Abu Ammar had given up on his relationship with Hafez al-Assad. As someone said, the two leaders had a chemical aversion to one another. From now on, it was clear when Abu Ammar was talking about independent Palestinian national self-determination, he was excluding Syria and making clear his rejection of Damascus's guardianship over the Palestinian cause and national movements.

Then he spoke about peace and said:

> Let us struggle together in order to achieve a just and permanent peace, the basis of which will be the liberation of our country and the restoration of our people's inalienable and non-negotiable rights, the right of return and the right to establish an independent state on our Palestinian land with Jerusalem as its capital." Then he said: "We declare this now, with absolute clarity, so that no party can have any possible illusions about an alternative homeland outside Palestine.

This was a cunning comment, which seemed to be aimed at Ariel Sharon, but was in fact meant to reassure Jordan and Lebanon about the Palestinians' rejection of naturalization in their countries. The last part of his speech was devoted to his visit to Cairo and his meeting with Hosni Mubarak. He tried to defend the fact that he had taken the decision by himself without consultation:

> I was in a place too remote to allow discussions with my brothers in the leadership. But it is a leader's right to take advantage of any moment or opportunity to make a decision and to be held accountable for this decision at a later date. This council now has the right to pass whatever resolutions it wishes on this matter, but it must bear in mind that the Executive Committee issued a resolution in 1983, reached in the presence of all its members, charging Abu Lutf and myself to make contact with Egypt whenever the circumstances allowed.

Who among the PLO Executive Committee members could have denied this claim or proposed a resolution condemning a position taken by the leader of the revolution? Abu Ammar was a master of such maneuvers, adorning his personal decisions with the cloak of democracy.

(3)

King Hussein then joined the opening session and delivered an address typed out on three dozen pages that took an hour and 20 minutes to read out.

After welcoming the decision of the National Council to hold its conference in Amman "with sentiments of extreme happiness and love," he said: "Your meeting today has achieved its quorum and you have defeated all attempts to establish guardianship over you. You have resolved to take matters into your own hands and confirmed the national unity of your people and your representation of your people."

King Hussein then gave a potted history of Jordanian–Palestinian relations since 1948, attempting to explain the reasons which led to their collapse and the bloody events of September 1970. He went on with his version of history until he reached 1972, when he said:

> We suggested that in order to escape from this crisis, we should prepare for what the Jordanian–Palestinian relationship would be after liberation. With that formula, we sought to balance between our national responsibility and our work in the international arena to recover the West Bank according to UN Resolution 242 and to confirm to our Palestinian brethren that Jordan recognized their national identity and had no designs on their land. We made three suggestions about this relationship for both the Jordanian and the Palestinian people to vote upon in the usual democratic ways in the event that the land was retrieved. The first choice was that the relationship would return to what it had been before the occupation [Jordan's pre-1967 annexation of the West Bank], the second was that there would be an equal federal relationship between the two countries, and the third was the establishment of an independent Palestinian state.

Then the king continued to expound upon his reading of our shared history. He spoke of the October 1973 war and UN resolution 338 which followed it, confirming Resolution 242, and the entry of the United States as a third party in the peace process. He mentioned Jordan's exclusion from the Geneva Conference, when Kissinger placed all his efforts on the Syrian and Egyptian fronts:

> The feeling grew among the Palestinians and some Arab brethren

that the PLO should take the place of Jordan regarding the West Bank, as it might make matters easier, given that Israel was saying Jordan had no right to ask for the return of the West Bank, because it was itself an occupying power there. In 1974, at the Rabat summit, we responded to the Arab decision to recognize the PLO as the sole legitimate representative of the Palestinian people.

Then King Hussein went on to deal with the stifling situation that had arisen in the current circumstances:

International opinion holds that it would be possible to return the Occupied Territories via a Jordanian–Palestinian formula outlining the obligations of both sides, which the world considers to be necessary in order to reach a just and balanced peaceful resolution. If you are convinced of this decision, then we are prepared to walk with you together down this road and to issue to the world a joint initiative for which we can secure support. The decision – whatever it may be – will always command our respect because it will have been issued by this venerable council which is the representative of the Palestinian people.

To utter silence, the King continued:

If you wish to choose the Jordanian–Palestinian formula, please allow me to present to you our vision for presenting this current situation to the wider world in order to secure renewed and effective efforts. The given facts in the Palestinian, Arab, and international arenas dictate to us that we should remain faithful to United Nations Security Council Resolution 242 as a basis for a peaceful, just solution according to the principle of land for peace. This principle is not a precondition; it is the framework within which negotiations will take place and is therefore non-negotiable. The negotiations, which we view as having to take place in the framework of an international peace conference, will center around ways and means, and the obligations necessary in order to secure the principle of land for peace.

The king concluded his speech saying:

This is our vision, but we do not hold you to it or force it upon you. The decision is yours and the matter is your responsibility.

We propose it to you because we share with you the same conditions of security and danger, and of benefit and harm."

King Hussein's address had struck most of the members of the PNC like a bolt of lightning. They had been banking on a resolution of the Syrian–Palestinian crisis, not the introduction of a new Jordanian initiative which would surely lead to a further escalation of the crisis, both within the conference hall and beyond.

Abu Iyad and Abu Jihad, both members of the central committee of Fatah, and the two most important figures after Abu Ammar, were the first to comment on the King's speech. Despite showing some courteous reservations, they were close to outright rejection of the initiative.

Abu Iyad said:

It is for the council to debate King Hussein's initiative and I shall not prejudge the council's decision. We understand that King Hussein's invitation is for mutual understaqnding and cooperation, but under what conditions? Our adherence is to the resolutions of the Fez Summit and the resolutions of the National Council. Those are what determine our relations with Jordan, as with any Arab country.

He also added:

The King's initiative centers on Resolution 242 and we reject that resolution absolutely. The solution lies in an international conference which would be a framework in which the two superpowers could participate, as well as the countries of the Security Council.

For his part, Abu Jihad said:

Joint Jordanian–Palestinian action is one of the issues proposed here in the National Council which are scheduled to be debated. We will take all that is said into consideration. As for Resolution 242, we have not, and we will not, accept this resolution. But that does not mean we are against any method to secure joint Jordanian–Palestinian action.

These two statements encapsulated the dispute that was taking place in the Fatah leadership on this matter. I think that Abu Ammar was upset by their comments because he was afraid they would delay the passing of a PNC resolution which would allow him a wide margin of freedom in making the anticipated Jordanian–Palestinian move.

As for the Secretary General of the PFLP, George Habash, he accused Abu Ammar of placing himself in the American camp through alliances with King Hussein and President Hosni Mubarak.

The other movements also denounced King Hussein's initiative and Arafat's position. The Syrian *Baath* newspaper took on the job of mobilizing opinion against the conference and its resolutions, saying that a new conspiracy was taking place, by means of which the whole region would be closed off for the benefit of the United States and Israel.

(4)

The opening session was extended late into the night, with the council taking a decision to relieve Khaled al-Fahoum of his post as president of the National Council and electing Sheikh Abdul Hameed al-Sayeh, who even before the *Nakba* had been one of the well-known personalities in the political struggle. He had already served as a minister in the Jordanian government.

There were some members of the National Council who did not sleep at all that night. There was no hotel in Amman that did not witness a meeting, seminar, or group gathering to discuss what had been said that day and what had been left out. After all the bitter experiences the Palestinians had endured, they started to suffer from paranoia which made them start all their discussions from a position of doubt and suspicion. This was reflected in the comments of the members in the session for general discussions.

My own contribution was delivered off the cuff though I had, as usual, written down the main points that I had wanted to discuss on a small piece of paper. Here is a summary of what I said:

Mr President, I cannot promise to adhere to the set time because I have a lot to say. I speak, sir, as a man who does not belong to any specific movement, organization, or régime, and I beg of you not to deprive me of this right which I had to snatch away from those who do belong.

First of all, the convening of this session in particular is a victory for the Palestinian national conscience, which believes strongly in democracy. ... This session is a victory for legitimacy ... It is also a victory for the Palestinian national opposition ...

It is not possible for this meeting be a continuation of our 16th session. Amongst you may be some who recall that, during that session, I alluded to and warned about what was looming on the horizon. I said that what had happened in Beirut and in Lebanon was a strategic event which required from us a reaction of the same caliber.

But the "movements," with Fatah at their forefront, decided to run matters as they have always done, so resolutions were formulated and recommendations were made behind closed doors. What we witnessed in the public meetings was a mere illusion. When we opposed this, some people stood up and said such opposition was tantamount to a call to break up the National Council. I wish we had chosen to confront our problems there and then, and aired our differences, as responsible, civilized people do when they disagree about a specific political issue. Instead, we have seen the whole arena explode once again, pouring fire onto our land and our refugee camps in northern Lebanon, where we complete the work that Israel was unable to do there ...

The simple fact of convening this session could be the salvation of the only Palestinian accomplishment of the past 20 years: the establishment of the Palestine Liberation Organization. ... That is our moral home. ... It is our point of reference and you in this session specifically are that point of reference, which must plan for us and throw light on our path and say to us: "This is the right path, go forth along it."

We want this council not so that we can give our support easily. We want this council to be a laboratory for the Palestinian mind. We want it to say to the world that our will is independent and free. We want it to say to the world that we are the ones who brought Yasser Arafat to this place, and we can get rid of him if we think that is the right thing for our struggle and its interests.

National unity is the secret of our strength. It is our path which we have no escape from, except to walk over its thorns no matter how much we suffer and how much pain we experience. ... We want national unity and a leadership that we can rally around and which is capable of telling us what it wants ...

Brothers and sisters, the relationship between our words and our deeds is a fragile one. I heard in Algiers about the courage of the revolutionary to criticize himself. And I heard again today those who are calling for self-criticism. But how long do we have to wait to hear any actual self-criticism? We know that our arena is full of mistakes and needs some courageous criticism. I can almost say that we need a revolution in this revolution, so that we can pursue our struggle and achieve the national goals of the Palestinian people.

Now, please allow me to make some observations about Palestinian–Arab relations. Firstly, let me warn you, once you have achieved what you call "independent national self-determination," to avoid any Palestinian chauvinism. I urge you to bear in mind our Arab relationships and our Arab depth. Without the Arabs, there will be no liberation, no Palestine. ... I fear an Arab reaction which will start speaking of an independent Jordanian decision, an independent Syrian decision, and so on, until there are 22 independent decisions, the same number as there are Arab countries. At that moment, we shall be the ones who will have brought about such behavior, which many of these countries wish to adopt. Never forget that any Arab regime is closer to its bitterest Arab rival than it is to the PLO ...

Let me discuss our relationship with Egypt. We all want Egypt to withdraw from Camp David, but how? Egypt cannot abandon Camp David simply because we ask it to do so. ... Camp David is a trap that Egypt has fallen into. How do we help Egypt escape from this trap? What happens after we cut our diplomatic relations with Egypt? Do we take down the Palestinian flag in Cairo, while an Israeli flag flies over an Israeli embassy?

The same thing goes for Jordan. Whether we like it or not, whether the Jordanians like it or not, we are in the same trench. We are the same people. We are related through family, history, geography, and destiny. ... No one can ignore the fact that there is no way into the West Bank except through Amman, or the fact that our people live on both banks of the river. The King of Jordan was very honest when he spoke to us. He did not promise us anything. Even when it came to political solutions, he said to us: "There is nothing." ... But he recognized the Palestinian national identity and the PLO as the sole legitimate representative.

He offered us his thinking and his position on Resolution 242, which we reject. ... I think that there should be discussions between us to find a formula through which we can cooperate to achieve political progress.

Brothers and sisters, I will also say a word about Syria. Syria is a geographical and political reality. Just as we speak of Egypt and its weight, the same goes for Syria and its history and Arab character. Despite the destruction that blighted our relationship, for this tormented Palestinian there is no alternative to seeking a return to normalized relations.

The simple fact of holding this conference here, my brothers and sisters, of achieving a quorum and opening the PNC's heart and arms to all Palestinian people, including all opposition movements and people who have split from us, has achieved its main goal – which is that the various movements in the PLO are present and that they are not simply a number that someone can erase. Nobody can erase them.

My intervention had not pleased Abu Ammar at all and he tried to interrupt me several times. After I had finished, he immediately demanded the right of reply. I answered by accusing him of having a poor understanding of the Arabic language because he could not see the difference between style and meaning. I was not surprised to hear later that he had opposed my nomination to the Executive Committee. But I didn't care because the position meant nothing to me and it never had. This is what time eventually revealed to Abu Ammar: there was nothing that I valued more highly than my freedom to speak my mind.

17

THE *INTIFADA* OF STONES

On Tuesday December 8, 1987, the news agencies reported the sad news of the death of four Palestinian workers and the wounding of nine others near the Erez military checkpoint in the Gaza Strip. No one expected that this would cause an overwhelming popular uprising, or *intifada*, to explode. But the spark was lit in Gaza's Jabaliya refugee camp and swept through the whole of the Occupied Territories. The *intifada* grew to become a turning point in the national struggle of the Palestinian people and one of the most important episodes in the struggle.

(1)

The Zionist invasion of Lebanon in 1982 and the events that followed had shown the impossibility of liberating Palestine and restoring its rights from outside its borders, or rather the ceasefire lines which had been demarcated in 1949 and then changed several times. This is why all the political conflicts we endured in Jordan, and then in Lebanon and Syria, transformed into armed clashes.

That invasion also revealed the enervation that the Arab world had suffered on both the official and popular levels, exposing its inability to help out any Arab country that was being invaded, or any Arab capital that was being taken over and its civilians murdered by many varied means.

When our people in the Occupied Territories launched their *intifada*, they were well aware of these new realities and had digested the lessons of all previous experiences of the struggle, recognizing the importance of setting out aims that were achievable and creating a new reality which would not succumb to intimidation.

The *intifada* was clear in its mode of combat, inspired by the reality under which our people lived, and aligned with their capabilities in the position that they found themselves in, unable to rely on outside support.

The people, all of the people, were the method of the *intifada*, the movements were the vanguards, not the alternatives. Their weapons were stones, with all the symbolism that stones inspired – a will that would not be broken and an insistence from which there would be no turning back from resisting occupation until the end.

It is no wonder that 1988 became known as the Year of the *Intifada*. It was a word that imposed itself on foreign languages as a description of a phenomenon that had not existed before. It was the *intifada* and nothing else that reduced the level of conflict between Syria and the Palestinians. It silenced the guns of the Camps War in Lebanon. It re-consecrated the PLO, this time from the land of Palestine itself, as the sole legal representative of the Palestinian people.

At the end of the first month of the *intifada*, the Central Council of the PLO convened in Baghdad on January 7 and 8, 1988, to hear the first official report on the uprising, written by Khalil al-Wazir (Abu Jihad), who would be martyred a few months later, at dawn on April 16, 1988.

> The *intifada* is a permanent decision and a daily exercise which reflects the true spirit of the Palestinian people and its renewed historical continuity. It came as the crowning moment of the national struggle, but it was not cut off or separate from the sum total of the struggle. It came as the natural result of the struggle led by the PLO.

On the aims of the *intifada*, Abu Jihad wrote:

> At a time when the immediate end to the occupation and rallying around the PLO and its aims was the aim of the *intifada*, its leaders were fully capable of meeting the tactical demands with immediately implemented measures. The aims include the cancellation of the Emergency Law issued at the time of the British mandate, which included powers of expulsion, administrative detention without trial, and house demolitions. They also demand the release of their prisoners.

Abu Jihad concluded his report by saying:

> No voice shall rise above the voice of the *intifada*. This is not an

arbitrary emotional storm; it is a new sacred march and a new reality which opens up the horizons of a new future. It has also reaffirmed the solidarity of the Palestinians inside and outside.

Jordan's response to the continuing *intifada* was to cut all legal and administrative ties between the Jordanian government and the occupied West Bank. The government stopped all development projects that had been initiated in the West Bank and dissolved all organizations it was associated with.

The leaders of the united national *intifada* considered this new reality as one of its most important political achievements; they demanded that the PLO leadership take on the responsibility of dealing with this new reality in a way that would ensure that it benefited from the movement, not only for the sake of the *intifada* itself, but for the whole Palestinian cause as well.

After more than 100 days of dialogue, maneuvers, and communications, the leadership of the PLO declared an emergency session of the National Council, which would be held in the Algerian capital, to discuss this vision and endorse it.

During that meeting, which was named the "*Intifada* Session," the most important and dangerous political decision in all the history of the Palestinian national struggle since its birth was taken – the decision by which the Palestine Liberation Organization changed from being a national liberation movement to a national independence movement. This is a decision that will remain a point of debate and conflict until the final result of our struggle is known.

(2)

After arguments that lasted three days and nights, at 00:40 Jerusalem time on Rabi al-Thani 6, in the year 1409 AH, equivalent to November 15, 1988, the Palestinian National Council unanimously ratified the Declaration of Independence. They declared the establishment of the state of Palestine with its capital in the holy city of Jerusalem. The political program to achieve this aim and allow the independent Palestinian state to exercise its actual power over its land was also ratified by an overwhelming majority.

When the moment came to vote, I left my seat. I had tears in my eyes and mixed emotions in my heart. A foreign journalist asked me if I was shedding tears of joy or sadness. I had to admit that they were both, but in a moment of anger, I said: "Thank God my father did not live to witness this day. I do not know what I could say to him if he asked me what was to become of his home city of Jaffa in this state that we have just declared!"

When the journalist asked me about my position and where my support lay, I said without any hesitation: "My vote would be for ratifying the document and the political program attached to it."

I do not think that I was the only Palestinian to feel this ambivalence. In fact I am sure that it was felt by of the vast majority of the people of Palestine. There is no doubt that, had it not been for the intifada and the confidence, self-worth, and ability to achieve miracles that it gave our people, this declaration would not have been possible – with all its allusions to the historical compromises we had made over our national rights, at the forefront of which was the liberation of all Palestinian soil.

But it is necessary to make it clear that this decision had a long political background in our struggle. The idea of a government-in-exile or a national authority over part of the Palestinian homeland had been current for a long time in the literature of the revolution. It dated back to 1974, when Abu Ammar had gone to the United Nations and the PLO joined the international organization with observer status. This implied the PLO's acceptance of the UN Charter and its binding resolutions. The admission of the PLO to membership of that international body was underpinned by Resolution 181 of 1947, which demanded the setting up of two states in Palestine, a Palestinian Arab one and a Jewish one.

Engagement with the UN was the start of the shift towards accepting a compromise. Allusions to this had been made tacitly in the resolutions of the National Council in the 12th and 13th sessions in 1974 and 1977.

The reader may well wonder why these concepts had appeared in such a roundabout way, instead of being voiced out in the open. The answer, I am convinced, is that the PLO leadership was not at that time able to offer a compromise that was in line with the principle of international law, which meant two states over the land of Palestine.

A resolution of such historical weight can only be taken in historical moments during which all the elements come together to allow it to take place, as happened after the intifada. That was the strategic shift that was necessary.

The text of the Declaration of Independence was written by Mahmoud Darwish and was a stunning example of linguistic and political rhetoric.

It is the state for the Palestinians wherever they are, in which they will develop their national and cultural identity, enjoy total equality in rights, in which their religious and political beliefs will be protected as well as their human dignity, under the auspices of a democratic parliamentary system, to be established on the bases of freedom, freedom of speech, and the freedom to form political parties, the guardianship by the majority of the rights of the minority and the respect of the minority for the decisions of the majority, on the basis of social justice, equality, and non-discrimination in public rights on the basis of ethnicity, religion, color, or between men and women, under the auspices of a constitution which guarantees the rule of law and the independence of the judiciary ...

It declared the establishment of the state on the basis of:

the natural, historic, and legal rights of the Palestinian Arab people over their homeland in Palestine, as well as the sacrifices of consecutive generations in the defense of their homeland and its independence, starting from the resolutions of the Arab summits, from the power of the legitimacy which is embodied in the UN resolutions since 1947.

When speaking of the legal basis, the declaration spoke of the:

historical injustice that befell the Palestinian Arab nation, with its displacement and its deprivation from the right to self-determination as a result of the UN General Assembly resolution number 181 in 1947, which divided Palestine into two states: Arab and Jewish." It then added that that resolution was "still the basis for the conditions of international legitimacy which guarantee the rights of the Palestinian Arab nation to sovereignty and national independence.

It was there that the historic importance of the political decision lay. This was the first time that a Palestinian leadership had frankly declared its acceptance of a resolution of the Palestinian question on the basis of two states: one, the already established Jewish state which is Israel, and another Arab Palestinian state whose establishment had been declared but which needed more struggle to establish it on the ground ... and still needs it.

One of the paradoxes of this sea-change was that some Palestinians rejected it because they considered it the beginning of the liquidation of the Palestinian cause, while many Israelis also rejected it, considering it to be the beginning of the end of the Zionist entity. Both scenarios were possible. This was part of the discourse of progress and change which had introduced new contradictions.

The support for this change among the people of the *intifada* was very encouraging. They expressed their support in demonstrations in favor of the declaration, and statements from the national united leadership welcomed it as an important step on the path towards achieving national independence.

After the *intifada*, our dream was no longer for a nomadic state. Our revolution was no longer floating without a place to land or drop anchor. The picture became clear after the *intifada*. There was a distinction between the strategic and the transient, yet to some degree a link between them was defined. The Palestinian mind had affirmed its ability to comprehend the inevitability of a struggle that was fought in phases, according to the circumstances of the moment. It had delineated its priorities and its agenda of resistance, which was open to all legitimate methods of struggle, at the forefront of which was the armed struggle.

The *intifada* masses had their own weight and this is why we considered their struggle to be a crossroads in the history of the modern National Palestinian Movement, and the PLO in particular, which was distinct from what had come before it, and which had now changed its struggle from a national liberation movement to a national independence movement.

(3)

It was no doubt true that the *Intifada* of the Stones was a revolution of men and women without names, and that it was the people as a whole, and the people alone, that was the heroic champion, the leader, the symbol of struggle. But there is another truth that cannot be hidden, that behind the people, giving support and sustenance to the *intifada*, was a brave leader whose history bears witness to everything that bestows honor on brave men – Abu Jihad, Khalil Al-Wazir.

If there was anyone among us who was ignorant of this truth, or who tried to avoid it, the Zionist occupation authorities were fully appraised of the significant role he was playing in support of the *intifada*. In reality, Israel's decision to assassinate Abu Jihad had been taken long before December 1987. He was not only one of the founders of the Fatah movement in the 1960s, he was one of the pioneers of resistance in Gaza in 1956 as well.

The operation to assassinate him was the culmination of extensive efforts at the top level of the Israeli armed forces. It required four naval vessels working in close cooperation, including a corvette patrol ship carrying two helicopters that could be used if assistance was needed. Another of the vessels was a floating hospital. They also had a command aircraft and a spy plane for identification and tracking. The operation's execution was supervised by several high-ranking officers, including Major General Ehud Barak, who later became the Israeli prime minister.

As soon as news of the tragedy was received in the land of the *intifada* on 16 April 1988, the streets witnessed the most violent demonstrations challenging the curfew that had been imposed on them. The day of farewell for this faithful son ended with the martyrdom of another 17 citizens, and 210 people were injured. Anger and sorrow engulfed all the cities and villages of Palestine, as well as all the Palestinian refugee camps in the diaspora, especially in Syria and Lebanon.

Khalil Al-Wazir, Abu Jihad, was buried in Damascus on April 20 and it was a notable Arab day. Hundreds of thousands marched in his funeral, people of all ages, men and women.

He was as generous in his death as he was in his life, and his soul was given comfort by the achievement of a wish he long struggled to realize – the restoration of national unity among the Palestinians and normalizing of Palestinian relations with Syria. There were meetings between officials from Fatah and Syria. Hafez al-Assad met Abu Ammar on April 25 and many people hoped that past conflicts would be forgotten, although it soon became clear that that would have to wait until another day.

(4)

As soon as the "*Intifada* Session" ended, I traveled from Algiers to New York to join the PLO mission at the General Assembly in order to publicize the political decisions taken by the National Council. I also wanted to find out how people would react to the PLO undertaking a political initiative inspired by the Geneva Declaration and the Declaration of Independence, establishing its definitive position on a solution of the Palestine question.

It was no secret that Abu Ammar had high hopes for his political achievement, secured with approval by the Palestinian National Council. At the time Arab rulers had been putting him under enormous pressure to move in that direction, with exaggerated promises about the prize he would receive from Washington. It was well known that the United States had undertaken not to engage in any contacts or communication with the PLO, and would continue to consider it a terrorist organization as long as it rejected Resolution 242 and refused to renounce terrorism. This is why there was a glimpse of optimism in Palestinian and Arab circles following the Declaration of Independence, despite the history of American administrations' reneging on their promises and commitments to the Arabs.

Even so, we were quite surprised at the negative attitude of the American delegation to the UN and the American media, as well as the position of the State Department and the White House. What we had considered to be a miracle breakthrough for the leadership – recognition that a solution should be founded on international law to establish two states on the land of Palestine – was received by the United States as if it were simply a maneuver by the PLO to play with words and hide behind obfuscation when only a clear statement would be acceptable.

What is more, instead of the prizes we were promised, the American administration began to ramp up its hostility towards the PLO by issuing orders that Abu Ammar should not be allowed a visa to come to New York. By taking such a position, Washington was going against the so-called headquarters agreement which guaranteed the rights of UN members and individuals to be given permission to enter the United States when all the necessary conditions were met.

At the PLO, we had spent years haggling with American embassies in Arab capitals so that we could represent our cause at the General Assembly or the Security Council. We often arrived in New York at midnight to begin our work the next morning. There were also stringent restrictions on our movements as members of the Palestinian delegation. We were forbidden to travel beyond a radius of 20 miles around Columbus Square. The same restrictions also applied to many delegations from socialist and Third World countries and national liberation movements.

Battle lines were drawn and tension increased. The Secretary General, Javier Perez de Cuellar, made an enormous effort to mediate with the American delegation but to no avail. Even some Arab countries tried to intervene, as well as some regional alliances, but the Americans remained stubborn and insisted on their position.

Further negotiations began and one of the things proposed to our delegation was to send Abu Ammar's speech on a pre-recorded videotape. We rejected the suggestion, so the next proposal was that we transmit the speech live via satellite to be broadcast on a large screen set up especially for this purpose in the General Hall. Abu Ammar refused.

Finally, the General Assembly took its decision to transfer all its sessions related to Palestine from its headquarters in New York to its headquarters in Geneva. It was decided that these sessions would take place on December 13, 1988.

When I arrived in Geneva with members of our delegation, I found the Intercontinental Hotel teeming with Palestinians waiting for the arrival of Abu Ammar.

When I was in New York, Abu Ammar had asked me to prepare the speech that he was going to give, highlighting a few points he wanted to emphasize. When he spoke to me, he told me that he wanted a historic speech, in the same style as the first one he had given in 1974. I promised him to do my best, despite the fact that I did not have the same friends around me as I had in Beirut then. The speech reflected very clearly the political turn that the *intifada* had brought about by transforming the Palestinian struggle from a national liberation movement into a national independence movement.

After an introduction in which he thanked the international community for showing solidarity with the PLO in moving UN operations to Geneva to overcome American arrogance, Abu Ammar expressed his feeling of honor that he was able to speak to the world on behalf of the people of Palestine and their glorious *intifada*, reminding people of what he had said 14 years earlier, that the war had started in Palestine and the peace would start in Palestine.

Then he spoke of the first Palestinian initiative to solve the Palestine question by setting up a secular democratic state in which the Muslim, Christian, and Jew would live together equally, and how Israel had rejected this without ever offering any counterproposal or initiative throughout these years for any kind of resolution.

Then he spoke of how consecutive American administrations had always adopted a position in favor of Israel. He wondered how Washington could explain its repeated non-compliance with resolutions adopted by the General Assembly. He highlighted Resolution 194, which stated that the Palestinians had the right to return to their homes and property and that those who did not wish to return should receive compensation. He asked how the United States was able to slice up international law and crush international legitimacy. Here, he pointed out the American position which recognized the state of Israel according to Resolution 181 in 1947, but at the same time rejected the establishment of a Palestinian state which drew legitimacy from the same resolution. He said:

> Our people do not seek a right which is not theirs and which is not in accordance with international law and legitimacy. It does not seek a freedom which oppresses others or a destiny that cancels out the destiny of another. Our people refuse to be more special than anyone else or have more privileges, they just want to be equal to all other people.

That was the first reference in the speech that was intended to send a message to the United States and Israel about the acceptance of two states.

From allusion, Abu Ammar went on to direct statement, the first of its kind. He said:

> The first decisive resolution of our National Council is to declare the establishment of the state of Palestine with Jerusalem as its capital according to the natural, historical, and legal rights of the Arab Palestinian people ... based on international legitimacy embodied in UN resolutions since 1947 and the ability of the Palestinian people to enjoy the rights of self-determination, political independence, and sovereignty necessary over its land.

He added that the National Council had:

> emphasized the necessity of an international conference on Palestine under the supervision of the United Nations ... and this international conference will be held on the basis of UN Security Council Resolutions 242 and 338, guaranteeing the national rights of the Palestinian people.

That was the second direct reference to the PLO's acceptance of Resolution 242 which it had long rejected.

Abu Ammar still had to make the point about renouncing terrorism and he made it by saying: "Our National Council has renewed its adherence to UN resolutions which confirm the rights of people to resist foreign occupation, colonialism, and racism, as well as its right to struggle for independence." He reiterated his rejection of terrorism in all its forms, including state terrorism, reaffirming his adherence to his past resolutions on this matter.

Then he added:

Mr President, this position is very clear and there is no ambiguity about it. Despite that, and as the leader of the Palestine Liberation Organization, I declare one more time: I condemn terrorism in all its forms. At the same time I salute all those I see before me in this hall, whose interrogators and occupiers accused them of terrorism during the battles to liberate their countries from the fires of colonialism. They are all honest leaders of their peoples and faithful to the principles and values of freedom and justice ... a salutary tribute to those martyrs who fell as a result of terror and terrorists, at the forefront of whom is my lifelong friend, my deputy, the symbol and martyr, Khalil Al-Wazir.

As Abu Ammar finished his speech, which had been repeatedly interrupted by enthusiastic applause from the floor, it seemed to me as if a great weight had been lifted from his chest. As far as he was concerned, it left no excuse for the United States to keep the PLO on its list of terrorist organization.

Reaction started to come in from all over the globe from media commentators and official spokespeople. Most expressed support for the speech and admiration for this step taken by the PLO towards a political resolution that accepted international law as the foundation for any negotiation.

But what was of most interest to everyone was the reaction from Washington, which, when it came, was disappointing and contrasted with our optimistic expectations. Abu Ammar's suite at the Intercontinental Hotel became a hive of activity, with throngs of Palestinian politicians and personalities as well as other foreign delegations, notably that of Sweden, whose foreign minister was undertaking the task of direct communication with Washington (and specifically George Shultz).

The summary of the position was that Washington had not liked the speech because it was not clear enough when it came to recognizing Israel, accepting Resolution 242, and renouncing terrorism.

Those around Abu Ammar were divided between people who refused to make any addition to the speech, as it would be giving too much away without receiving any promises in return that Israel would recognize the inalienable rights of the Palestinians. A group of Palestinian businessmen were trying to influence Abu Ammar in the other direction, with the aid of some of the more naive Palestinian leaders and those in a hurry to find a solution, any solution.

When we parted at the end of the night, it was clear that Abu Ammar was still weighing the advantages and disadvantages of accepting the American demands. He had declared his intention to hold a press conference in which he would declare the PLO's final position and answer all questions. The circle around him became reduced to a very small number – I was not among them. They started to consider phraseology which Abu Ammar could use in his press conference that would satisfy the American administration. It was said that one of the businessmen had received a text prescribed by the US State Department for Abu Ammar to read out. He had translated into Arabic himself and it had been approved by the Americans.

The next day, Abu Ammar held his press conference and read out this text. As soon as some journalists began to ask some questions in order to clarify some issues, Abu Ammar said with some anger: "Enough striptease!"

He then flew to Vienna and might have been still in the air when Abu Ja'far called to tell him that the US ambassador in Tunis had informed him of Washington's decision to remove restrictions on dialogue with the PLO and of his desire to meet some PLO officials.

18

RETURN TO THE EXECUTIVE COMMITTEE

After a round-the-world tour of media engagements, I thought seriously of tendering my resignation to the PLO and returning to journalism, the love of which I had never lost. I had begun to wonder whether my continuous calls for change and reform would always fall on deaf ears. I did not want to be like those senior PLO officials who had been infected by the disease of silence which made them put their positions and personal interests above their principles. I had also started to have contradictory feelings about Abu Ammar. My love and friendship for him were undimmed, but at the same time I could not tolerate some of the things he was doing as a leader who held the fate of an entire nation in his hands.

(1)

By this time, at the beginning of the 1990s, Lebanon had signed the Taif Agreement (1989) and was struggling to put its problems behind it. The PLO office was still shut and neither Lebanon nor Syria wished to see it reopened. The PLO leadership was not in a position even to discuss the subject. I therefore found myself in an invidious position, facing all sorts of problems, yet with no way or possibility of helping beyond the written word in articles or participating in closed seminars.

The days passed slowly and miserably until 25 August 1991, when I went to Algeria to take part in the 20th session of the Palestinian National Council. On the agenda was a debate about what position to take towards the US initiative suggested by George Bush Senior in a speech to Congress after the "liberation" of Kuwait. He said: "It is time to find a solution to the Arab–Israeli conflict, including the question of Palestine."

Moscow was on the verge of the *Perestroika* revolution and was quick to approve the initiative, on condition that it would be the one to convene the conference that would be held to announce the beginning of the negotiations, based on international law and the principle of land for peace.

Of course, the Arab countries could only hail the initiative and declare their prompt acceptance of it. When Damascus and the PLO tried to make some conditions, James Baker, the US Secretary of State at the time, said that those who had been defeated were in no position to demand conditions; in Baker's view the whole Arab world was defeated, even those countries which had sent troops to participate in the war against Iraq.

Israel, which did not want peace and could not see any need or advantage in it, did not dare to reject the initiative publicly. But it did try to derail it by making demands about who represented the PLO at the conference, on the pretext that "their hands were stained with Jewish blood." It also ruled out negotiations with a united pan-Arab delegation representing all Arab countries, saying it preferred separate agreements similar to those that had been signed with Egypt in Camp David.

Finally, James Baker was able to find a formula which gave Israel what it wanted. He agreed to reject the idea of a pan-Arab delegation and persuaded the Palestinians to operate as part of the Jordanian delegation. The members of this delegation had to come from the territories occupied in 1967 and had to be acceptable to the United States.

(2)

I was certain that the National Council would agree to the American initiative so as to ward off an even worse outcome for us, for it would have been utter madness to defy Washington, particularly at that time.

But I had no idea of the surprises awaiting me at that PNC meeting. After the opening session, speeches were given by Ahmad Ghazali, the Algerian prime minister, and Abu Ammar. Then the leadership of the Council made sure that there was the legal quorum required and it was decided that the oldest and youngest members, Father Ibrahim Ayyad and Muhammad Subayh, should preside over the meeting while it elected a speaker.

I was sitting at the back of the hall, next to my friend Abu Ja'far, when Father Ibrahim called on the members to propose their nominations for the Presidency of the Council because Sheikh Abdul Hameed Al-Sayeh's term had ended. I was surprised when Brigadier Ziad Al-Atrash, one of Fatah's well-known cadres, nominated me for that position.

My immediate reaction was to stand up and hold up my hand to signal that I was declining the nomination. Abu Ja'far dragged me down to my seat again. "Why are you refusing?" he said. "Let's wait and see what happens." I replied: "I don't want this position and I am not qualified for it. It requires a patience which I lack." Abu Ja'far replied: "I know that, just as I know that you will not get this post, but let's see what effect this nomination has."

He pointed to Abu Ammar and said: "Watch what he is going to do." Abu Ammar seemed just as surprised by the nomination as I had been. It was extraordinary that a member of Fatah would make such an important suggestion without consulting him first. I could feel Abu Ammar's anger from where I was sitting. I knew that he wanted to renew Sheikh Al-Sayeh's presidency for another term.

There were many nominations, but a number of people stood down and we were left with only four candidates. They were: Sheikh Al-Sayeh, Yasser Amr, Khaled Abdul Ghani, and myself.

Then Abu Ammar decided, for the first time in the history of his chairmanship of the PLO, that there would be a democratic election for the presidency of the National Council, conducted with a secret ballot.

I did not move from my seat. I did not try to contact any of the leaders of the organizations. I even sent away anyone who came to offer their support. All I said was that my intention in accepting the nomination was to bolster the principles of democracy and, personally, I was going to vote for Sheikh Al-Sayeh.

The secret ballot took place and Sheikh Al-Sayeh won with 238 votes. I got 102 votes while the second runner up got 54 and the last candidate got six. Saleem Al-Zaanoon and Tayseer Qub'a became the vice-presidents, and Muhammad Subayh the secretary.

After the results were announced and Sheikh Al-Sayeh returned to the podium, I went over and hugged him, congratulating him on winning the trust of the members. I tried to tell him briefly that I did not stand in order to oppose him but in order to emphasize the principle of elections. He assured me that he understood that and thanked me for my sentiments. On my way back to my seat, Abu

Ammar stopped me saying: "Why didn't you tell me you wanted to be nominated for the presidency of the Council?" He said it in such a way as to make me understand that there was never a clear path to any position unless he had been consulted and given his approval. So I replied: "Abu Ammar, if I had asked you then it would have been your say and not that of the members of the Council. ... I wanted them to decide for themselves. And I think I have succeeded, because they have done so, as I hoped when I accepted the nomination."

I walked away, knowing that now I had to resign because Abu Ammar would not forgive and would not forget.

(3)

Discussions continued in public for two days, ending with a positive response to the US initiative that was announced in the final political communiqué. The conference welcomed the positive aspects of the US president's initiative and the invitation extended by Presidents Bush and Gorbachev to convene a peace conference. It was understood that, to ensure the success of efforts to convene that conference, we would have to work with other parties in order to achieve the following principles:

1. The peace conference should be based on international legitimacy and the decisions that the UN had already made, including Resolutions 242 and 338, and that there should be an undertaking to implement them. These resolutions included a guarantee of a complete Israeli withdrawal from all occupied Arab Palestinian land, including Jerusalem, the realization of the principle of land for peace, and the national and political rights of the Palestinian people.
2. Jerusalem was to be considered an inseparable part of the occupied Palestinian territories and therefore all decisions made for the Occupied Territories should include Jerusalem, in line with the UN Security Council and General Assembly resolutions.
3. The would be an end to settlements in the Occupied Territories, including Jerusalem, as a requirement for the beginning of the peace process, with international guarantees to secure this.
4. The PLO, as the only legitimate representative of the Palestinian people, had the right to form the Palestinian delegation from inside Palestine and outside, including Jerusalem, and to determine the

formula for its participation in the peace process on a par with all other concerned parties.

5. The Arab positions had to be coordinated in order to secure a comprehensive solution and the rejection of individual solutions, in accordance with the resolutions of all Arab summits.

6. There had to be a guarantee of coherence between the stages of the settlement so as to reach a final and comprehensive solution according to international resolutions.

The declaration reiterated, so that there could be no confusion, that the PLO would start from these principles with the aim of achieving the following: to secure the right to self-determination for our Palestinian people; to guarantee their right to freedom, national independence, and sovereignty over land, water, and natural resources, all political and economic affairs; to resolve the problem of Palestinian refugees who had been forced out of their country, according to the resolutions of the United Nations, especially Resolution 194 which was ratified by the UN General Assembly. Finally, the participants in the conference repeated their demand for full guarantees for efforts to remove the existing settlements, considering them illegal and in violation of international legitimacy and resolutions, including Security Council Resolution 465.

(4)

I was satisfied with that position, and the conditions that it set down to meet this new challenge, the challenge of the battle for peace. I was convinced that our organization, and with it the concerned Arab countries, had enough ammunition in its armory of conviction to sink the Israeli position, which lacked international legitimacy and the most basic standards of human rights.

I was careful to leave the hall as the time for discussing the election of a new Executive Committee approached. Abu Ja'far, Basel Aql, and I went to visit the Algerian minister, Lakhdar Al-Ibrahimi, hoping to consult him on possible work opportunities for myself in the Arab League. Mahmoud Darwish had intended to come with us as he was determined not to be involved in the Executive Committee again, but Abu Ammar had grabbed his arm and physically held him back. He was always very careful to keep Mahmoud at his side in order to benefit from his popularity.

A few minutes before the final session was about to end, we went back to the big hall. Mahmoud Darwish greeted me with excitement and said: "Congratulations on becoming a member of the Executive Committee." I felt as if I had walked into a glass door. I shouted at Mahmoud, as if he was responsible for what was happening: "Congratulations? Hadn't we agreed that these posts are pointless? Instead of us getting yourself out of the committee, you've got me into it?"

My friends surrounded me and prevented me from going into the hall to reject the appointment, claiming that it would grab the attention of the press and media and shift the focus from the real cause. Over a cup of coffee, I learned from those who knew what went on behind closed doors that I had been nominated to the membership of the committee by more than one organization as an independent figure, and that the only one who had opposed my nomination was Abu Ammar. They said that the discussion had grown heated more than once, with Abu Ammar insisting on saying no. Then I was told that Mahmoud Darwish had said to Abu Ammar: "If you don't want Shafiq, then I refuse to be a member of a committee that he is not part of." That was when Abu Ammar gave in, in order to secure Mahmoud's continued membership, not because he wanted me on the Executive Committee, as he later tried to convince me.

Thus, after 23 years, I was a member of the Executive Committee of the PLO again.

(5)

Instead of returning to Beirut, I headed for Tunis, the headquarters of the Executive Committee, where I attended my first meeting after this long hiatus.

I was surprised when I noticed that an item I had expected to be on our agenda was not there: handing out portfolios so that each of us knew which specialist field he was to be responsible for and which department he would be supervising.

Personally, I did not desire a portfolio that would mean that I had to stay in Tunis, especially that I still held the position of PLO representative in Lebanon. I therefore suggested to Abu Ammar that he allow me to concentrate on Palestinian–Syrian relations, adding my own efforts to what Abu Lutf was trying to achieve in that area, which was normalization of relations and attempting to put relations back to where they should be in terms of coordination and solidarity. I told him that I intended to return to Beirut via Damascus. I knew that this might be a bit of an adventure, given the experiences I had suffered in Beirut during the 1990s. I had lived for years under virtual house arrest and my home had been subjected to a raid by Syrian forces that truly broke my heart, as it reminded me of the Israeli raid in 1982. Despite that, I was determined to bridge the gap in relations between Syria and the PLO, because I have always believed solemnly and sincerely that the Palestinian cause cannot make any advances in isolation from the countries that surround Israel, especially Syria.

Before my departure, I paid a friendly visit to the Syrian ambassador in Tunis to introduce myself. I told him of my desire to visit Damascus in my official capacity as a member of the Palestinian leadership, and asked him to make me an appointment to meet the Syrian foreign minister, Faruq al-Shara'. The proposal appealed to him and he promised to do what was necessary to achieve it.

My first visit to Damascus caused a frenzy of excitement in both the Palestinian and Lebanese media, including as it did successive meetings with Faruq al- Shara' and Vice President Abdul Halim Khaddam.

As was to be expected, I left my first meeting filled with optimism and my second in a slough of despair, for Khaddam's tongue was as sharp as ever in his criticism of Abu Ammar. As for the Palestinians, I received great support and encouragement from the different organizations. Of course, there were always those elements who feared for their personal interests or the interests of one foreign power or another when it came to the normalization of Palestinian relations with Damascus.

In the first week of January 1992, I got the signal from President Hafez Al-Assad's office that Damascus had no objection to my returning to work in Beirut as the director of the PLO office and the representative of the Executive Committee. This news attracted positive and negative reactions in equal measure. Representatives of all sides of the conflict, Syrian, Palestinian, and Lebanese, made their presence felt.

In Lebanon, for example, the Lebanese Forces' magazine *Al-Maseera* published an editorial which contained at least one vicious lie, rumor, or incitement in every paragraph. The people behind *Al-Maseera* were horrified that the PLO should return to Lebanon. They fulminated that the government had accepted "an ambassador from a certain side who was imposing himself on the country without his accreditation papers being offered to the Ministry of Foreign Affairs or the President of the Republic."

On the other hand, Sameer Attallah wrote in *Asharq Al-Awsat* welcoming back Shafiq al-Hout, "the symbol of Palestinian–Lebanese ties with all their mutual pain ... the man who is loyal to both, passionate about both, and filled with love for both Palestine and Lebanon."

In Palestinian circles, my return also raised mixed feelings, except among the ordinary folk who expressed their true feelings whenever they gathered in large numbers. Some factions which still had representatives in Lebanon were less than pleased to see me return, especially those with ambitions to take over the office of the PLO in Lebanon themselves.

My problem with Syria was one of trust. Syrian diplomacy always started from a position of skepticism in order to reach the truth, with the PLO as with everyone else. Whenever we visited Damascus, we were accompanied by a number of Syrian minders, all of whom were of course from the Mukhabarat intelligence service. As our visits became more frequent, there grew between us a sense of friendliness and understanding. One of their fathers had been a friend of mine, and I had the utmost trust in him. One day during a conference at the Sheraton Hotel, he began to tell political jokes about some Syrian officials, though not the president of course. He noticed my neutral reaction to his jokes and asked me why I was not laughing. I replied: "No matter how hard you try, I will not give you the chance to write a report at the end of this evening saying I laughed at a joke about someone or other." My response turned out to be the best joke of the night, and everyone burst out laughing.

This reminds me of another story. During one of the meetings the Palestinian leadership had with President Hafez Al-Assad, I took the opportunity to take a break from talking about official matters, and said: "Mr. President, please give me two minutes because I wish to tell you about a personal problem I have."

He smiled with surprise and said: "I hope to God it is nothing too serious." I said to him: "My wife wants to divorce me!"

His smile got wider and he was quite intrigued. I continued: "You alone can save the situation." Everyone stared at me in genuine surprise until they heard me say: "Sir, you have allowed me to return to my position in Lebanon through the gates of Syria and you are quite aware of the tragic scars the war has left on our people in Lebanon. There is no household that has not suffered. Since my return, there has been a line of needy people about half a kilometer long outside my home. My home, sir, has become more than an office, it has become an open convention center and my wife can no longer tolerate it."

At this point Khaddam interrupted and said: "No problem. Divide the house into two parts, a home and an office."

I resented the implication of this comment and retorted: "My dear chap, you go back and forth to Beirut all the time, why don't you honor me with a visit one day and see how I could divide the palace that I live in!"

At that point President Assad intervened and said seriously: "You have to be a little patient. The Lebanese leaders are still suffering from their difficult experience. Anyway, we will speak to them when the time is right." This meant that the subject of reopening the office was to be postponed to a later date which would be decided by the President.

(6)

During that meeting, I proposed the idea of an Arab high committee to liaise between Syria, Jordan, Lebanon, and the PLO on all the negotiations that were taking place in Washington with Israel. Assad declared that he was prepared to accept this coordination, starting at junior levels and going up to a committee of heads of state. However, Abu Ammar ignored my suggestion. He remained impassive and started fiddling with his headdress as if he had not heard what had been said. There was at the time someone who was whispering in the ear of the Palestinian leader that Syria might do a deal at the expense of the PLO, and convinced him of the need to make a quick decision, accepting what Israel had put on the table. There were also those who were whispering in Syrian ears, accusing the Palestinians of preparing to reach a separate peace deal in isolation from Syria and Jordan.

The next day I had a meeting with Abdul Halim Khaddam to continue a discussion which we had started about the situation of the Palestinians in Lebanon. In his office I met Muhsin Ibrahim, who also had a meeting at almost exactly the same time. He was one of the stalwarts of the Lebanese National Movement, and a man close to Abu Ammar.

After the meeting was over, I agreed with Muhsin that we should go back to Beirut together. He got in the car provided by the Syrian president for his guests during their visits to Damascus. As we approached the Lebanese town of Anjar, the headquarters of Ghazi Kanaan, the man responsible for supervision of the Syrian forces in Lebanon, Muhsin asked me: "Are you going to stop and see Brigadier Ghazi Kanaan?" I replied that I had only met the man once, when the

Syrians made their decision to accept my return to work in Lebanon as the director of the PLO office. I told him the story of that meeting:

> I was on my way back from Damascus, on a day like this, in the president's car, without which I would probably never have reached his office. It was crowded with all sorts of prominent Lebanese political figures. I greeted him and told him who I was and why I was visiting, to get to know him and to coordinate our efforts to find mutually beneficial solutions to our problems in Lebanon, at the forefront of which was our common cause. The man welcomed my visit with kind words and expressed his honor at meeting me and getting to know me. He assured me of his readiness to offer all the support that I needed in improving the relations between Syria and the PLO. That was my first and last visit.

(7)

As for my program in Lebanon, the first priority was to visit government officials. This was not just for the sake of protocol, as was the norm, but also to build firm fraternal relationships.

The first visit I made was to the President of the Republic, Elias Hrawi, at the temporary presidential headquarters in Ramlat al-Bayda on January 13, 1993. I delivered a letter from Abu Ammar which confirmed the PLO's belief in the need for the frontline states to coordinate on the process of negotiations which were taking place at that time in Washington. When the journalists asked me about the Palestinian diplomatic position in Lebanon and where the PLO office was now, I answered: "The PLO office is still there and the Lebanese government has never taken a decision to close it. The PLO leadership has also not withdrawn its delegation from Lebanon."

On 17 January 1992, I had my second meeting with the leadership. I was received in his office in parliament by Hussein Al-Husseini, the speaker. I delivered to him a similar message from the leadership of the PLO. I made it clear to journalists after the meeting that I was seeking to rebuild the bridge of trust between the Lebanese and Palestinian leaderships and to confirm that the PLO recognized that Lebanon was free and had sovereignty over its own land, and was the master of its decisions when it came to politics and security.

In the government palace in Sanayeh I was received by Prime Minister Omar Karami. I told him what I had told Presidents Hrawi and al-Husseini. I assured him that the PLO would not be an obstacle to the state asserting its sovereignty over its own territory, but that the PLO was demanding that this government take responsibility for protecting the Palestinians who lived on its land and to remove the political, social, and economic constraints on them.

On 13 February I met with Faris Buwayz, the foreign minister. I delivered to him a message from Tunis asking what Lebanon's position was towards the second round of bilateral negotiations which was to be held in Washington. The meeting was also attended by the Secretary General of the Ministry of Foreign Affairs, Suhayl Shammas, the head of the Lebanese negotiating team in the peace talks.

After visiting the officials, my next task was to seek the blessing of the popular leaders. My first visit on February 28, 1992 was to Sidon, a city I had not been to for ten years. I arrived at noon and immediately had a meeting with the PLO's political leaders in the south and inspected the Ayn Al-Hilwa refugee camp. There was an important discussion on the suffering in the refugee camp because of the lack of security, armed clashes, and assassinations.

After the meeting was over, my colleagues, the members of the leadership, and I visited the head of the Nasserite Popular Front, Mustafa Sa'd, at home. I spoke to him of the deep roots and fraternal ties that linked him to the PLO. Sa'd replied to our initiative with kind and honest words. He renewed the promise to fight the enemy until Palestine and all occupied Arab lands were liberated. We visited several eminent leaders in Sidon, but the climax of that day came during the public meeting which took place in the Abu Hassan Salama Hall in Ayn Al-Hilwa refugee camp. The hall was full. There were some welcoming words, together with demands and complaints, and we parted on the basis that we would continue our struggle, which would not stop until our people had regained their land and their rights.

19

NO FINAL SOLUTION WITHOUT A SINGLE DEMOCRATIC PALESTINE

One of the paradoxes of the *Intifada* of Stones, which was responsible for redirecting the path of the modern Palestinian national movement towards political negotiations over the fate of part of Palestine, was that it also produced two new movements, the Islamic Resistance Movement (Hamas) and Islamic Jihad, that reinvigorated the notion of "complete liberation of all Palestinian soil" with "resistance and the armed struggle" as the means to achieve that aim.

Both those movements declared their rejection of a compromise and the programs associated with compromise, including the Declaration of Independence which the Palestine National Council of the PLO had issued in 1988 in conjunction with a political program aiming to establish a Palestinian state over part of Palestine, the part which was occupied in 1967, including East Jerusalem.

Despite the fact that these two movements emerged 20 years after the establishment of the PLO, they were able to forge a wide popular appeal on the ground. This brought back memories 0f the Palestinian political scene in the 1970s with all the disputes and clashes on the same issue, arguing between what I call the "just solution," which appears to be impossible as it entails the liberation of all Palestinian soil, and the "acceptable solution" which appears to be possible, establishing a state on part of that territory.

(1)

It would be no exaggeration if I said that the PLO embarked on its peaceful engagement with the enemy in exactly the same way that it had engaged in its military engagement, that is with no fixed strategy or any political agenda comprising a list of priorities, mechanisms, or tactics.

After its groundbreaking decision to announce the establishment of a Palestinian state, the leadership behaved as if it had done all it was supposed to do and it was now up to others, such as the major powers, the UN, and the Arab League, to implement this decision and turn it from a wish into a tangible material reality.

The leadership promised to form an interim government which would act as the official voice of this state. A president and a foreign minister were elected, but that was it. The government was not formed. Why? No one knows. The relationship between the structure of this state and the leadership of the PLO was also never established or clarified. All that had changed was that Abu Ammar and Abu Lutf had two new titles to go with all their others. So Abu Ammar became the president of this putative state as well as being the Chairman of the Executive Committee of the PLO, the General Commander of the Armed Forces, and the Leader of the Fatah movement. Abu Lutf became the foreign minister, in addition to being the President of the Politburo of the PLO and the Secretary General of the Fatah movement.

More than that, the PLO delegation at the UN asked to change its official name to Palestine instead of the PLO, without explaining the reasoning behind this. In my view that was wrong, because we had chosen a title which did not reflect our reality and a position which deprived us of our rights as a national independence movement without bestowing on us the rights of a state.

(2)

Seven years before the Declaration of Independence was issued, I wrote a detailed study, which was published in several installments in the al-*Anba* newspaper in Kuwait, in which I asked the question "What Palestinian state do we want?" I later included that study in my book *So We May Sow the Land* in 1986. The study was based on three beliefs.

The first was that the basis of the Arab–Zionist conflict went further and deeper than simply one over "land" and "borders." It is a conflict between two opposites on all levels and the only historical solution was to return Palestine to its geo-historical reality, as an inalienable part of its Arab surroundings, historically and in the future: that is to establish a democratic state of Palestine.

The second was that the achievement of this strategic goal needed the right objective circumstances to guarantee victory. This meant that we, as Arabs in general and as Palestinians in particular, should plan our long-term struggle and become adept in carrying it out according to the demands of each stage.

Thirdly, this "Palestine," which we believed could be established at some point in this struggle alongside its counterpart, "Israel," had to have specific features which would guarantee its survival and its role as a stage in the continuing path towards the final solution.

I summarized these features as follows:

- **The name of the state**: Palestine, without any description attached to it, is the most suitable, precise, and truthful title, and the one that is required. The name Palestine embodies a historical reality which goes back to the Canaanite period. It also carries the dreams of the future – to restore the unity of land and people. Palestine will always be the name that stands in contradiction to Israel and to all that racist name has tried to misappropriate.
- **The borders of the state**: any identification of the borders of the state entails, in an indirect way, the understanding that those borders are not final and that accepting this current state does not mean that we surrender our strategic goal; the state and the goal are two things that deserve every possible effort. In case the ultimate goal proves to be impossible, there should be a special appendix issued by the Palestinian side declaring that the establishment of this state does not prevent the Palestinians from their right to struggle through peaceful means to establish a democratic Palestinian state over the entirety of Palestinian national territory. This is exactly what the Federal Republic of Germany did when it issued an appendix after recognizing the German Democratic Republic over its right to continue the struggle towards German reunification.
- **The capital of the state**: any Palestinian state in any part of Palestine that does not have Jerusalem as its capital is a failed state even before it is established. Only Jerusalem can give the Palestinian state symbolic, existential, and historical meaning. Jerusalem alone is capable of drawing the world's attention. Without it, the state will be empty, of no consequence except that it is a place for Palestinians to gather. We have to guarantee the rights of the followers of all three religions to be able to reach their holy places and to practice their religions freely.

- **The geopolitical situation of the state**: this state will always be dominated by the geopolitical factor imposed upon it by its prime position as the arena for the war of civilization between the Arabs and Israel. In the absence of the armed struggle, Zionist propaganda will concentrate on the Israeli lifestyle and will claim it is more modern, more developed, and more progressive than the Arab way of life. So it will try to steal attention from the Palestinians and to present itself rather than the Arabs as a model for progress and development as well as other factors that determine the way people live.

  Thus it becomes clear to us that, despite its small size and lack of natural resources, and its division into the two parts of the West Bank and the Gaza Strip, this state will have, right from the beginning, to play a very important and pivotal role: confronting the Zionist cultural war as a doctrine and Israel as the state that embodies that doctrine. This would be achieved by establishing institutions, including scientific, intellectual, cultural, and artistic academies at the most advanced levels, which are able to draw on the best Arab brains which realize the nature of the cultural clash and its implications, and which know how to deal with it and are able to monitor the fallout of the clash on both sides of the divide. Knowledge, intellect, culture, and art are for Jerusalem like bread and oxygen, and are located on the frontline of this conflict.

  It is this role which in the end will determine what a Palestinian state will become. It might become our gateway into the very heart of Zionism or a bridge over which Zionism will cross in order to realize its remaining dreams of power and expansion.

- **The population of the state**: the establishment of the state of Palestine will first and foremost mean the restoration of Palestinian national identity. This will by necessity draw a line under the tragedy of the refugees. It would be natural for the constitution to allow the right of return to all Palestinians who want to live in their own homeland and carry a Palestinian passport.

  We have to guard carefully and diligently against imperialist-Zionist (and sometimes Arab) attempts to establish a distinction between the "people" and the "land" and to resist all attempts to naturalize our people outside Palestine.

- **The two parts of the state, the West Bank and Gaza**: we must recall the danger and significance of the geopolitical situation caused by this state being made up of two parts, connected by a corridor passing through Israel. The geopolitical aspect here is of utmost importance. It means that the necessary decisions and procedures have to be put in place right from the beginning.

The Gaza Strip has two paradoxical features, one positive and the other negative. One is that it is connected by land to Egypt, as well as being the window of the Palestinian state on the sea. This feature has its own strategic importance when it comes to establishing and developing the security of the state.

As for the negative feature and the Achilles heel of the Strip, it is that its only connection with the rest of the state, the West Bank, is through a corridor passing through Israel. The state should therefore constantly consider how it would respond if that corridor were cut. This can be done by preparing means and guarantees of bringing rapid and effective pressure on Israel when necessary.

As for the West Bank, the center of the state and the place of its capital, as well as being the principal arena in the struggle as we have shown, it is in direct contact on the eastern side with the Hashemite Kingdom of Jordan, which means there must be close relations between the two states which have to be managed in the best national interest of both peoples.

I used to believe that such an understanding of the "acceptable solution" need not clash with the "just solution," but was just one point on the path to it. My intention in this study was to unify the two most prominent Palestinian viewpoints, which was proving to be an obstacle to national unity at that time. This is an argument I later repeated before the Oslo Agreement and I think it holds true to this day.

(3)

At that time, our position internationally was every bit as perilous as the threats we faced internally.

On 2 August 1990, Saddam Hussein committed the sin of his life by invading Kuwait and declaring its annexation to Iraq. I will not go into the details of that war, its causes and reasons, but what is important to me here is to illustrate its consequences for all the Arabs, and especially the Palestinian cause.

Whatever has been said in defense of Abu Ammar's position, by appearing to align himself with Saddam Hussein, and by the policies which he pursued in order to remedy the situation, there is no doubt that he added more problems to our existing predicament. A huge tragedy occurred for the tens of thousands of Palestinians who had lived in Kuwait, peacefully and securely, and who became refugees within the space of a week.

It is perhaps enough to record for the purposes of this history that, on January 17, 1991, the armies of an alliance between the United States and some Arab countries began waging a war against another Arab country.

Separately, we were in for another shock, another earthquake which had repercussions around the entire world: the collapse of the Soviet Union. The world changed after *Perestroika*. It put an end to the prevailing international order based on the existence of two superpowers and a balance of fear between them. The United States became the sole superpower, with no counterbalance.

In my opinion, this was the origin of the split inside the PLO between those who surrendered in their own minds when confronted by these new realities and came to believe there was no solution other than through Washington, and those who refused to give up although they understood these global changes and knew the drastic effect they would have on the struggle. The former group viewed this refusal as absurd and idealistic. Nonetheless, the latter group decided to carry on with the struggle, believing that the Palestinians and their Arab allies still had some cards to play and that the "acceptable solution" could still be achieved on the basis of international law and UN Security Council Resolutions, including 242 and 338. There was also a third school of thought gaining currency and it was not one to be taken lightly: its adherents rejected anything other than the "just solution," the comprehensive liberation of Palestine, even if that seemed impossible at the time. At the forefront of these were Hamas and Islamic Jihad, and to these were added other movements which sprang up after the failure of the Oslo accords.

(4)

After the PLO accepted the invitation to participate in the Madrid conference in late October 1991, the Palestinian leadership set up an operations room in Tunis to organize the negotiations. Mahmoud Abbas, known as Abu Mazen, was appointed to lead this work for two main reasons: the first was that he was the keenest of all

Palestinian leaders to seek a political solution through negotiation, and the second was that he had long experience of dialogue with Israelis, beginning in the late 1970s.

A follow-up committee was set up from members of the Executive Committee and some leading cadres from Fatah, whose mission was to liaise between the delegation in Madrid and later in Washington and the leadership in Tunis. The negotiating team was made up of Dr Haidar Abdul Shafi as president and the following as members: Ilyas Freij, Dr Zakariyya al-Agha, Mamdouh al-Ikr, Mustafa al-Natsheh, Dr Nabeel Qassis, Sami al-Kilani, and Ghassan al-Khatib. All of them came from the West Bank and Gaza as Israel had insisted. More than 45 men and women joined them to participate in subcommittees and the public affairs offices.

Even though I had been working in the field of diplomacy since 1964, I have to admit that between 1991 and 1992 I learnt more about the diplomatic arts than I had in the previous 37 years, especially the art of negotiation.

The Israeli team, headed by Dr Elyakim Rubinstein, tried dominate every minute detail in order to put obstacles in the path of these negotiations. For the first month, the Israeli and Palestinian teams were in effect negotiating in the corridor outside the meeting room over procedural matters. Whenever any of the negotiators felt tired of standing up, they went to sit on a nearby sofa. This is why these meetings were jokingly called the "corridor" or "sofa" negotiations.

It is impossible at this point to write down my memories in detail. There are dozens of documents, thousands of pages long, recording what was said between the two teams, and these were conveyed to us in the follow-up committee. I just want to mention three examples of what was going on. The first argument was about the Palestinian representation and the description under which it was to attend the conference when it came to discuss the issues concerning the question of Palestine. Would it be included under the umbrella of a Jordanian delegation, or would it be independent? There was also the issue of the relationship between the different delegations and the different peace tracks, given that there were now three delegations and two separate tracks: an Israeli delegation, a Jordanian delegation, and a Palestinian delegation; and an Israeli–Jordanian track and an Israeli–Palestinian track.

The second argument concerned the goal of the negotiations. While the Palestinian delegation focused on solving on finding a solution to the political conflict, demanding that their legal national rights be dealt with, the Israeli delegation insisted that the dialogue would be restricted to the issue of "self-rule" with all other questions left to the final settlement which would be reached in three years.

Thirdly, the Israelis were wrangling about where the negotiations would take place. Although Washington was the capital of their biggest ally, they were suggesting that negotiations should be held in Israel, or "our country" as Rubinstein called it. If that had passed without any objections from the Palestinians, it would have been a free goal for our enemy. Rubinstein knew that, but he used it to test the vigilance of the Palestinian negotiators.

While the arguments were going on in the corridors, the forces of the occupation were devouring more Palestinian land to build settlements for Jews. They also arrested and exiled the Palestinian inhabitants and implemented other measures that violated international law and the Geneva conventions. Between the convening of the Madrid Conference and the start of negotiations in Washington alone – just two months – Israel confiscated 2,240 *dunum*s, more than 2.2 million square meters, of land in the West Bank and started building three settlements, one of which was close to the city of Nablus in the heart of the West Bank. They also established a new settlement in the heart of the Golan Heights.

On January 14, 1992, on the second day of a meeting taking place away from the corridor, the Palestinian delegation presented a note entitled: "The continuation of Israeli settlement activity threatens the negotiations over interim self-rule of the Palestinians." (We still hear the same phrase uttered by the current chief negotiator, Saeb Erekat, and his boss, Ahmad Qurei.)

The note covered everything, from every aspect, including the authority of the negotiations, the Fourth Geneva Convention of 1949, and Clause 43 of the Hague Convention of 1907, as well as all the Security Council resolutions declaring that the building of settlements on occupied land is illegal. But it did not include any threat to withdraw from the negotiations or suspend them if Israel continued to build settlements. We in the follow-up committee were divided on this matter, and similarly in the PLO Executive Committee. Some argued that we should continue negotiating because, from the beginning, it was Israel that wanted to hold up the process and we should not let it succeed. Others saw this matter as pivotal to the whole process, because it was obvious that Israel would continue to gobble up Palestinian land and build settlements on it, while procrastinating and using delaying tactics in the negotiations at the same time. One day we would wake up to find that the land we had come to reclaim had been stolen in front of our very eyes, because we had remained silent from the beginning.

I was in the latter camp, which was led by Dr Abdul Shafi. Most people took the other view, however, which was advocated by Abu Ammar and his small coterie. The war of notes continued without any result and the process broke down in the first week of December 1992, after eight rounds of talks. Israel's policy of devouring Palestinian land and building settlements has continued to this day.

(5)

As the negotiations continued in Washington, slow, stumbling, and fruitless, it became clear that Israel was determined not to reach a peaceful political solution. The fate of the other tracks fared no better than the Palestinian track, even though the media continued to portray it as a "race" between countries towards peace and to spread rumors that each negotiating team was vying to reach a solution first at the others' expense.

After the fourth round of talks, I headed for Tunis to participate in a meeting of the leadership committee for the negotiations, to evaluate the results of that round, and to prepare for the fifth.

I arrived at Carthage airport on March 8, 1992. Some friends were waiting for me in the VIP lounge and I found them to be uncharacteristically serious and somber. One of them came up to me and told me that he had received a phone call from Beirut with the news of my mother's death. She had been ill for some time.

In the evening, I received Abu Ammar and all the leaders who were in Tunis, who came to offer their condolences. Haidar Abdul Shafi was among them and I understood from an informative chat with him that the Washington negotiations were nearing an end. Indeed he believed that they had to end before they became a smokescreen behind which Israel could continue all its practices which contravened international law governing times of both war and peace. I learned from him that the last negotiating session had ended without any date or place being set for the next round. It had been left to the American and Russian sponsors to decide on that.

I also recall from what Dr Abdul Shafi said was that the Israelis were behaving according to the principle that the land was theirs. As for the population there, the Israelis would determine their fate by allowing them some administrative authority. In this way, they were trying to go from a temporary occupation to a final annexation with Palestinian agreement.

I returned to Beirut the next morning on board the same plane that had taken me to Tunis, hoping to get there in time for my dear mother's funeral. Sadly, I was too late, so I headed to the place where she was buried near the Martyr's Cemetery and read the *Fatiha* for her soul. I felt like an orphan, as if I was ten years old, not an old man of over 60. I did not love her more than I loved my father, but my grief for her loss was greater.

At the end of March, Beirut was preparing for a meeting of the Arab foreign ministers from the countries taking part in the negotiations. The Lebanese foreign minister, Faris Buwayz, was delighted with this occasion, which confirmed Beirut's success in restoring itself to its role in Arab affairs. A joint statement was made at this meeting which confirmed that the ministers were committed to participating in the achievement of a just, permanent, and comprehensive peace according to UN Resolutions 242 and 338, on the basis that Israel would withdraw from all Arab land and guarantee the legitimate political and national rights of the Palestinian people. It must also withdraw completely from all occupied Lebanese land, implementing UN Security Council Resolution 425. The assembled ministers also confirmed their positive response to the invitation by the sponsors of the Madrid conference to undertake a new round of bilateral negotiations in Washington. The meeting postponed a response to the US Secretary of State's letter about where the bilateral negotiations would be held in the future, resulting from Israel's insistence that the negotiations take place outside the American capital.

The reader may be puzzled by this position taken by Israel despite its strategic relationship with the United States. But it can easily be explained: it feared Arab competition in political dealings with Washington which might lead to the development of bilateral relations between the United States and the Arabs, especially the PLO. It also feared that the discrepancy between its position and that of the United States would be revealed, even if it was just in the matter of methods and tactics in the negotiating chamber. For its part, Washington wished to avoid guaranteeing any agreement which might in the future prove embarrassing for its relations with Israel or its Arab allies.

20

THE NIGHT OF ABU AMMAR'S PLANE CRASH

There is no doubt that Abu Ammar was a believer who performed his religious duties regularly. He never became fanatical although the political and social environment in which he was raised could have easily made him so. During times of crisis or when difficult decisions had to be taken he often used to meditate and seek God's guidance and intercession.

I recall a meeting of the leadership in the mid-1980s when a plan for an agreement with Jordan was under discussion and there was a sharp division of opinion involving, among others, members of the Executive Committee from the Fatah movement. Abu Ammar wanted the plan to go through and tried hard to gain unanimous approval for it. The meeting was in Tunis, in the house of our ambassador, al-Hakam Balaawi. After midnight, Abu Ammar called for a recess and excused himself, saying he had to perform all the prayers that he had missed during day. When he came back about half an hour later he did not call the session to order again. Someone asked whether we were going to continue the debate that night or postpone it until the following day and he replied: "No, it's over. I have made my decision and put my faith in God. I have meditated and the reply has come in favor of the agreement."

On the basis of this experience, one could describe him as having been an extreme fatalist who was willing to put all his faith in the Almighty. One might also observe that he sometimes used to create this impression so that he could impose his own personal will without consulting his mortal associates.

(1)

Abu Ammar flew off to inspect the PLO units stationed in Yemen, before stopping off in Sudan to see their comrades there. This was his habit on the main Muslim holidays, *Eid al-Fitr*, which ends the fasting month of Ramadan, and *Eid al-Adha*, the feast of sacrifice after the *Hajj* pilgrimage. On April 7, 1992, he left Khartoum on his way to Tunis on board an old Russian-built Antonov military plane belonging to the Palestine Liberation Army. As members of the Executive Committee, we were scheduled to meet him later that night, but before sunset we heard rumors that contact had been lost with the plane after it entered Libyan airspace over the southern desert. Word of the rumor reached the media and we began to be inundated with questions about what had happened to the plane with Chairman Arafat and his companions on board; the Politburo also started receiving calls from all the units and cadres of the PLO in Tunisia; it was decided that Abu Lutf would handle all the enquiries and media relations, as well as liaising with our allies among the Arab states.

The 15 hours between the plane's disappearance and its discovery the following morning were probably the most difficult that we faced, if not also the most perplexing. What if Yasser Arafat was dead or if the wreckage of the plane was never discovered? It was a question that no one dared to ask, because there was no answer. The reason was that, many years earlier, Abu Ammar had unofficially ditched the role of deputy chairman of the Executive Committee of the PLO. The last person who had occupied that post was Ibrahim Bakr, during the fifth Executive Committee, between 1968 and 1970. Even within the Fatah movement itself, the hierarchy was far from clear and so there was no consensus on who was Abu Ammar's designated successor. Abu Iyad was known in the media as Arafat's Number Two, but it was Abu Jihad who enjoyed more popularity in Fatah, including greater support among the powerful military wing. Meanwhile, Khaled al-Hassan, known as Abu Said, would often tout himself around as the most suitable man to govern Fatah.

But those 15 hours proved beyond doubt the truth about Abu Ammar's status within the Palestinian revolution. The grief and trauma felt by the communities inside and outside occupied Palestine showed that he was not just the chairman, but the leader. How could his comrades in Fatah, or any other faction, fill the void we feared he was leaving? Even the international community seemed to have arrived at the conviction that the ongoing negotiation process was in danger if Arafat was lost.

No one slept that night. We all followed the progress of the search and rescue efforts. Even during those critical moments, some people sought to exploit the situation for personal gain. They came out with stories about how the United States and other world powers were prepared to step in with assistance. However, on the following morning, I learned that the plane had made an emergency landing in the Libyan Desert, where it had broken up into three pieces. By God's supreme will, Abu Ammar and most of his companions were saved, but there were two victims: the pilot Mahmoud Darwish and co-pilot Ghassan Yassine, God bless their souls.

Happy as we were for the leader's survival, there was also some anger and recrimination as Abu Ammar's temporary absence had exposed the deficiencies of his one-man show. Nothing could be done without his signature, whether it was to sign internationally binding treaties or to purchase spare blankets for the troops.

We headed immediately to visit Abu Ammar in Tripoli where, despite the disaster, we found him in an excellent psychological state. On April 10, he returned to Tunis and went straight back to his normal work schedule. He also received visits from all his companions and loved ones, in addition to the floods of people who came from all over the world to congratulate him on his deliverance. Two weeks later, he decided to call an Executive Committee meeting.

(2)

As a result of the plane crash and everyone's desire to congratulate Abu Ammar on his safety, the Executive Committee meeting was packed. They were also keen to address the succession procedures, especially concerning the chairmanship. It was felt that this was the only way to guarantee the continuation of the Palestinian revolution. But as this topic was clearly sensitive, it was agreed that our comrades in Fatah should initiate the discussion, and then all the other representatives of factions, as well as independent members like myself, would chip in.

When I entered the hall, Abu Ammar grabbed my hand and led me to the seat next to him. This was a violation of protocol and common practice and I had no idea what he was doing. The session began and it quickly degenerated into a party to celebrate the chairman's survival, with a series of speeches, some in rhyme, some in prose, in his honor. Abu Ammar did nothing to impose discipline on the meeting – it suited him down to the ground to preside over this renewed pledge of allegiance, which let everyone understand, within Fatah or without, that there was "no chairman but the Chairman." If anyone had any doubts about the matter, he'd better relinquish them now.

I waited for someone to make the first move – anyone, Abu Lutf, Abu Iyad, Abu Said, or any other of the *abus* – to indicate in words or even facial expression that there were lessons to be learnt from this experience: that the destiny of the PLO, indeed of the entire Palestinian revolution, had been teetering on the brink.

That was when I realized why Abu Ammar had grabbed my hand and made me sit next to him. But I refused to take part in this conspiracy of silence. I requested the floor and saluted Abu Ammar, saying: "Brother Abu Ammar, may you be blessed, the day you were born, the day you disappeared, and the day you returned to us safe and sound. May God bless your safe return." I then launched into a brief summary of the paralysis and bewilderment that had confounded both our people and the leadership on the day he disappeared. I requested permission to speak openly, as that was a more honorable course than whispering in private rooms while being silent in public, and said: "First of all, I want you to be assured that I consider you my leader and my president." As though sensing my intentions, Abu Ammar interrupted me, saying in an ironic tone: "What, with all my good and bad points?"

I was silent for a moment, but then went on to recount the great loss that the Arab nation had suffered in 1970 with the death of Abdul Nasser and, less than one year later, the principles of the July 1952 revolution had been diverted away from the natural revolutionary course. I said that, recently, we had been on the brink of a similar disaster when "Abu Ammar, your plane crashed and had it not been for God's care, you might not have survived. Tell us, Brother Abu Ammar, for God's sake, what did Almighty God say to you when He took you away and then delivered you to safety? Did you hear His message about what you should conclude from this experience, from this test?"

I went on to remind him and the Committee members that everyone had been extremely worried about what might happen to Fatah or the PLO had he not returned. "In your briefcase, which you were carrying with you on that plane, you have all our secrets, addresses, plans, everything related to our people. How long are we going to keep this system? Isn't it time to implement one that guarantees the succession of authority in a regular and healthy manner, without a crisis, without letting power fall into undeserving hands, to people who may abandon the original revolutionary principles, as happened with the July Revolution?" By the end of my speech, Abu Ammar was furious. Instead of addressing me, he began talking directly to his comrades in Fatah, intending no doubt to quash any chance that they might agree with me. His anger took me by surprise; I had thought that his experience over the Libyan desert might have left him more humble and forgiving.

I was even more surprised to see that, instead of controlling his feelings, he started flagrantly to lash out in defense of his unilateral behavior. Regarding the issue of the "safe," (as we referred to the national treasury), he exclaimed loudly to Jawid al-Ghussein, President of the Palestine National Fund: "Jawid, do I ever write a check without your signature?' "Never, Abu Ammar," replied Jawid. Then he turned to Ahmad Qurei and asked him the same question, except in reference to the Fatah treasury, and Qurei's reply was identical to Jawid's. The low point of this performance came when he turned to his brother, Fathi Arafat, and said dramatically: "Listen, Fathi. If anything should happen to me, please remember that Fatah owes me 500,000 dollars!"

Because I held the man in high esteem, I concluded with some anguish that Abu Ammar had become a different person after the plane crash. Contrary to what several of his loyal friends had hoped, his behavior became far more autocratic. He labored under the illusion that he was infallible, a man of vision, under the direct protection of God. He also began to confuse fiction with reality by believing that his identity and that of Palestine were one and the same.

I have never understood what possible harm it could have done had Abu Ammar named a deputy in the Executive Committee. And why did he obstruct the creation of a straightforward system in Fatah that would facilitate the transfer of the leadership? Did not such attitude, which was unjustified either at the political or the administrative level, betray a suspicious imbalance in the man's psychological make up? Self-confidence is a positive quality, but vanity and conceit are not, while the illusion that one is indispensable is a state of mind requiring medical intervention. The patient needs to be reminded that perfection and immortality are the exclusive preserve of God Almighty.

Abu Ammar was of course not the only Arab leader with this affliction. Several others have contracted this malady in our time:

some have already paid for their mistake and fallen, while others remain in power. Their time has not yet come. There is a popular saying in Arabic: "Pharaoh, who made you a pharaoh?" [Translator's note: the well-known implied response is: "Because no one stopped me.']

(3)

During this period, the talks in Washington were suffering from stagnation because of Israel's intransigence and the unacceptable conditions it wanted to dictate to the Palestinians. Israel's position was reinforced by the US administration's refusal to exercise any kind of pressure against its spoilt brat of an ally. The remainder of 1992 went by with no progress, and the Palestinians' internal mechanisms underwent a number of upheavals, as the Americans had managed to wear down the negotiating team and its supervisors in Tunis. As if Abu Ammar was not paranoid enough already, with his insistence on keeping all the cards in his hand and remaining the sole decision maker, some people started whispering to him about the possibility of an alternative leadership in the Occupied Territories.

Stormy days passed, and regrettably we began to hear conflicting statements from the negotiating team, who all came from the Occupied Territories, and Tunis. One famous incident almost led to the unanimous resignation of the members of the delegation. According to one of the negotiators, US Secretary of State James Baker met members of the team during a visit to the West Bank and pressed them on a matter that was still pending; he asserted that their position was in conflict with the policy of the leadership in Tunis. To back this up, he produced an official Egyptian document purporting to express Abu Ammar's view on that particular issue. I recall that, despite Abu Ammar's attempts to downplay the issue, the negotiators were in uproar. They accused him of trumping their efforts – from his privileged position, far from the Occupation, surrounded by bodyguards and escorts – by claiming to adopt more radical positions than theirs while he secretly agreed to what they had publicly rejected? Did he want them to be attacked by their own people for being too soft with the Israelis?

As a member of the follow-up committee, I began to sense that we were no longer receiving all the documents relevant to the negotiation process. One day I arrived early for a meeting and found Hassan

Asfour, who used to work in Abu Mazen's office, removing one of the documents that had been distributed at the negotiating table. I asked him why he was doing this but he was unable to give me a straight answer. In addition, Abu Ammar's behavior with the members of the Executive Committee became intolerable. He often used to leave us sitting around the table, while he would busy himself signing papers or reading letters. I had no doubt that we had been neutralized and our role had been completely sidelined. I once opened the subject angrily with Mahmoud Darwish, whose response was both harsh and true. He said: "Abu Hader, this is a revolution tailored to Abu Ammar's requirements, and you either have to accept the status quo or quit." From that moment on, the idea of resignation remained on my mind.

Our meetings had become more like social get-togethers than serious political debates, and were held in a different location from the operations room. I recall one occasion during a session, when I was sitting at one end of the table where it was permitted to smoke, and Abu Ammar was signing papers as usual. I started to ask those around me, Mahmoud Darwish, Abu Mazen, and Yasser Abed Rabbo: "If the Israeli delegation were to offer to withdraw from the Gaza Strip, what should our delegation do? Should we accept or refuse? And what would be the grounds for either decision?" Apparently, Abu Ammar's auditory capabilities remained acute despite his being tied up with his paperwork, and he suddenly dropped the pen and shouted: "What are you saying?" I repeated my question. His tone became even sharper and he pounded on the table: "That's a trap and I shall not fall into it! Remember that Rabin already offered Gaza to Mubarak, and he declined it. He told Rabin the last thing he needed was more Muslim Brotherhood members." I asked: "So what will you say to our people? Will you tell them that we turned down the opportunity to lift the Occupation?" He was silent for a moment, but then continued: "No ... we'll take it ... but through a third party, through the United Nations for example." The discussion, if one can call it that, ended. Abu Ammar went back to his papers, and the rest of the colleagues remained as they were: silent, jovial, absent-minded, or distracted by the television!

Little did I know then that a new channel had opened up, far away from Washington, and more in harmony with Israel's previous and ongoing demands. I felt disenfranchized when some months later I learned that while I was looking to Washington for a solution, things were actually being cooked up in Oslo. I was very upset with some of my comrades, who had known what was going on but had kept quiet about it. They and Abu Ammar could at least have told me there was an attempt to work through another channel that offered more hope than Washington, and that it was in our national interest to maintain secrecy until the time was right. That was possible, and perfectly legitimate in the diplomatic world. But it was quite unacceptable to keep things under the table, because of their lack of confidence in the correctness of the steps being taken.

I decided to start reducing my visits to Tunis as much as possible. Whenever I did go, I made sure not to stay long, preferring always to return to Beirut, despite the many problems there. There were financial strains on the PLO and a continuous failure to cover our basic expenses, for example the salaries of the martyrs' families, or the costs for the treatment of chronic medical cases, such as open heart surgery and kidney dialysis, treatments perhaps considered too much of a luxury for Palestinian refugees.

21

RESIGNING IN PROTEST OVER THE OSLO AGREEMENT

At the beginning of 1993, the list of crises the PLO was facing became even longer. Renewed pressure was exerted with the aim of taming the people of Palestine and their organizations, breaking the strength of their resistance, and tempering their rejection of unacceptable peace agreements.

It became apparent, suddenly and with no prior warning, that all the departments of the PLO and its affiliated organizations and agencies were at risk of paralysis because of an unexpected shortfall in the Palestinian National Fund. The Fund was unable to meet its financial obligations because it lacked sufficient financial resources. We were surprised to hear this crisis had not only affected the PLO and its subsidiaries, but had also hit Fatah and the groups associated with it. As far as we knew, Fatah's budget was many times greater than that of the PLO, the umbrella organization. Since the fate of tens of thousands of Palestinians depended in one way or another on the PLO's multifarious organizations, the public, both inside the Occupied Territories and outside, was very anxious about the grave consequences if this crisis was allowed to continue without a solution, and a speedy one at that.

(1)

I was unable to get to the bottom of this crisis. Was it the result of political or administrative failures, or had it been concocted in order to focus people's attention on the need to put food on the table, so that they would be prepared to accept any solutions they were offered? It is sad that by this time, any transparency in the financial sector had disappeared as a result of the marginalization of the National Fund under the pretext of the revolutionary struggle's need for "secrecy."

This crisis caused powerful shockwaves of concern about corruption within the higher echelons of the Palestinian revolution and the handful of parasites who had turned the cause into a profession. There were many stories about companies and investments set up by phantom organizations in the name of the PLO. All, without exception, were said to have gone bankrupt. A few names were bandied about and accused of theft and deception and being in cahoots with senior officials.

It was perfectly natural that the reverberations of this crisis would reach the Palestinians in Lebanon. There was unrest in the refugee camps. Blockades and demonstrations took place in front of my own home – as if the matter were in my hands. Things got so bad that one day the Mothers and Sisters of the Martyrs broke into my home and threatened to stage a sit-in until they were paid their dues.

I took the first plane to Tunis, hoping to find a quick, even if temporary, solution, because ordinary people's lives had reached an unbearable state. There were a number of medical emergencies which had to be funded. I remember with much sorrow and pain that during this crisis ten men out of 14 who had been suffering kidney failure died because we were unable to fund their renal dialysis.

(2)

In Tunis, I felt as though the leadership was on another planet and that there was now what resembled a shadow administration of "advisors" and people who had insinuated themselves into the PLO. They were solution brokers and godfathers of secret communications. Their movements and declarations began to appear in the media in the form of test balloons of public reaction. There were also whispers about communications which some of those men had undertaken with Israelis who claimed to be academics, but who were in reality from Mossad.

To be honest, I was sure that Abu Ammar was conscious of what was going on around him. I would even go as far as saying that it was taking place with his encouragement. It is well known that Abu Ammar's method in politics is not to object to any bridge set up between him and any other party because, in his view, you never know when it might come in handy.

In addition to the new financial crisis, there remained the chronic historical dilemma, the problem of national unity. The organizational formula that had governed the path of the revolution since the factions took over the leadership of the PLO in 1968 was no longer adequate for managing things in the 1990s, in the wake of the *Intifada* of Stones, when two new organizations had appeared in the Palestinian arena, with a specific ideology and a well-known methodology. They began to exercise their roles and this had consequences for the political movement as a whole. It would have been impossible for Hamas and Islamic Jihad to stay outside the fold without causing an imbalance or embarrassment to the leadership which then controlled the PLO.

This matter was raised many times in the meetings of the Executive Committee. Many decisions were taken to emphasize the importance of engaging with the two fraternal organizations in order include them in the same framework as the other Palestinian movements. My impression was that, after all the attempts and the meetings that took place, the situation had not developed sufficiently for this necessary step to be taken, no matter how much time was available, and that both sides were both responsible for this failure to reach an agreement.

(3)

On August 22, 1993, before any information of secret talks taking place in Oslo was leaked, I took the decision to suspend my membership of the Executive Committee. I explained my position in a press statement and I sent a copy of that to the Vice President of the National Council because he was the responsible authority. The statement read as follows:

> The political, financial, and administrative crises which the PLO is suffering are no longer a secret. Responsibility for those crises lies in the hands of the current leadership, in other words what is known as the Executive Committee. It has become an urgent national duty for all the Palestinian agencies, organizations, and factions which work within the framework of the PLO to ensure the Palestinian National Council is called to an emergency session, in the shortest possible time, in which all these crises can be discussed in order to find suitable solutions for them. After that, a motion of confidence in the current leadership should be proposed after a discussion of its general performance in terms of politics, finance, and administration. As a member of the current

Executive Committee, I have to admit that I and other colleagues can no longer take responsibility for decisions that are passed in our name but of which we have no knowledge. This has led the committee to lose its authority. The same thing has happened to other institutions in the PLO, especially the National Fund Committee, which has not met for more than two years, and whose president has been marginalized. Since he was chosen, he has only attended one or two meetings of the Executive Committee and has not said a word about the so-called financial collapse that has blighted the PLO.

More dangerous than any of this is the marginalization of the Executive Committee in the negotiating process. Negotiations are being carried on by people who do not belong to the Executive Committee, are not appointed by the Committee, and are not answerable to it. The process has come to be dominated by people with posts and titles that do not exist within the formal structure of the PLO, who then appear to go on to become decision makers while the leadership, represented by the Executive Committee, is sidelined and unable to influence the negotiations. This cannot be accepted and responsibility cannot be taken for it, especially as we get closer to the stage when existential decisions will have to be taken. What we hear today from those so-called advisors, with their sophisticated declarations and attempts to blur the line between what is strategic and what is tactical, no longer washes with anyone. We, like the rest of our people, have started to sense the dangerous consequences of the risky and complacent politics being played by the leadership in the name of the Executive Committee.

At our National Council we agreed to enter negotiations after delineating our positions and red lines. But today we see that these positions are threatened to their very essence and that we have already crossed those red lines. Therefore, it is necessary to call for an emergency extraordinary meeting of the National Council and to seek the participation of all the active forces in this arena without any exceptions in order to build a united position for which all can be held responsible as they represent the people. As we await the convening of this meeting, and call upon every Palestinian to demand it, I am forced to suspend my participation in the affairs of the Executive Committee. I promise all who have known me and who know me that I will remain the same faithful soldier for the Palestinian cause and the PLO. I have the honor of being one of those who established the PLO and I find it hard to bear witness to its destruction and the liquidation of its organizations and the driving away of those who work in them. The PLO was built to last and it will last until it achieves the goals that it was set up to achieve, to establish an independent Palestinian state and to close the file of the Palestinian refugees with the return of all refugees to their free and sovereign homeland.

(4)

The day after I made the statement, Abu Ammar phoned me from Tunis. We spoke for more than half an hour during which he was unable to change my mind, while I was not able to convince him of the need to convene the National Council. More important than this failure to agree was that he did not inform me, even by insinuation, of the secret negotiations which had been taking place for months and which were about to reach their conclusion. It also emerged that these negotiations had been carried out without the knowledge of several colleagues in the Executive Committee.

At the beginning of September 1993, Beirut was about to host a meeting of the foreign ministers of Arab countries linked to the peace negotiations in order to evaluate the negotiation process and to coordinate the positions of all the Arab delegations. I was shocked to receive a directive from Abu Ammar in Tunis to join the Palestinian delegation participating in this meeting, along with Abu Lutf and Saeb Erekat.

Of course, I refused to participate. But that did not stop me from meeting my two colleagues and talking to them about what was going on in the PLO and the crises it was facing which had led me to suspend my membership of the Executive Committee. I would not be revealing any secrets if I said that neither Abu Lutf nor Saeb had been told about the secret negotiations in Oslo. They were being honest when they denied knowledge of any secret negotiations when speaking to the Arab Foreign Ministers during that official meeting.

It was natural that news of my suspending my work for the PLO would raise the interest of the Arab and Lebanese press. I gave several interviews in which I tried to explain the reasons for my anxiety over the rumors that were circulating of a secret agreement between the PLO and Israel. The Lebanese press was mainly concerned with the fate of the Palestinian refugees who lived in Lebanon after the agreement was signed, and whether the danger of naturalization had increased or there was hope that the refugees would return to their homes and properties.

After less than a week had passed, on September 9, news of the mutual recognition letters between Yasser Arafat and Yitzhak Rabin was announced. Several media outlets began to speak of a secret political agreement which had been signed in Oslo under the headline: "The Israeli–Palestinian declaration of principles: the Gaza–Jericho First Agreement."

On September 10, I made an announcement to the effect that I was resigning from the Executive Committee and from my position as the PLO representative in Lebanon.

At the beginning of October, I received an invitation to attend an emergency session of the National Council to ratify the Agreement. It had been signed on September 13 in a curious ceremony on the White House lawn.

I headed for the Tunisian capital, taking with me my reasons for rejecting the Gaza–Jericho First Agreement, which later became known as the Oslo Agreement.

(5)

The Palestinians in Tunis, like the rest of the Palestinians scattered over the Occupied Territories and the lands of the diaspora and exile, were bewildered, anxious and nervous. It seemed to me that there was not a single Palestinian who was not suffering at that moment a crisis of choice in deciding between two possibilities when it was very difficult to decide which was worse and more evil.

The cadres of the organizations and their members knew exactly what the consequences of such a decision would be, and the radical effect it would have on the fate of each and every one of them. Their dilemma was all the worse because the overwhelming majority of them knew they had no refuge other than the PLO, not only in terms of the national cause but also as a sanctuary and a source of income for them. Thirty years after the establishment of the PLO, they had become like nomadic Bedouin, following their leadership literally wherever it went.

This is why I was aware of the tension with old comrades who began to hover around me as soon as I arrived to discuss the matter

of my resignation. They were on my side when it came to rejecting
the Agreement but they argued that it was better for me to keep my
position rather than resign, so that I could stay close to the source
of decision making, and be able to continue to observe matters
closely and rectify the political process. Convincing them that my
position was the right one was not easy. Despite their experiences
and the knowledge most of them had about the conduct of our senior
officials, they could not see the truth: that effecting any change from
the inside had become impossible. I had had two experiences of this:
the first had been at the time of the establishment of the PLO with
Ahmad al-Shuqayri and the second was with Abu Ammar. Power
tempts one to cling on. It confers status and prestige in society and
the media. It could also offer material gain for those who wanted
to exploit their position and to trade on it. Staying put would have
meant pledging loyalty to the person who held the key to the safe. I
am sorry to say now something which I have never said before: that
I lived to see leading colleagues of mine kiss the hand of Abu Ammar,
not because of any faith in him or as an expression of loyalty or
love, but because he had approved their personal requests which they
knew went beyond any boundaries of what was acceptable. Among
them were men on the Executive Committee who had sometimes
tried to trump me and others with their intractable and extremist
positions. When it came down to it, they sided with the man who
would guarantee their survival in their positions and they continued
to trade on the cause of our homeland.

I met Abu Ammar and we were left alone for a while. After a brief
discussion, I told him in all honesty: "Abu Ammar, you are at the
beginning of a huge gamble, but I cannot bear to share any responsibility for it unless there is real participation in the process by the
National Council – not the Council you intend to convene tomorrow
or the day after [I meant the Central Council]. You know it has
no authority to take existential decisions in place of the National
Council. It is simply an advisory council, nothing more and nothing
less."

In the end I suggested that, if this step had to be taken, he should
set up a leadership council made up of people from the West Bank
and the Gaza Strip which would take responsibility for the policy
and monitor its consequences. I also said to him: "As for you, I
suggest that you retire to a cottage on a Tunisian hillside, and remain
as the leader of your country and the chairman of this organization,

the final authority for the people of Palestine. That way if your gamble succeeds, it will be a victory for all of us. But if it fails, you will have at least saved yourself, the PLO, and the cause."

Abu Ammar did not interrupt me once during all our time alone, even though sometimes his face betrayed traces of mockery. He could not imagine himself away from the central stage for one second, because he believed that if he stayed away the cause would be in danger. It was the identification of the person with the cause.

I did not stay long. I left him in the company of the group of hypocrites who were going to build him Hong Kong and Singapore on the sands of the Gaza Strip and the hills of the West Bank. There was no choice left but to part company. I decided to make use of the platform of the Central Council to say what I had to say and to explain why I was against this agreement: to put on record, with others, for the historians of the future, that this agreement was not ratified unanimously by the representatives of the Palestinian people and that there were those who stood up and said no.

(6)

At noon on October 6, my turn came to speak. My colleague, Ahmad Sidki al-Dajjani, famous for his impeccable manners, soft expressions, and his care not to hurt the feelings of others, had gone before me. He gave a calm yet decisive speech that was clear in its rejection of the agreement. Then Abu Adeeb, the Deputy President of the Council, called me to the podium. My address lasted about an hour. I reviewed the clauses of the agreement, the exchange of letters, and even the preface. Abu Ammar interrupted me half a dozen times, but he failed to provoke me into anger or to silence me. He was extremely irritated by the applause that I received from the audience for my criticisms of the agreement. Below are extracts from my speech taken from an audio recording:

> Mr President. We are facing an event of existential importance, which touches on our past, our present, and our future. We are not engaged here in a self-indulgent intellectual argument. We are discussing our destiny.
>
> To begin with, on the matter of form, this agreement has been termed a "declaration of principles" regarding prepara-tions towards interim self-government. There should have been

a declaration of principles regarding the whole issue and all its consequences, so that preparations for the interim period could have come as part of a whole, with everyone agreeing on the principles governing them. Furthermore on studying this agreement, we discover that there are no principles at all in this declaration of principles – there are only vague insinuations which have no authority apart from Resolution 242, but even that has been dropped as a legal reference and turned into an appendix for the conclusion of the final status negotiations. This means the results of the negotiations have become the legal reference, instead of the international resolution. Upon reading other clauses, we find that we have already conceded that our land is no longer occupied and that we are satisfied to enter negotiations as a means to achieve what is termed withdrawal.

Abu Ammar interrupted me: "Of course, that is only your opinion."

I replied: "I can only say what is my opinion." After this exchange I said:

The text says in the preface that the government of Israel and the Palestinian team in the PLO agree on what follows, after the mutual recognition which has taken place between the PLO and the Israeli government ...

For my part, I will point out the importance of this recognition. Firstly: the recognition was not limited to Israel's right to exist, it was linked to its right to peace and security. There is nothing like this in any recognition agreement between two sides anywhere in the world.

Abu Ammar interrupted me: "Even Resolution 242 – which, Shafiq, all the Arab countries have agreed to – dictates secure recognized borders. You are saying things which are not true."

There was an argument between us during which I pointed out that the new agreement speaks of rejecting violence and abandoning terror as well as disciplining those who do otherwise, implying that we are the terrorists, while we are resistance fighters and people with a right. I went over what the preface said about the two parties agreeing that the time had come to end decades of confrontation and conflict, and to recognize each other's legal and political rights.

I said: "Words are like gold. I am only saying that the political and legal rights of Israel are well-known. It is a sovereign country that issues identity cards and passports. It has navies and complete sovereignty." I asked about our own legal and political rights. What were they? "They are unclear rights? So what are we signing up to?" Then I assured my colleagues that I would not comment on all 17 articles in the agreement and would restrict myself only to certain points.

The subject of the issues which were left unresolved in the agreement was one of the most important issues I raised. At the forefront of these issues was Jerusalem. Refusing to limit my concern to the churches, the mosques, and the sacred places in East Jerusalem, I said: "I would not give up an inch of land from the East Jerusalem of 1967 because it was all just as sacred as the al-Aqsa Mosque and the Church of the Holy Sepulcher."

The fate of the refugees was also one of the most prominent issues left hanging in the air. The agreement only promised to discuss – if there really was to be a discussion – the issue of refugees exiled in 1948. The reality was that the refugees in the diaspora lived in great anxiety over their fate. The displaced people of 1967 are not in a much better position. I clarified: "Despite the statements made by my brothers and their assurances that it will only be months before hundreds of thousands of displaced people return to our occupied land, a joint Egyptian, Jordanian, and Israeli committee has been set up to discuss criteria for which individuals – individuals and not groups – would be permitted, a certain category of human beings."

Here, Abu Ammar interrupted me and said: "This is not true." We had a discussion, during which my point of view relied on the actual documents.

Then I turned to the way the agreement was made and I highlighted my objection to it:

> It would have been my wish to see this council convened before going to Washington. That would have been practicing democracy. It was my wish that we, being a people who have been deprived of our homes, would not be deprived of our right to express ourselves within our own frameworks. This is too much! Too much!
>
> Also, and I hope, Abu Ammar, that you keep an open mind when I speak of the performance at the signing ceremony. All of us, all the people of your nation were watching you on the television. Abu Ammar, we deserved – indeed our martyrs deserved and

your people who brought you to the White House deserved – at least one word which contained some sort of a message to us, as Rabin spoke for his people. This made it look as if we were the ones who had been the aggressors, that we were the ones who were spreading lies and that we were the ones who were doing the killing, not showing that the opposite had been happening for 45 years of our lives ...

In conclusion, I said:

> In keeping with my principles and because of my conviction that I am not a man for all seasons and all political programs – to go from belief in liberating the land from the river to the sea, to any independent Palestinian state, and now to the Gaza–Jericho Agreement, with all the new challenges that that brings – I confess, without trying to upstage anybody, that I have decided to reaffirm my resignation from the Executive Committee and from my representation in the PLO until we find out what will happen and what will be the fate of this organization. I thank you all.

(7)

More participants who spoke after that; some were supportive and some were against. Then it was time to vote. I had no illusions that the agreement could be scuppered or that it would not be ratified, but I was surprised that only eight members out of 120 or more voted against it. It saddened me greatly to see some members holding up their hands, but lowering them when our eyes met, only to raise them again.

Perhaps you could hardly blame many of them for looking out for their own interests and their dues, but those who really deserved the blame were those who belonged to the leadership of Fatah and were members of the Executive Committee. I had spent years listening to their extremism and one-upmanship, even having to bear their taunts for my "moderate" positions. They had made a complete U-turn. They had not only supported the agreement, but had raised their voices in its defense. There is no need to name names because many of them were later exposed and their true colors revealed.

The next morning, after a sleepless night, I made a tour of several offices and departments to say good-bye to friends and comrades, most of whom I had known for decades. On the very day of my resignation, I had entered my 30th year with the PLO in which I devoted myself to the political struggle.

Before heading for the airport, I dropped in on Abu Ammar in his office in Yoghurta Street. He stood up and greeted me as if nothing had happened. We exchanged looks that indicated there was no need to talk about it. It was what fate had brought to the struggle and no differences of opinion about it would overrule our friendship.

However, I still felt that I should say a quick word despite the sensitivity of the moment, so I said to him: "Brother, Abu Ammar, you know the depth of our friendship and the countless shared memories that hold us together. I want to reassure you that I will not taint this friendship with malice. I shall oppose you politically, according to my way of doing things which you know very well. That is to say, honestly and without treachery. So please do not believe the whispers of unscrupulous people or listen to the plots of conspirators."

At this point we hugged each other and he said to me: "May God help you. You will find the situation in Lebanon in chaos, but I have no fear you can handle it."

I left, wondering if we would ever meet again, and if so when and where?

22

AFTER THE RESIGNATION

Despite my conviction that I had been right to resign from my position in the PLO in protest against its leadership signing the Oslo agreement, I still had doubts that were now keeping me awake at night. The popular reaction to this agreement had not been as decisive as I had predicted. I was genuinely surprised when I realized that many Palestinians had supported the leadership's position, especially among our people in the Occupied Territories but also in the diaspora. This is why I was very careful, in the first few weeks after my resignation, to try to find out the real position of the Palestinian populace, especially those in Lebanon, and the reasons behind their unexpected support.

(1)

After some research and analysis, making direct and indirect calls to those in the know in the political movement, the organizations, and the popular unions, I came across a most important document: a comprehensive and objective poll carried out by the Institute for Administrative Research under the supervision of Maurice Khouri two days after the agreement was signed. The poll sought to assess to what extent the agreement was accepted or rejected. It surveyed 600 people, chosen at random from all the Palestinian refugee camps in Lebanon, with the exception of those in Ba'albek and its environs. The most important results of this poll, as pointed out in the report, can be summarized as follows: 63 percent agreed in principle to peace negotiations between the Palestinians and the Israelis, against 35 percent who did not; 59 percent believed that the PLO represented all Palestinians, against 39 percent who did not; 56 percent believed that despite signing the agreement, the Palestinians still had the negotiating power to regain the West Bank and Jerusalem, against 36 percent who did not. The overwhelming majority, 86 percent, were optimistic that the agreement would allow all or a proportion of the displaced people of 1967 to return. What was interesting about the poll was that the majority, 63 percent against 36 percent, admitted that the agreement was an abandonment of Palestinian rights. Out of those, 31 percent said that it meant relinquishing Jerusalem, 44 percent thought it meant relinquishing the rest of the Occupied Territories, and 31 percent said that it abandoned the right to self-determination. Seventy percent of those polled believed that the agreement would lead to the total or partial naturalization of the Palestinian refugees in Lebanon, while 14 percent did not.

During the past 20 years, I had always discussed affairs and exchanged opinions with three friends who were prominent activists in the Palestinian cause, Ibrahim Abu Lughod, Edward Said, and Iqbal Ahmad. The four of us agreed to reject the agreement and to declare it detrimental to the rights of the Palestinian people. More important than that was our consensus that the agreement had no future and would fail to produce either a settlement or peace. However, we disagreed on the methods that each of us chose to express our positions.

Edward had already gone further than Ibrahim and me on a radical path because he was convinced that it was impossible to cooperate with the leadership of the PLO. He ended up placing all responsibility for the consecutive defeats which blighted the Palestinian struggle on Abu Ammar, because he had appropriated the decision-making process and lacked a clear strategy. This had become evident a few months before the signing of the Oslo Agreement. Edward announced his resignation from the National Council and began a relentless media campaign, declaring that the solution lay in establishing a secular, democratic, and united Palestinian state which included both the Palestinians and the Israelis in the land of historical Palestine.

Just before the agreement, Ibrahim had also taken a decision that was hugely important for both his personal and political life, deciding to return to Palestine. He was able to do so because of his US nationality, which he had acquired after more than 40 years of living in the United States. He resigned from Northwestern University and moved to Birzeit University, which had become the most significant seat of culture for the Palestinians in the Occupied Territories. The comprehensive Arab collapse that Ibrahim had witnessed in the last few decades had alarmed him, and he began to warn of a future similar to those of the countries of Central America, which all spoke the same language but were disunited and weak. He emphasized the need for Palestinian steadfastness in the land of Palestine, believing that demography would win in the end and would strip the Jewish entity of its ethnic character. He did not sever his relationships with the PLO, but he preferred to work with institutions of civil society such as the Welfare Association and the Abdul Mohsen al-Qattan Foundation, concentrating on education and cultural affairs.

The same thing happened to Iqbal Ahmad, who was Pakistani by birth but Palestinian by belief and universal in his way of thinking. He argued that it was necessary to strip the agreement down for all to see, and to oppose it by using all the platforms available to him. Because he had no Palestinian roots, his only way to support the cause was the written word. He also decided to leave the United States and return to his place of birth, Islamabad, to work on a major educational project, setting up the Khaldunian University because he believed in the anti-imperialist role which could be played by the education sector.

As well as rejecting the agreement, I also rejected what was known as the "National Number." This referred to an Israeli decision that the government would agree to my return to Palestine if I was to declare, one way or another, that I no longer rejected the agreement. As I explained to many of my friends and comrades at the time, I did not reject it because of my stubborn disposition or because of any attempts at one-upmanship. I rejected it because of my personal conviction that what I could offer to our cause from my position in the diaspora was much more important to me than what awaited me if I returned to the homeland. That was especially true because I was a refugee from Jaffa, whose population had been divided between those who remained steadfastly there, whom I would not be able to reach, and the majority who now lived in the diaspora in Jordan, Syria, and Lebanon.

Based on all this I began a new stage in my political struggle, turning away from official work in the PLO, trying to focus on the importance of restoring the balance between the patriotic struggle and the national struggle and of reaffirming that there were no other solutions to the central problems of our nation except those of the national solution. In that context, there was a need for serious hard work to increase the nation's awareness of the democratic dimension, the respect due to the Arab human being, and the rejection of unilateral regimes.

On the Palestinian level, after I had resigned from the PLO, I could not find the right position within the framework of the existing opposition organizations. They all had the disadvantages that were intrinsic to the leadership of the PLO. With the exception of the Popular Front for the Liberation of Palestine, the leaders of those organizations had remained the same over the past four decades, with no changes. I also could not find among the opposition any practical political programs that tempted me to cooperate with them, just old revolutionary words and slogans, as if nothing in the world had changed.

(2)

My first appearance as a member of the opposition to the leadership of the PLO from outside its framework was at a lecture I gave at the American University of Beirut Alumni Club, where the Palestinian Cultural Club used to hold weekly seminars every Tuesday evening. Dr Anis Sayigh, who established this club in the early 1990s, was an old university friend whom I had known since the 1950s. Our friendship became stronger when the PLO was established and he became the head of the Research Center in the mid-1960s. Anis Sayigh was one of the strongest opponents of the Oslo agreement. His disagreement with Abu Ammar went back several years before the agreement was signed, and had ended with Anis resigning from the center and later from his position as the head of the board of directors of the *Encyclopedia of Palestine*.

About 100 Palestinian personalities made up the membership of this Palestinian Cultural Club. You could say that they were the intellectual élite of those who lived in Beirut and the refugee camps surrounding it. It also included a considerable number of well-known cultural and economic experts as well as a number of the up-and-coming young people who were concerned with many cultural and social issues. The lecture was on the Oslo agreement and I gave it the title of "The rejected solution."

I tried as much as I could to avoid using the platforms of the Palestinian organizations and kept them all at arm's length. That was because of the unwritten agreement between us, which was I could be relied on as the spokesman for Palestine on national occasions because I was independent of any organization. But now I had enough time to participate in national activities, particularly in the National Arab Conference and later in the National Islamic

Conference. I was elected more than once to sit on the board of directors of the former and to the membership of the follow-up committee of the latter. I also participated in the establishment of the Al-Quds International Institution as one of its trustees, as well as taking part in the National Forum.

(3)

A few days after my resignation, Dr Hala Maqsoud, the head of the Arab-American Anti-Discrimination Committee (AADC), called me from Washington. She asked me if I could participate in the committee's annual general meeting and speak to its members about the Oslo agreement and the reasons why I had rejected it. I said that I would love to do it if I could get a visa to enter the United States, because they usually held up our visas every time we wanted to go to the United Nations to discuss resolutions that concerned our cause.

Hala promised to try her best and I in turn tried to get a visa through the usual channels. I was surprised when an official at the United States embassy in Tunis asked if I had really resigned from the PLO and was therefore no longer one of its active members. When I replied that I had, he asked me to wait for a moment. He returned a few minutes later carrying my passport stamped with an ordinary visa; there were no notes on it, no restrictions or warnings as had been the norm previously. What was the secret of the American U-turn? But there had been no such thing. Simply, the point was that, according to their laws, I was no longer a member of a "terrorist organization," the PLO. I am sad to say that the PLO is still viewed as such to this day despite the signing of the Oslo agreement and the toasting of peace between the Israelis and the Palestinians in the Rose Garden of the White House.

The AADC was one of the most effective organizations among the Arab community in the United States. It rightly took over that status from The Arab-American University Graduates (AAUG), which had been led by some of the best Arabs living abroad, people such as Edward Said, Ibrahim Abu Lughod, Fuad Moghrabi, Baha al-Din Abu Laban, Samih Farsun, Rasheed Khalidi, Naseer Aruri, Elaine Hagopian, Khalil Jahshan, and others. As for the AADC, it was headed by the Arab-American Senator James Abourezk, Hala Maqsoud, and Mary Awkar.

One of those who participated in this conference was Azmi

Bishara. I had got to know him through his writing but had not met him yet. He had started to rise as a Palestinian political activist of a new kind. It was my chance to salute him and shake his hand.

Because my lecture succeeded in dissecting and refuting the Oslo agreement, Hisham Sharabi invited me to another seminar to have a discussion with other Arabs and Americans who were concerned about the situation in the Middle East. That seminar witnessed a very animated discussion, especially because Hisham had not yet declared his final opinion of the agreement and seemed to be going along to a certain extent with the chaotic and mendacious discourse of peace.

And here I feel that I should praise the steadfast patriot, Clovis Maqsoud, who was Arab to the core. He was never tempted by the luxuries of life, and no earthquake could shake his commitment. He remained the same as when I had got to know him in the 1950s, fighting for his convictions with all the power he could muster to find the right words, even if he had to sculpt them out of thin air.

Before returning to Beirut, I decided to go to New York for a farewell visit. It was difficult not to love that city no matter how harsh, careless, or breathless it seemed. I had been visiting it on average two times a year since 1974 and there was something inside me that made me long for it. Places, corners, restaurants, museums, universities, and the mixture of people of all colors, origins, and creeds.

Both my daughters, Hanine and Syrine, were studying there. That year, Hanine, who had just graduated with a PhD in education from Columbia University, was living in Amherst Massachusetts with her husband, Marwan Gharzeddine, who was working on his doctoral thesis in clinical psychology. Syrine was preparing to submit her thesis in comparative literature at Colombia University, where her supervisor was Edward Said.

I have tried my best when writing these memoirs not to distract the reader with my personal life. I have made the event, rather than my person, the center around which my story has focused. I was afraid that if I were to become personal my sentiments towards some people, be they negative or positive, would appear to be excessive, saying more than I meant to, exacerbating sensitivities which have no place here, especially because I feel honored by the opportunities and occasions I have had to meet many people and to call them my friends.

But I want to apologize for now straying from my rule to salute five people I always think of when I think of New York or the United States. They are Ibrahim Abu Lughod, Edward Said, the Yemeni ambassador Abdallah al-Ashtal, the Syrian abstract artist Hadi al-Turun, and Reja-e Busailah.

I want to start with a quick word about Ibrahim Abu Lughod, whom I have already mentioned several times in these memoirs. I can only say that he is one of the few people I can call a lifelong friend. We were born in the same city, in the same area, and we went to the same school. We parted ways after the *Nakba*, he going to the United States and I to Lebanon, but we were reunited by the Palestinian Liberation Front and then the PLO, and by all the branches of the Palestinian cause, its institutions and activities. We remained bonded. Our last meeting was when he visited me in hospital in Washington in 2000, only for him to pass away in 2001. He was buried where he wished he had lived his whole life, in his beloved Jaffa, whose love he was always faithful to.

I met Edward Said through Ibrahim, who had discovered him when he was a student at Princeton after the 1967 war, which had a huge impact on the consciousness of the Arab-Americans, making them come face to face with the reality of their position in the United States compared with the Jews and the Zionist Movement. I really do not need to write anything about who Edward Said was, for he has become one of the most famous people on this planet and one of the most important modern intellectuals, penetrating the American consciousness with force and putting the Palestinian cause on the agenda for intellectuals and academics from the West all the way to the Far East. If I was to name the most precious gift that I have ever received, I would say without hesitation that it was Edward's dedication of his book *The Politics of Dispossession* to my wife and me, and his declaration that I was a man who was incorruptible. Edward's remains have now mingled with the soil of a Palestinian olive tree on top of a hill in Brummana in Lebanon.

I got to know Abdallah al-Ashtal as a young man at the American University of Beirut before he joined the Yemeni revolution in the southern Arabian peninsula. In 1974, he was the ambassador of South Yemen to the United Nations. He remained in that post until he achieved his dream of uniting the two halves of Yemen and became the ambassador of Yemen, north and south. Without Abdallah Al-Ashtal and his hospitality, I would have found my stays in New York boring even though it was New York. Much more important than that is that in defending the Palestinian cause he often went way beyond the lines drawn for him, sometimes even surpassing the Palestinian delegation itself. He was a fine diplomat who presided over the Security Council with expertise, wisdom, and good sense. I will never forget how Abdallah al-Ashtal and his wife threw a wedding party for my daughter and her husband, inviting many friends and colleagues. Abdallah, like our mutual friend, Edward, was snatched away by cancer. He was buried in Sanaa in 2005. There is truly nothing more kind to a man than the soil of his own country, so what is the man who has no country to do?

Hadi al-Turun, the painter whom circumstances had driven away from his home, had remained in New York after he finished studying there. He worked in the Arab League office then went on to work for one of the UN agencies. Hadi was the epitome of the witty Syrian Arab and had an unparalleled ability to come up with satirical remarks. Aside from his job, he put on several exhibitions of his work, and in the last few years his reputation has begun to rise on an international scale. Hadi was my special "advisor"; when I had any anxiety about taking a position I would consult him, and he always proved firm but also flexible.

Finally, Reja'e Busailah, my friend from the days of the Ameriyah School in Jaffa. I was halfway through secondary school when Reja'e came from Akka. He was a distinguished pupil in his manners and energy. He was one of the first people I met who had lost their eyesight but he had not lost his insight. Exile brought us together in Kuwait, but he then went to the United States to carry on with his graduate studies. He became a professor of English literature. Reja'e did not live in New York, but he was one of the few people with whom I was always in touch. He was not satisfied with just teaching; he became a reference source for anyone who asked and one of the most prominent Palestinians in the diaspora. He was a sensitive poet, who wrote in English. In the last few years, it made me very happy to have some time to record for him the poetry of Mahmoud Darwish, Samih al-Qassim, and a number of other contemporary poets on cassette. I hope that his memoirs about Akka and Palestine see the light. There are many who have lost the pleasure of sight but have the ability to give light to others. Reja'e is one of those people.

I apologize to the reader for this digression about my very close friends.

When I left New York, doubting that I would return to it any time soon, I thanked God that my son, Hader, had left the United States that year, having finished his studies at Northwestern in Chicago and Madison in Wisconsin. Something that worried me seriously was the temptation for our children to remain in America when they compared the environments of the United States and the Arab world. I cannot blame the Arab youth for emigrating when the governments of their countries failed to offer a respectable alternative, even if I would rather they came back and reformed those regimes.

In the Arab world, I could not move around with the freedom I had hoped for in order to accept the invitations I was receiving from most of the Arab capitals and major cities. The difference between the declared and real positions of those governments meant that my movements would be restricted. I had created some enmities with their regimes through my journalistic work before I gave it up to work for the PLO.

(4)

Life continued at this pace until May 11, 2006, when I received an invitation which read as follows:

> The representative of the Executive Committee of the Palestine Liberation Organization in the Republic of Lebanon, Abbas Zaki, is honored to invite you to the opening of the Palestine Liberation Organization Representation offices on Monday May 15, 2006.

Abbas Zaki was one of the old guard of Fatah. He spent most of the years of the struggle as a representative of the PLO in the Popular Democratic Republic of Yemen, and then became a member of the Executive Committee. My immediate reaction was that I could now say that the charge that I had received 42 years ago and had protected with all the care, power, and wisdom I could muster had found someone who could carry it on and take over its guardianship.

At about 6 o'clock in the evening that day, the day of the reopening of the PLO office which had been closed since 1982, I was on my way to the new offices when memories took me back through 42 years.

I thought of how we had clashed with the Lebanese authorities about the flag of Palestine which we insisted on displaying from the balcony of the offices on the day they opened. I remembered how the Soviet ambassador, Surgar Azimov, surprised me with an unexpected visit which caused a traffic jam on the Cornish al-Mazraa that lasted about an hour. He said laughingly that the only reason for his visit was to make the world aware of Moscow's interest in the PLO and their respect for it – and he had succeeded.

How could I forget when the Mossad agents shelled my office with rockets twice, and how it was only God's care that saved myself and my colleagues from certain death? How could I forget those friends to whom I am forever indebted for the years during which they dedicated themselves, for the sacrifices they made, and their efforts to build this temple to Palestine which was worthy of consecration – the PLO.

At the forefront of those was Abdul Qader al-Daher, the deputy director, the dynamic administrator who never stopped. He had resigned from his job in UNRWA at a time when Palestinian youths dreamed of finding a job there, preferring adventure to stability. Shawqi Armali, the devoted son of Shafa Amr, who had experienced the evils of the Zionists in childhood when they attacked his home and terrorized his family, resulting in his mother losing her mind and displacing the rest of the family to the mountains. Shawqi, a lawyer who had recently graduated from the Jesuit University, was the legal advisor in the bureau and became a prominent defense lawyer for Palestinian causes in Lebanon and abroad, where he took on the defense of several freedom fighters who had undertaken operations abroad. Shawqi became the PLO representative in Athens and then in Brussels at the European Union. Today he is at the Vatican.

I cannot forget the efforts made by those people who always go unnamed and never enjoy the spotlight, people such as "Colonel" Haleema Hourani, Najia Hammoud, Adnan Sanjaq, Salwa al-Hout, Khaled Abadi, Taha Hammad, Khaled Ajjawi, Nadia al-Bayraqdar, Mahmoud al-Iraqi, Ibrahim al-Natour, Yolande Sarrouji, Abu Othman, Muhammad Fayyad, Mahmoud Baraka, and many more.

I remember with honor Brigadier Muhammad al-Shaer, who worked as a military attaché then became the PLO ambassador to Moscow. He was one of the brave officers of the Liberation Army and had a huge role in the training of the cadres of "Palestine Liberation Front – the Road to Return" in the 1960s. I also cannot forget the friendship of the modern artists Ismail and Tamam Shammout, who took over the cultural-artistic section in the PLO bureau and did a wonderful job. Their continuous efforts have had a great effect on modern art in our cultural life to this day.

My memories were interrupted by my arrival at the new offices, where Abbas Zaki was waiting to receive me along with members of the Fatah leadership in Lebanon and a number of representatives of other organizations. The Lebanese government, including its three top figures, was present, and so were the representatives of the various forces and political factions in Lebanon.

I almost remarked how like yesterday tomorrow looked. But I was determined to push away the pessimism I was feeling and to give my last official speech in the way required by my responsibilities.

After congratulating the new representative on his position, I said that I was not very happy for him because his role was not an easy one. It was full of problems and the field was full of contradictions. I advised my colleague and successor from a position of great experience, perhaps taking longer than I should have, to be careful to balance three spheres. The Palestinian sphere, where much work was needed to achieve national unity and secure a minimum of coordination. The Lebanese sphere, where I advised him to adhere to a form of language that was acceptable to all the Lebanese groupings and would therefore avoid one Lebanese faction mobilizing the Palestinians against a rival, and to stick to the rule of "we will befriend those who befriend us." As for the Arab sphere, I advised him not to forget, even for one moment, the importance of the Arab role in the Palestinian cause, especially that of Syria, the eternal neighbor of Lebanon, and the importance of realizing this truth and of remembering that the Palestinian people are the ones who have the greatest interest in the unity, coordination, and solidarity of the Arabs.

I therefore consider May 16, 2006 to be the first day of a holiday I had dreamed of for 42 years, a holiday from the PLO but not from the struggle for the cause, because the cause was not a job, it was fate.

23

MY HEART REBELS

The decision to stop smoking may be an easy one to take, but seeing it through is a different matter. I knew it would be tough for me when I – or rather my doctor – decided that I must give up tobacco. But I had no idea how much control those accursed cigarettes had over me, physically and psychologically. After five days of not smoking, I stood in front of the mirror to shave and was surprised to see that something about my reflection had changed. I inspected myself closely to make sure it wasn't a trick of the light or the sleep in my eyes, and I suddenly noticed that my neck was swollen. There was no pain or discomfort, but it looked as though I'd swallowed two hard boiled eggs which had now lodged in my throat. This new condition scared me and I rushed to my doctor – the same one who had ordered me to stop smoking a short time before. To my surprise he laughed and told me not to worry. He explained it was a side effect of nicotine starvation, affecting the pituitary gland and hypothalamus in particular, which had caused my tonsils to relax and my neck to drop. He told me that there would be other weird symptoms, pain, and disturbed sleep, but I shouldn't worry about them. He was right – my ears, my stomach, my bowels, my joints all suffered, not to mention the disease of gluttony which I contracted, meaning I was unable to leave the table unless a huge balloon had been filled up between my belly button and my esophagus. So a new battle had to be joined – the battle of the bulge.

And then there was the wolf in the wilderness, howling for just that one cigarette, or just one puff of a cigarette. Had the doctor not told me that a single puff would bring everything I had struggled for crashing down, I would not have been able to resist the wolf's cry.

(1)

But the wolf did not stop howling and my efforts did go to waste. I wrote the preceding paragraphs during my first attempt to stop smoking in the spring of 1985. It did not last and I went back to smoking more eagerly and addictively than ever. In fact, I started smoking three packets a day instead of just the two, and in the end my breathing became so wheezy it kept me awake at night. On June 13, 2000, I was invited to dinner with my friend Muhammad Oweis on the last night of a visit to Washington, where I had been invited to give a speech by the American-Arab Anti-Discrimination Committee (AADC) on the situation of Palestinians and in Palestine after seven years of the Oslo Agreement. Muhammad came to my hotel an hour before dinner to take me on a tour of Washington landmarks. I felt uncomfortable in the car. I could feel pain in my chest and I had difficulty breathing, so I asked Muhammad to park and let me get out to breathe some fresh air. We were in a beautiful park overlooking the river. I got out to walk a little and fill my lungs with oxygen.

Muhammad came up to me and asked if I was OK and I said yes, I was sure it was just a momentary feeling that would soon go away. But instead of walking along the river bank as I had planned, I headed towards the first park bench I could find. I slumped down on it, took out my packet of cigarettes and lit one up, inhaling until my lungs were filled with smoke. Then I exhaled triumphantly, like a steam engine, feeling a strange kind of relaxation. Muhammad was standing there anxiously, looking at the streams of sweat running down my face. I told him that I wasn't in any pain, I was just feeling a little uncomfortable, and I suggested we go straight to dinner as I wanted to have an early night to prepare myself for the long flight the next day.

At the restaurant, it became clearer to me that what I was experiencing was not just a passing phase and I said maybe I should go to see a doctor after all. Muhammad told me he had been hoping I would say that, and he would have mentioned it himself, but for the fact that it's not the kind of thing a gracious host tells his guest just before dinner. As I was sitting there at the table, I started feeling all kinds of new pain, light and bearable at first, but as time passed and we were on our way to the hospital they got worse and worse. One sensation was like a heavy weight pressing down on me, another was sharp as a bee sting. I was sapped of all my energy and my skin felt as though it was being jabbed repeatedly with a blunt object.

(2)

Fortunately, the restaurant was not far from George Washington University Hospital. When we arrived, Muhammad told me to wait in the car while he fetched a wheelchair. I told him there was no need for that but he insisted, saying it would help me be seen more quickly and without any fuss about health insurance, or awkward questions about who I was and what I was doing in Washington.

The emergency team arrived with a wheelchair and took me into the emergency room. As I was being examined and given some initial treatment, a succession of hospital staff asked me the same questions over and over again, about my name, my age, my symptoms, and whether I had any history of serious medical conditions, such as a stroke or a heart attack. By I had gone through all these questions for the third time, I was feeling exasperated, though I realized later it was a deliberate technique to make sure the information I had given was consistent. I burst out: "Sir, in my country it is considered a shameful sign of weakness to cry out, but I'm not sure I can stand this for much longer. Please stop asking me questions and give me a painkiller or a sedative, anything to reduce this pain. I don't want start screaming because it would embarrass me." The doctor replied that I was already receiving the maximum permitted dose of morphine, in fact he was surprised I was still conscious – apparently the dose I'd been given was enough to knock out a camel! He urged me to have patience while they carried out the required scans and tests.

Finally, came the dreaded question. "How long have you been smoking?" I thought for a moment and said, feeling ashamed at what I had brought onto myself, "Fifty years."

The doctor shook his head sympathetically and said: "I'm afraid you have had a heart attack and are going to need surgery. We can't operate immediately because your heart has been weakened, but we are going to perform a catheterization now and put a stent in to widen your artery and help the blood flow. In a few days, we will perform a quadruple bypass."

An hour later, they moved me to the operating theater and the stent was fitted. I was conscious for most of the time, and was able to watch what was going on a TV screen provided for me. Then I either slept or lost consciousness, I am not sure which. I awoke the next morning strapped to my hospital bed, hooked up to all sorts of tubes and wires and with an oxygen mask over my mouth and nose. There were several familiar faces around me, including Muhammad Oweis, who had spent a busy night on the phone to Beirut, as well as making arrangements for my treatment. Next to him was my nephew Jamal, who lived in Chicago and whom I had not seen for

20 years. Muhammad told me he had spoken to my son, Hader, who had broken the news to my long-suffering wife, Bayan.

The next day I awoke to hear an unusual commotion outside my room, and a few seconds later the door opened and Abu Ammar strode through in his trademark khaki suit and black-and-white headscarf. He sat down beside my bed and took my hand in his and stroked it gently, while he mumbled some words. I could not hear what he said properly, but it was something full of love and emotion – one of those moments when all the negative feelings that have built up over years between two people can be swept away on a tide of forgiveness. I treasure that encounter, which came during one of Abu Ammar's many flying visits to Washington in the midst of the death throes of the Oslo process. It was our first meeting since Oslo had caused the rift between us and it was to be our last before he passed away.

A few hours later, I was surprised by another visit, this time from Abu Mazen and Saeb Erekat. I was a bit more myself by that time and began to criticize them forcefully for the damage they had inflicted to our cause, Abu Mazen interrupted, in a loud voice but without anger: "Brother Shafiq, we wanted to come and see that you were OK, but I can see that there's nothing wrong with you! The nurses said you were semi-conscious – if only it were true!"

We all laughed and our laughter cleared the air. When they got up to leave, I called after them: "I wish you *bad* luck." Saeb came back for a moment and whispered in my ear: "If only you knew how bad the positions of some of the others are, you'd change your mind about Abu Mazen." Then he was gone. I began to ponder whether there really was any difference between the bad and the worse.

(3)

The date for my open heart surgery was set for June 19, and the day before I was made to read and sign all kinds of lengthy contracts that the hospital administration required to protect itself in the event of anything going wrong during the operation, God forbid. During my time in hospital I was inundated with visits and phone calls from the Palestinian and Arab communities in Washington and beyond. Abdallah al-Ashtal and his wife Vivian traveled to see me from New York, and Ibrahim Abu Lughod came from Chicago. I had not expected the visit and it was the last time I saw him.

On evening of June 15, Bayan arrived after a grueling 24-hour journey from Beirut. She entered the room trying to be as composed as possible. But, as soon as I saw her, I was overwhelmed by feelings of guilt and regret about everything I had put her through over the years. I was at a loss about what to say to her. Apologize? What words could I use to express myself? All I can say now – as I recall the dozens of difficult episodes of our lives – is that had it not been for this dear woman I could not have achieved my lifelong dream to struggle for Palestine and for the restoration of our rights. And despite the burden of being my wife and a good mother who knew how to protect her family, she has also been able to offer her own contribution to the struggle, with four books that have become essential references for any student researching the Palestinian cause and its history.

The arrival of Bayan did not relieve Muhammad Oweis from his daily round of duties, receiving visitors, answering the phone, checking papers, and monitoring my medical progress with the hospital staff. His most important job was to raise morale and disperse the boredom of hospital life as we waited for the big operation, something he was more than qualified to do, being one of the wittiest men I know.

The night before the operation everything was calm and normal, with no discussion about what was to come. I can say honestly that I wasn't afraid of dying or even thinking about the possible that I might die. But I have to admit that I was concerned about the pain after surgery. I went to sleep like a good boy, surrendering to the pills and injections I had been given, and placing my faith in Him who created the earth and the heavens. I woke up at dawn to find the nurse taking samples of my blood. After that a succession of nurses came and performed their duties on a man no longer in control of his own destiny.

They moved me to the operating theater at about 7:30. The anesthetist spoke a few reassuring words to me and, as I waited, I recited the opening chapter of the Qur'an and asked for God's forgiveness and His protection for my family and my loved ones. I closed my eyes for a moment and saw the image of Raya, my grandchild who was not yet three years old, then the clarity of the vision faded away and I could no longer see her or my other grandchildren, the thoughts of whom had filled my mind at the hospital; this was a sign that the sedatives they had given me were working. When I opened my eyes again, I saw Bayan standing beside me and with a last wave to her they wheeled me into the recovery room.

Being put under anesthetic is not like sleep, with its dreams and moments of consciousness. It is oblivion, a temporary death. It had to be, because while I was unconscious they opened my chest and took out my heart, sliced through my left leg from top to bottom and removed enough arterial tissue to replace the four arteries around my heart that had mutinied and ceased to work properly.

(4)

My recovery was slow and fitful. I was not able to speak at first because of all the tubes in my mouth and nose. My nights were troubled with bad dreams and my days passed in painful boredom. Bayan and Muhammad were with me all the time to help me through the experience. Little by little I was able to get out of bed and move to a chair. But one day I experienced a terrible pain in my chest which sent me into convulsions, bringing the nurses and doctors hurrying over to see what was wrong. Apart from that single relapse, however, my condition improved and I was soon walking around, pulling along my intravenous drip. Sometimes I would get tired and have to stop, but my strength was returning and my spirits were always raised by encouraging words from patients and staff I encountered on my trips around the hospital.

It remains for me to end this chapter with same subject that I started with – the scourge known as the cigarette, the lone wolf that inhabits the smoker's lungs and never stops howling for more nicotine. I had forgotten about smoking while I was in hospital and I did not dare to remind myself for several weeks afterwards – not because of any self-control on my part, but because of the effects of the surgery and the fact that breathing was still difficult. Then one morning, I heard the wolf's cry again, as I was having breakfast with the smell of fresh coffee in my nostrils. At that moment, and with no inner conflict, I decided that I would never smoke again. It was a habit that I had to put behind me completely. I knew I had tried before and failed, but this time I was fortified by the experience of those agonizing pains that I had felt during and after my heart attack. I am happy to say I won. To this day I have not puffed even once on a cigarette, cigar, or hookah pipe. Nevertheless, I believe the wolf is not dead. He is in a coma and I hope he never wakes up from it.

24

COMING OUT OF A DARK ABYSS

After I had finished the last chapter and started making notes about the areas I wanted to concentrate on in this concluding chapter, I heard news of the death of a friend of mine, the artist Ismail Shammout. He was not just my friend, but a unique character among my group of lifelong friends, a brother by a different mother, if you like. He was one of the generation of Palestinians for whom the *Nakba* of 1948 had been like a stab in our hearts, disrupting our young lives and taking over our destiny. He was an artist committed to Palestine; his brush strokes found their colors in the wounds of the Palestinians and in the beating of his own heart. Until his heart stopped beating. We had been together since the 1950s, as colleagues in the PLO office in Beirut and drinking companions during long nights of merriment, few as those may have been.

He died on Monday, July 3, 2006. The news did not come as a surprise, as I had been fully aware of Ismail's poor health and his heart problems for several years. Nevertheless, I felt as though I had fallen into a dark abyss. It is strange how we refuse to come to terms with death, no matter how often we witness it around us or how many different reasons lie behind it. Despite our understanding of its inevitability, many of us reject the very concept of death. I cannot say I am very different in my thinking, except that my experience of facing death in all its forms has made me more at home with the idea of my own demise. It no longer scares me as much as intrigues me, leaving me curious to know what comes afterwards. Perhaps like the early Arab poet Zuhayr Bin Abi Salma, I have become like the 80-year-old who grows "weary of the burdens of life" – though I have not reached the age of 80 quite yet. Had the poet known about the tragedies that would befall the Palestinians and the Arabs in this evil time, he might have been able to tell of those who grow weary of the burdens of life today before the age of 20, preferring martyrdom and control over their own fate in an unjust and oppressive world.

Photo 8 The author in his last years when he wrote his memoirs.

(1)

When Ismail died I stopped writing and all my efforts to emerge from the abyss came to nothing. Total depression overcame me, overwhelming my private and public existence. I began to delve into the past and compare it with the present, looking at the times when we made mistakes and when we had done the right thing. I began to wonder whether this decline and fall would ever end. The more I thought about what our nation had gone through since the first Camp David agreement, the fall of communism, the Gulf wars, the Madrid conference, and Washington negotiations, the Oslo agreement, the Israeli–Jordanian treaty and ... and ... right up to the present day with massacres in the West Bank and the Gaza Strip, massacres of human beings, trees, and even stones, I sank deeper into this slough of desperation. I began to feel I was sinking into quicksand, or that the abyss I had fallen into had no bottom or floor. The only glimmer of hope was in the heroic stance taken by the free people of Lebanon in the south, where the struggle against the Israeli occupiers was still alive, while Arab leaders sat in their palaces, spineless and subservient.

Then came July 12, 2006 – a historic moment in our struggle that shone out like a bolt of lightning. The Zionist enemy tried to extinguish this light by waging a cowardly and deceitful war against Lebanon, under the illusion that their aims would be achieved in a few hours or days. But it lasted 33 days, the longest Arab–Israeli war since the *Nakba* and the establishment of the state of Israel. Not only was it the longest of those wars, but it was the first in which Arabs came out victorious and Israel's army was defeated. When I say Arabs, I do not mean the Arab states, I do not even mean the Arab peoples. I mean a group of Arabs of Lebanese origin, the men of Hizbullah.

(2)

I was born before Israel and I will always be a few years its senior – a witness to its grim history of racist crimes and mass murder from its foundation. I have lived through its wars, from the *Nakba* to the *Naksa* (setback) of 1967, and the puzzling conflict of October 1973. I have lived through our people's revolution with all its victories and defeats. At the end of every cycle in this conflict, I joined my compatriots in refusing to admit defeat and clung to the belief that "that which does not kill us, makes us stronger." There is no doubt that there were those who fell by the wayside, those who got side-tracked, who fell into despair and surrender, and there were those who professed pragmatism in order to hide their surrender. Relations between ourselves and these "pragmatists" have always been tentative and awkward. No one ever dared debate or interrogate the difference between our two methodologies and patterns of behavior. Even at the official level, most Arab governments remained too embarrassed to lay out their real position, preferring instead to hide behind deceit and falsehood in their public statements and political decisions. It has become worse in the last few years, after the Palestinian leadership fell in to the trap of the Oslo agreement. The methodology of surrender came to fore and the methodology of siege and resistance, which the American media managed to brand as terrorism, became narrower, as if humanity had never before watched a national liberation movement act out its plans. This is surprising given that the past century had almost entirely been taken up with the defeat of colonial imperialism around the world.

But those like me, whose fate saw them through the experience of the Arab revolution during the time of Nasser, who were able to follow closely the liberationist revolutions and coups which seized independence in Yemen, the Gulf, Algeria, Tunisia, and Morocco, who knew and met men like Gamal Abdul Nasser, Ahmad Ben Bella, Tito, Sukarno, Castro, Guevara, and others like them who were figureheads in the struggle for freedom, we realized, with much sorrow and heartache, the difference between what we had once been and what we had become. That was especially true in the Palestinian struggle, in both the political and popular frameworks. For us there was no longer any comparison between our situation in the 1960s and 1970s and where we were in the 1990s, after the Oslo agreement and the intellectual and political heresies which came after it, and the decline in our goals and values.

So it was not Ismail Shammout's death that had pushed me into the dark abyss. He was just one in a long list of comrades and friends who had gone before him, after which I had always been able to continue along the path with my head held high. What had pushed me into the abyss and sowed doubt in my soul had been my realization of the succession of events that we had lived through and the defeats we had suffered. My nerves were shattered. I was tired. I despaired. I was weary. But I had never given up until then, even though I was like a lost spirit, caught between the two methodologies without ever being able enjoy solace from either of them. Then came the summer of 2006, a season that was so different from all the others that had preceded it since the *Nakba*. The men of Hizbullah pulled me out of the abyss, with their stunning victory over Israel. Their dream conquered my nightmare. The promise was renewed, that Palestine would return to us and that we would return to it. There is nothing in the world to compare with that feeling of being delivered from a pit of despair, nothing better than the space, the sunshine, and the blue skies of freedom.

On October 29, I traveled to Amman to take part in a memorial service for Ismail. There I declared, to the multitudes on both sides of the River Jordan, that resistance, in every philosophical and practical sense of the word, was the only way that we could open the gates of freedom, peace and justice. The path of resistance was the only path of return. I went back home and started writing again.

(3)

Going back to writing for me meant going back to living. Writing is my profession and my hobby. Above all, it is my weapon and battle standard in our fight for the justice and liberation which our people seek generation after generation. I therefore consider myself lucky, despite all the suffering, difficulties, and agonies that have afflicted my life, because in the end I have lived long enough to see in 2006 that Israel's existence is not permanent and remains a passing phenomenon. I hope I do not appear overly dramatic or romantic when I say this. In reality, life in its essence is one long, continuous struggle governed by the laws of human and physical contradictions. It is in this struggle that the secrets of progress and change lie. What distinguishes humans from other living and inanimate things is that we are reasonable and thinking beings. This is why the human is created "more argumentative," as it says in the Qur'an. Intellectual argument is based on the struggle between Good and Evil and the collision between them. As soon as they are prized apart, confusion returns and the struggle recommences. I suppose what I want to say here is that the most important thing that distinguishes one human being from another is how successfully they distinguish between truth and an illusion.

There is a story of a boy sitting in the prayer niche of a mosque asking God: "Almighty God, enlighten my mind with the truth." When he had finished his devotions and was about to leave, an old man stopped him and asked: "Why did you ask to be enlightened with the truth, son?" The boy replied: "So that I can uphold it and spread it among the people." The old man said: "Then you should ask God to give you the courage you will need to uphold it." The boy prayed as the old man had told him and then left the mosque. Outside a second old man stopped him and asked what he had been doing. When the boy told him the story, he said: "Son, go back to the prayer niche and ask God to strengthen your faith by making truth victorious, no matter how long it takes. Do not despair if death comes to you before the victory of truth. But make sure you pass on the flame to him who comes after you."

If you were to ask me about my own success in distinguishing between truth and illusion, all I can say is that I have tried, and I am still trying, and it is enough for me to continue doing so.

INDEX